Philip Roth and the Body

Philip Roth and the Body

Jewishness, Gender, and Race

Joshua Lander

BLOOMSBURY ACADEMIC
NEW YORK · LONDON · OXFORD · NEW DELHI · SYDNEY

BLOOMSBURY ACADEMIC
Bloomsbury Publishing Inc
1385 Broadway, New York, NY 10018, USA
50 Bedford Square, London, WC1B 3DP, UK
29 Earlsfort Terrace, Dublin 2, Ireland

BLOOMSBURY, BLOOMSBURY ACADEMIC and the Diana logo
are trademarks of Bloomsbury Publishing Plc

First published in the United States of America 2025

Copyright © Joshua Lander, 2025

Cover design: Eleanor Rose
Cover image © Erik Von Weber / The Image Bank / Getty Images

All rights reserved. No part of this publication may be reproduced or transmitted
in any form or by any means, electronic or mechanical, including photocopying,
recording, or any information storage or retrieval system, without prior
permission in writing from the publishers.

Bloomsbury Publishing Inc does not have any control over, or responsibility for, any
third-party websites referred to or in this book. All internet addresses given in this
book were correct at the time of going to press. The author and publisher regret
any inconvenience caused if addresses have changed or sites have ceased
to exist, but can accept no responsibility for any such changes.

Library of Congress Cataloging-in-Publication Data
Names: Lander, Joshua, author.
Title: Philip Roth and the body: Jewishness, gender, and race / Joshua Lander.
Description: New York: Bloomsbury Academic, 2025. |
Includes bibliographical references and index.
Identifiers: LCCN 2024019665 (print) | LCCN 2024019666 (ebook) |
ISBN 9798765104842 (hardback) | ISBN 9798765104835 (paperback) |
ISBN 9798765104859 (ebook) | ISBN 9798765104866 (pdf)
Subjects: LCSH: Roth, Philip–Criticism and interpretation. | Jews–Identity–In literature. |
Human body in literature. | LCGFT: Literary criticism.
Classification: LCC PS3568.O855 Z756 2025 (print) | LCC PS3568.O855 (ebook) |
DDC 813/.54–dc23/eng/20240513
LC record available at https://lccn.loc.gov/2024019665
LC ebook record available at https://lccn.loc.gov/2024019666

ISBN:	HB:	979-8-7651-0484-2
	ePDF:	979-8-7651-0486-6
	eBook:	979-8-7651-0485-9

Typeset by Integra Software Services Pvt. Ltd.

To find out more about our authors and books visit www.bloomsbury.com
and sign up for our newsletters.

Contents

Acknowledgments		vi
List of Abbreviations		vii
Introduction: The Word as Flesh		1
1	Reading Roth's (M)Others	23
2	The Jewish Stain	49
3	Jews in the Garden	81
4	Black Skin, Jewish Masks	117
Conclusion: Goodbye, Philip		153
References		156
Index		172

Acknowledgments

Thanks to the following people:
Aimee and Maren, for your time, advice, and encouragement.
Chris and Mia, for the support and supervision during the PH.D.
Sophie and Calum, for keeping me logged on.
Beth, for the joy, japes, and love.
Mum, for everything.

Abbreviations

AL	*The Anatomy Lesson*
AP	*American Pastoral*
CL	*The Counterlife*
D	*Deception*
EF	"Eli, the Fanatic"
EG	*Exit Ghost*
GW	*The Ghost Writer*
HS	*The Human Stain*
N	*Nemesis*
OS	*Operation Shylock: A Confession*
P	*Patrimony: A True Story*
PAA	*The Plot against America*
PC	*Portnoy's Complaint*
ST	*Sabbath's Theater*
TF	*The Facts: A Novelist's Autobiography*
WW	*Why Write: Collected Nonfiction 1960–2013*
ZU	*Zuckerman Unbound*

Introduction: The Word as Flesh

This book is a focused study and analysis of Philip Roth's fictional bodies, unconcerned with the Philip Roth we do or don't know. This monograph parses the symbolic functionality of the corporeal in his main works by looking beyond the usual dichotomies of whether Roth is an American or Jewish writer or is Roth writing autobiographically. Instead, the book offers close readings of Roth's prose to explore the subject of the body and embodiment, analyzing how the author's fictional bodies throw into doubt the body as a coherent, stable entity. In doing so, this monograph seeks to illuminate the abject in Roth's prose, analyzing how his fiction unsettles racial, gender, and national borders that are so often denoted through the body.

In 1983, Roth was featured in *People* magazine, where he claimed to be fascinated by "the body and its plights" (qtd. in Shostak 2004: 20). This interest proved to be a thematic constant for the author, whose fiction exhibits a repeated and consistent intrigue in the breakdown and transformation of bodies. *Goodbye, Columbus and Five Short Stories* (1959), *Letting Go* (1962), *When She Was Good* (1967), *Portnoy's Complaint* (1969), *The Great American Novel* (1973), *My Life as a Man* (1974), "Zuckerman Bound: A Trilogy and Epilogue" (1979, 1981, 1983, 1985), *The Counterlife* (1986), *The Facts: A Novelist's Autobiography* (1988), *Deception: A Novel* (1990), *Patrimony: A True Story* (1991), *Operation Shylock: A Confession* (1993), *Sabbath's Theater* (1995), "The American Trilogy" (1997, 1998, 2000), "The Kepesh Trilogy" (1972, 1977, 2001), *The Plot against America* (2004), *Exit Ghost* (2007), and "The Nemeses Tetralogy" (2006, 2008, 2009, 2010) are all either instigated, shaped, or thematically inflected by the subject of a body or bodies in crisis. Simply put, the body cannot hold in the Rothian imagination. The body's "volatility"—a term I borrow from Elizabeth Grosz—is this book's primary focus; I argue that Roth's representation of the body as a volatile "site" enables him to create an aesthetic that destabilizes identificatory categories (in a Butlerian manner) pertaining to gender, race, religion, and sex.

Although Roth's fiction has often been positioned as misogynistic and—more recently—racist, I ask to what extent Roth's fictional bodies *undermine* white masculinist, patriarchal, and racist society his characters exist within. This book considers to what extent Roth can be read as a writer whose fiction resists the homogenizing force of white masculinity by parsing the meaning of Roth's porous, unstable bodies, and the political and aesthetic implications Roth's fiction presents vis-á-vis his slippery, slimy prose.

By broaching the topic of embodiment in Roth, the book approaches the author through a framework that interrogates how gender, race, and religion emerge in the author's representative bodies. It is important to note here that Roth's narrative framing is almost always exclusively male and Ashkenazi, which is significant in terms of discussing how women and people of color materialize in Roth's pages. Concurrently, I consider what Roth's fiction teaches us about what it means to physically occupy space as a Jew living in predominantly non-Jewish spaces. Effectively, the book is shaped and determined by the following question(s): Whose bodies matter in Roth's fiction, and what do the author's bodies tell us about America's racial and social politics?

Given the breadth and scope of Roth's literary career, combined with the expansive topic addressed here, the book analyzes Roth through an "eclectic theoretical pluralism" (Hillman & Ulrika 2015a: 2). In other words, my book parses Roth's fiction through an array of theoretical approaches—pivoted around bodies—that examines and allows for the multiplicity and complexity of both Roth's prose and the topics of embodiment and the body. I do not address topics such as age and/or disability explicitly (though both do come up, of course); rather, I bring Roth into conversation with Annette Kolodny, Frantz Fanon, and George Yancy, and glue the book together using Julia Kristeva's theory of abjection, a recurrent and consistent theoretical tool in my approach to Roth's fiction. The author's oeuvre and the topic of bodies and embodiment are yoked together by their slippery indeterminacy; neither can be neatly categorized or defined.

Conversely, this monograph *does* question to what extent Roth can be read as a writer whose fiction resists white supremacy. The term "white supremacy"—to lean on Charles Mills's definition—is "the unnamed political system that has made the modern world what it is today" (1997: 1). This omission, Mills explains, "is not accidental. Rather, it reflects the fact that standard textbooks and courses have for the most part been written and designed by whites, who take their racial privilege so much for granted that they do not even see it as *political*, as a form of

Introduction: The Word as Flesh 3

domination" (1997: 1). Roth, as a Jew, *does* see the racial politics underpinning the racial domination of American society; his fiction questions, complicates, and condemns the power dynamics Mills outlines. My positioning of Roth as a resistant and/or rebellious writer conjoins and departs from Roth scholarship that precedes this monograph.[1] This book's entry into Roth studies is timely, as there is an argy-bargy brewing regarding the politicization of Roth's fiction.[2] Roth's literature—specifically *The Plot against America* (2004)—has received newfound interest in the aftermath of Donald Trump's presidency. Roth has been credited—somewhat inaccurately—with prescience that has been egregiously overstated regarding the repugnant rise of Trump's political career.[3] However, there have been excellent scholarly outputs on the subject of reading Roth in the aftermath of Trump.[4] Brittany Hirth, for example, argues that *The Plot against America* "offers its readership an insight into America's uncomfortable history of oppressing minority groups, a historical past that has rhetorically reemerged through the political platform of President Trump" (2018: 71). I agree with Hirth, although I would point out that the oppressiveness she highlights is only re-emerging for certain minorities (Jews, for example); other groups have been continuously living with America's racial oppression daily. Andy Connolly—in part—responds to Hirth (and others), questioning the "tendencies to see *The Plot against America* as somehow illuminative of the moral anxieties defining our historical period" (2022: 62).

My interest is in Connolly's broader thesis regarding "how Roth's formal concerns with issues of ambiguity, irony, and contradiction resist the corralling

---

[1] Roth scholarship has blossomed in the last twenty years or so. Debra Shostak's *Countertexts, Counterlives* (2004) remains a must-read for any Roth scholar. Shostak leans on Lacanian psychoanalytical theories to illuminate how Roth's "books talk to one another as countertexts in an ongoing and mutually illuminating conversation, zigzagging from one way of representing the problems of selfhood to another" (2004: 3). Her in-depth analysis and close-readings remain enormously influential in Roth Studies. Elsewhere, Aimee Pozorski's *Roth and Trauma* (2011) is an illuminating and significant exploration of Roth's depiction of trauma. Another important work is David Brauner's *Philip Roth* (2007), which highlights the significance of paradox in Roth and his relationship with contemporary American authors, while David Gooblar's *The Major Phases of Philip Roth* (2010) provides a comprehensive overview of Roth's fiction. Patrick Hayes's *Philip Roth: Fiction and Power* (2014) offers a sophisticated Nietzschean analysis regarding how "Roth's importance lies in the depth and sophistication with which he has explored the ramifications of a distinctively post-Nietzschean way of valuing literature" (2014: 3). Finally, Andy Connolly's *Philip Roth and the American Liberal Tradition* (2017) examines "the conflicting manner in which hallowed ideas about the outright separation between the aesthetic and the 'worldly' are, at one and the same time, both upheld and transgressed" in Roth's prose (2017: 2).

[2] See Berlinerblau (2023: 82–91). Berlinerblau responds to a number of reviewers of his book, which I discuss hereafter, challenging their accusations regarding his methodology and close readings.

[3] On both matters, see Connolly (2022: 60–92, 65–7).

[4] I refer to Hirth (2018: 70–93); Kaplan (2020: 44–72) and Sherwood (2021: 3–25).

of his fiction to suit any particular ideological aspiration" (2022: 60). This is a commonplace opinion in Roth scholarship, and it is often noted how dialogical and cacophonic Roth's fiction is, suggesting that because there are a multitude of voices within Roth's prose, there is a discernible *lack* of political standing. Or rather, it is difficult to locate the author's view (especially on matters pertaining to Israel) because of the multiple political viewpoints on show. It is as though Roth cannot be pinned to a particular ideology because his novels are slippery, slimy beasties. My approach risks vandalizing Roth's fiction, by asking how his work undermines and destabilizes the homogeneity of racial and gendered borders.

Roth has repeatedly expressed wariness around the mispositioning of his work; just ask Bryan Zanisnik (Tracy 2012), whom Roth sent a cease-and-desist letter to for using his novel in a performance piece. Don't forget the time Roth wrote an open letter to Wikipedia after he was unable to correct a description of *The Human Stain* (Roth 2012), and as Ira Nadel discovered, he was particularly precious regarding the publication of his memoirs. Nadel received a letter informing him that he did not have permission to quote from any of Roth's work, nor would any of Roth's friends or associates cooperate with Nadel (Boyagoda 2021). Roth was skittish about labels, sharing Saul Bellow's uneasiness regarding the moniker "Jewish-American Writer," preferring instead the four-syllabled "American." The preference reflects both the privilege and precariousness of American Jews like Roth had; on the one hand, the author was free to self-identity as an American, but at the same time, his proclamation felt weighted. As Adam Kirsch wryly observes, "an American Jewish writer's denial of Jewishness can be considered a deeply expressive Jewish act" (2019: 18). This double bind reflects Tanya Golash-Boza's point that "[w]hile whites self-identify as Americans, non-white Americans recognize that they are not Americans, but African-Americans, Native Americans, Asian Americans or Latino/a Americans. In this sense, how one becomes American or how one assimilates into American society depends in large part on one's racial status" (2006: 28). I suggest there is—underpinning Roth's queasiness surrounding the term "Jewish-American"—a recoiling from an identity that has been derisorily demarcated as other.

In seeking to avert being sublimated into a political position, Roth effectively flees into another. Cynthia Ozick expresses a similar view in her essay "America: Toward Yavneh," arguing that "[t]he Jewish writer, if he intends himself really to be a *Jewish* writer, is all alone, judging culture like mad, while the rest of the culture just goes on *being* culture" (1994: 25, italics in original). Ozick's use of the word "culture" is rather unclear here, but I suggest it serves as a strawman symbol for white America. In Ozick's view, Roth's desire to be recognized as American signals an unconscious yearning to be included within white American culture, one that seeks to expunge Jewish religious and cultural differences. To submit to the neutral, non-hyphenated American serves as a kind of purification: "to say 'I am not a Jewish writer; I am a writer who is a Jew,' … turns out to be wind; it is precisely those who make this distinction whom Diaspora most determinedly wipes out" (Ozick 1994: 26). The elision of Jewish difference is prescient in Roth and Bellow's refutation of the title: Jewish writer. Of course, their skepticism was not monolithic in its origins and Roth had a famously rancorous reception from certain factions of America's Jewish communities, which will have no doubt fueled his reticence in being marked out as a figurehead for the mythical Jewish community. Nevertheless, whiteness remains a powerfully alluring concept precisely because it is perceived to be a neutral "space," one without the tensions and fractures that demarcated and dominated American-Jewish life.

Roth—as writer and a man—has always elicited strong reactions from readers and public commentators. *Goodbye, Columbus* (1959), Roth's first publication, was frostily received by certain corners of America's Jewish readership for its supposedly offensive portrayal of Jews. One reader wrote to Roth accusing him of having "done as much as all the organized anti-Semitic organizations have done to make people believe that all Jews are cheats, liars, connivers" (*WW* 50). Another asks, "[W]hy don't you leave us alone? Why don't you write about the Gentiles?" (*WW* 50). Then came *Portnoy's Complaint*. The novel's satirical depiction of Jewish American lives vis-à-vis a singular psychoanalytic session produced an impressive backlash from literary critics. Irving Howe famously wrote that the "cruelest thing anyone can do with *Portnoy's Complaint* is read it twice" (Howe 1972: 75). Marie Syrkin condemned Roth by suggesting there is "little to choose between [Joseph Goebbels] and Roth's interpretation of what animates Portnoy" (1980: 333). The philosopher and Kabbalist Gershom Scholem goes even further, declaring: "with the next turn of history, not long to be delayed, this book will make all of us defendants at court. … This book will be quoted to us—and how it will be quoted! They will say to us: Here you have the testimony from one of your own artists … an authentic Jewish witness" (qtd. in Cooper 1996: 110–11). The anxiety Roth's work produced tellingly articulates the various fears surrounding how Jews wished to be seen. For Scholem, Roth's

6 *Philip Roth and the Body*

novel runs the risk of validating antisemitism's pernicious stereotypes and serves as an authentic testimony of Jewish degeneracy.

Roth had a knack for eliciting disgust from his readers and detractors. Jacqueline Susann, for example, commented on *The Tonight Show* that she would very much like to meet Roth but would not shake his hand (the implication being that he was too dirty to touch) (Pierpont-Roth 2014: 64). In 2011, Roth received the International Man Booker Prize, which led to Judge Carmen Callil's resignation. Callil bemoaned Roth's repetitiousness and lack of imagination: "[H]e goes on and on about the same subject in almost every single book. It's as though he's sitting on your face and you can't breathe" (Flood 2011). This wonderful complaint encapsulates the disgust and repulsion Roth's fiction can elicit from his readership, one that highlights the physicality of the author's prose.

The corporeality of Roth's fiction is gendered in terms of its focus and framing. Following his death in 2018, several articles were published attacking the author for his sexism and misogyny. Dara Horn wrote an article for the *New York Times* entitled "What Philip Roth Didn't Know about Women Could Fill a Book" (2018), while Sandra Newman, writing for the *Huffington Post*, published, "Stop Treating the Misogyny in Philip Roth's Work Like a Dirty Secret" (2018). Elsewhere, Brett Ashley Kaplan expresses frustration at his problematic "representations of women but also with his attacks on feminists, his queasy-making depictions of queer women, not to mention the totemic manner through black characters are consistently plunked throughout his texts" (2013: 187–8).

These concerns regarding Roth remain today.[5] Indeed, this monograph follows on from Jacques Berlinerblau's *The Philip Roth We Don't Know: Sex, Race, and Autobiography* (2021), a book that has caused quite a ruckus among Roth scholars, as he employs a "reverse biography" that seeks to locate the author in his protagonists: "Roth's autobiographical bent raises a delicate question: what is the relation between all that male rage-y prose and all those scenes of predation on the one side, and Roth's personal experiences with women on the other?" (Berlinerblau 2021: 13).[6] Connolly's review is unequivocal in its assessment of Berlinerblau's efforts: "In thus capsizing the space between the writer's output and his life, Berlinerblau manages to flatten Roth's body of writing to the moral

---

[5] I, too, find Roth a difficult writer to read at times. Although his explorations of Jewishness were revelatory for me (a Scottish Jew without much connection to my religious identity), I am often sighing at his portrayal of women, his warring against perceived political correctness (see *The Human Stain*), and his questionable depictions of African Americans. The sex scenes, too, often leave me cringing.

[6] See Vanderwall (2022: 92–8).

apostasies of what he describes as a cringingly outmoded, 'cis-gendered,' white male privileged has-been" (2023).

While I share Connolly's concern regarding Berlinerblau's methodology, I find the latter's discussion on Roth and race significant. The most provocative point in Berlinerblau's book emerges in the first chapter, as he argues Roth's "fiction fails to capture the unyielding structural racism that thrust Blacks into Jewish neighborhoods in the first place" (2021: 30), and more recently has stated that "Roth confronted many issues with originality and intelligence; race was not one of them" (Berlinerblau 2023: 84). These claims are challenging, especially as Berlinerblau argues that American Jewish racism goes unopposed in Roth's main novels, raising questions regarding to what extent Roth *can* be read as a writer who resists white supremacy.

Berlinerblau contends that Roth fails to portray the issue of race with nuance, arguing, "Roth's representation of African American characters can be neither sympathetic nor thoughtful" (2021: 22). As a non-Black scholar, I feel it inappropriate to simply dismiss this claim outright; indeed, at certain points, I found myself nodding along with Berlinerblau, particularly in his discussion of "Goodbye, Columbus" and *The Great American Novel* (1973). I was left wanting, however, in his analysis of *The Counterlife*, *I Married a Communist*, and *Patrimony* (Berlinerblau 2021: 30). Berlinerblau makes three dashing references to each of these novels, before signing off the subsection with a quote from Larry Schwartz: "Roth the hard-edged, thoughtful, and ironical realist, becomes a conservatist 'utopian'" (2005: 1). Schwarz's article—excellently researched and written—makes a compelling argument regarding Roth's portrayal of African Americans, as does Jung-Suk Hwang's "'Newark's Just a Black Colony': Race in Philip Roth's American Pastoral" (2018), as both explicate how deracialized readings of Roth's novel and the author's portrayal of Newark have rendered "African Americans … subalterns whose voices remain unheard" (Hwang 2018: 184). Berlinerblau, however, fails to unpack the structural racism represented and portrayed in Roth's novels, which stems—in part—from the critic's reverse biography. Distracted by his pursuit of the author, Berlinerblau skirts over the complexities of the racism he identifies.

My aim in this monograph is to offer a response to Berlinerblau that does not rescue or rehabilitate Roth; instead, I aim to parse the bodies that emerge in his fiction and what they represent. However, I do not intend to follow Berlinerblau in his ill-advised quest to find Roth or his views in the pages of his fiction. More than enough has been written on the life and times of Philip Roth. More work, however, is needed on the fiction and essays of Philip Roth *the writer*.

As such, I intend to follow from scholars such as Brett Ashley Kaplan's excellent *Jewish Anxiety and the Novels of Philip Roth* (2015), which has had an important bearing on this project. Kaplan examines how Roth's books "teach us that Jewish anxiety stems not only from fear of victimization but also from fear of perpetration" (2015: 1). This illuminating work underscores the ways in which Jews inhabit a "doubled view of America" (Kaplan 2015: 10) that is perpetually marked by the "specter of Nazi occupation, the threat of the Holocaust, [which] ... haunts numerous characters and heightens the sense of the doubled America" (2015: 11). My intention here is to develop Kaplan's examination by further probing the ways white supremacist conceptualities of Jews and African Americans overlap and differ vis-à-vis the body, and how Roth's (Jewish) bodies destabilize and resist the homogeneity white nationalism fetishizes.

Surprisingly, there has been no monograph-length study of the body in Roth Studies to date. *Philip Roth and the Body* therefore aims to fill this lacuna but joins a rich array of scholarly conversations and discussions on the topic of bodies and embodiment. As I noted above, Debra Shostak's *Countertexts, Counterlives* (2004) highlights the importance of the body in Roth's oeuvre: "One of the first things a reader notices in the fiction is the emphasis Roth places on his protagonist's body and bodily consciousness, because the body often acts seemingly in defiance of the mind's control" (2004: 21). Shostak reads Roth through Lacanian theories to illuminate the role of the corporeal, stressing how bodies are inscribed on: "[T]he circumcised penis is the instrument that writes the Jewish body, a body traditionally conceived of as *male*" (2004: 67). I diverge from Shostak in that I excavate the abject imagery in Roth (a topic she addresses, but given the expansive approach undertaken, does not attend to fully), and I place Roth into dialogue with a broader range of theorists to consider race as well as gender.

My monograph joins and adds to these discussions by drawing out the connections between gender and race and how these messy monikers play out through the body. I don't intend to redeem or rescue Roth; rather, I wish instead to consider the author's leaky bodies, and what these illuminate about Jewishness, race, and gender in American society. I intend to close-read Roth's fiction, without trying to locate the specters of Roth in the process. The man has haunted me long enough .... Before that, though, I shall provide a brief history of the Jewish body to contextualize Roth's writing.

The Jewish Body

In *The Cambridge Companion to the Body in Literature* (2015), David Hillman and Maude Ulrika highlight how "the body has always been a contested site" (2015a: 1) and that within "the Christian and Humanist traditions, it has often been seen as a mere auxiliary to the self, a vehicle or object that houses the mind" (2015: 1). Descartes's dualistic theory is predicated around this idea that the body and mind are separate. As Katherine J. Morris explains, Cartesian "conceptions of the body [treat] it as pure *Körper* [the body-object], rather than as 'the lived body' (*Leib*)" (2012: 49). The term *Körper*—roughly translated as "body-object"— illuminates the peculiarly detached manner Descartes conceived the body through; that is, he read the body as a machinic, lowly entity. Phenomenologist Edmund Husserl challenged this idea, arguing that the "lived body" is "the *medium* of *all perception*; it is the *organ of perception* and is *necessarily* involved in all perception" (*Ideas* II §18, qtd. in Morris 2012: 49, italics in original). This line of reasoning was developed and expanded on by Maurice Merleau-Ponty, who claimed "[t]he body is our anchorage in a world" ([1945] 2012: 146). In *The Phenomenology of Perception* ([1945] 2012), *The World of Perception* ([1948] 2004), and *The Invisible and the Invisible* (1968), Merleau-Ponty—inspired by Husserl, Martin Heidegger, and Jean-Paul Sartre—"located the body as the primary locus of subjectivity and argued bodily experience organizes our perception of the world" (Roth 2022: 5).

The prioritization of the body as *the* locus point of perception is an essential component of Philip Roth's writing.[7] *The Dying Animal*'s epithet encapsulates the Merleau-Pontian philosophy underpinning Roth's own approach to fiction: "The body contains the life story just as much as the brain" (2002: n.p.). For Roth, the body is the story. However, the body is not simply the center of perception; it is the nexus unto which the self is encoded. In other words, the body is a politically contested space. Bodies are not shaped or formed neutrally; nor, for that matter, is perception universal. As Michel Foucault has highlighted, "the body is also directly involved in a political field; power relations have an immediate hold upon it; they invest it, mark it, torture it, force it to carry out tasks, to perform ceremonies, to emit signs … the body becomes a useful force only if it is both a productive body and a subjected body" ([1975] 1995: 25). Foucault presents the

---

[7] For more on the relationship between Roth and Merleau-Ponty, see Trepanier (2023: 130–44).

body here as a writing surface (Grosz 1994: 117), a site used to mark, demarcate, and dominate citizens. Foucault's theory helps elucidate how the body operates as a space that identities are mapped onto; indeed, Elizabeth Grosz explains how bodies "are fictionalized, that is, positioned by various cultural narratives and discourses, which are themselves embodiments of culturally established canons, norms, and representational forms" (1994: 118).

The Jewish body has been a wellspring for both Jews and non-Jews in defining and establishing Jewish identities. A core text in Jewish studies, Sander Gilman's *The Jew's Body* (1991) explores how "certain myths reflect basic cultural and psychological ways of dealing with the difference of the Jews" (1991: 4). Gilman highlights how there are "'realities' of the Jewish body, such as the practice of infant male circumcision, which also become part of the social construction of the Jew's body within the mythopoesis of Western culture" (1991: 4). Jews have stereotypically been defined as "the People of the Book," yet, as Barbara Kirshenblatt-Gimblett has highlighted, there has been a corporeal turn in Jewish studies that has sought to stress the role of the body within the religion.[8] Howard Eilberg-Schwartz highlights how the stereotype of Jews as a "People of the Book" threatens to privilege "certain dimensions of Jewish experience at the expense of others" (1992a: 1). The collection of essays brings to focus the embodied existence of Jewish religious and secular cultures.

The body is a symbolically contested site used to define real and imaginary Jews. While Judaism's ritual of circumcision marks and defines the (male) body as Jewish, external forces also use the body as a means of conceptualizing the Jew as a figure of otherness. The Jew's corporeality is weaponized to racially, religiously, and biologically create a conceptual Jew that is fundamentally different. By doing so, racists create a prototypical Jew that serves to demonize and separate the Jews from non-Jews. The Jew is never static, though; anti-Jewish imaginations have constructed a myriad of contradictory Jewish phantoms that often reflect the political, cultural, and social anxieties and consternations of the given epoch.

The strategy of differentiation through the body became prevalent as ethnic nationalism developed within the modern era. Jon Stratton highlights how "the modern nation was considered to be made up of a single people, manifested in one culture, one language, and limited in membership to one race, identified

---

[8] See Kirshenblatt-Gimblett (2005: 447–61).

Introduction: The Word as Flesh 11

usually by colour and physiognomy" (2000: 119). Toward the end of the nineteenth century, Jews in Western Europe and America began to achieve equal rights.[9] The integrative process, born from the slow and tumultuous adoption of emancipation, enabled Jews to enter political and cultural areas from which they had historically been excluded. David Feldman emphasizes how in "western and central Europe Jews acquired, broadly speaking, the same political, civil and legal rights as other subjects and citizens" (1998: 172). Subsequently, Jews in Western Europe and America flourished as lawyers, scientists, journalists, artists, and as musicians. In other words, the emancipatory period brought about a newfound prosperity and cultural flourishment that saw an evolution in Jewish cultures and identities.[10]

Nevertheless, Jewish entry into Western society was perceived as threatening.[11] Jewish expansion into European culture and the secularization of Judaism meant Jewish "differences" were increasingly obscured. Zygmunt Bauman writes that "[m]oderntiy brought the levelling of differences—at least of their outward appearances ... Differences had to be created now, or retained against the awesome eroding power of social and legal equality and cross-cultural exchange" (1989: 58). The body was essential for the creation and maintenance of differences. As Jay Geller explains, "scientific disciplines endeavoured to administer the increasing overlap of the gender-differentiated bourgeois order and racially differentiated imperial order by affixing an identity to the body, especially to the body of those menacing others" (2007: 7). Modern antisemitism was a distinct form of anti-Jewish prejudice that sought to transfix Jewish difference as immutably biologic.

The term itself is a modern phenomenon, which Albert Lindemann defines as "a potent mixture of fantasy and reality, of crude caricatures of Jews constantly nourished by daily perceptions and often accurate portrayals of them" (1991: 11).

---

[9] Jacob Katz highlights how the "process of naturalization was interrupted and even reversed; rights that had been given to the Jews were limited or cancelled" (1980: 2). It is useful to note the political strife and varying degrees to which Jews were granted an emancipated status in society, oscillating according to their geopolitical positions.

[10] Yet as Calvin Goldscheider and Alan S. Zuckerman state, "modernization created new forms of Jewish cohesions as it destroyed old forms. In particular, the socioeconomic redistribution of Jews continued to distinguish them from non-Jewish and create conditions of ethnic solidarity" (1984: 80).

[11] Albert Lindemann explains that white Christian Europe's concern regarding the surge in Jewish involvement in Western Europe's culture and politics was because "Jews were in truth encroaching on arenas that had previously been exclusively Gentile, and Jews were helping to make life as those Gentiles had traditionally experienced it difficult or impossible" (1991: 12).

The Jewish body became an integral source for producing and maintaining a myriad of racist conceptions of Jewish differences that proved not only the Jew's inferiority but their foreignness. Jews could not belong to the nation because they were fundamentally (i.e., biologically) different.

The pseudoscientific markings of difference were structured around ideas that Jews were social degenerates, diseased, and deviant. In 1903, Otto Weininger published *Sex and Character* (1903), an enormously popular work of literature that proposed the human body was made up of male and female chemical elements. Weininger stated the masculine was responsible for morality, decisiveness, and complex thinking, while the feminine comprised passion and emotions. Subsequently, Weininger contends, "the woman of the highest standard is immeasurably beneath the man of the lowest" ([1903] 1906: 302). The Jew, Weininger argues, is "saturated with femininity to such an extent that the most manly Jew is more feminine than the least manly Aryan" (1903: 306). Weininger's text was enormously influential and was read by intellects and writers such as Sigmund Freud, James Joyce, and Gertrude Stein.[12] The book's scientific language meant *Sex and Character* was perceived as a legitimate text that was used to justify prejudices against Jews because Weininger's book proved they were an inferior race.

The use of scientific rhetoric to validate anti-Jewish ideologies was a common strategy in the modern period. Jean Martin-Charcot, a French neurologist considered to be one of the most significant researchers of hysteria, believed the Jew was susceptible to the condition because of their genetics; the Jew was feminine, therefore prone to hysteria.[13] Gilman highlights how "the etiology of the Jew's hysteria, like the hysteria of the woman, was to be sought in sexual excess" (1991: 76). The Jew's excessive desire linked to ancient stereotypes pertaining to Jewish avariciousness traceable to the medieval period. Gilman contends that "[t]he perversion of the Jew ... lies in his sexualized relationship to capital" (1991: 124). The Jew's relationship to money has been a wellspring of anti-Jewish stereotypes. William Shakespeare's Shylock in *The Merchant of Venice* is the most obvious example, as Jews have stereotypically been associated with moneylending. Recently, however, Julie L. Mell has contested the common historical narrative of the Jew-as-moneylender, stressing the ways in which this became a philosemitic narrative in the nineteenth and twentieth centuries as a way

---

[12] For more on Weininger and his influence, see Robertson (1998: 23–40).
[13] For more on Charcot, see Geller (2011: 233–56).

Introduction: The Word as Flesh 13

of responding to political antisemitism.[14] While the moneylender myth may be a "metanarrative" (Mell 2017: 6) within Jewish studies, the stigmatic associations that have linked Jews with money and power remain deeply embedded in antisemitic conceptualizations of Jews. The Jew-as-moneylender became a prominent stereotype following Thomas Aquinas's decree that Christians could not partake in usury. Subsequently, Jews became associated with the collection of loans, fueling racial stereotypes that the Jewish people, who famously rejected Christ as their savior, were immoral. As Gilman writes, "Jews, in taking money, treated money as if it were alive, as if it were a sexualized object. The Jew takes money as does the prostitute, as a substitute for higher values, for love and beauty. And thus the Jew becomes representative of the deviant genitalia, the genitalia not under the control of the moral, rational conscience" (1991: 124). The Jew comes to be defined as a figure of corruption whose ethics exist outside of the Christian doctrine and is thus deemed deviant. The connection between Jew and prostitute is unclear, but Mia Spiro usefully explains how both "Jews and prostitutes allowed men to imagine themselves, and their relationship to their property (including money and wives), as virtuous" (2012: 151). The Jew, in contrast, was greedy and selfish; the wealth they procured they kept for themselves, and this meant that the Jew was seen to be a social pariah who would not contribute to the wellbeing of Christian societies. "By extension ... Jews were depicted as 'polluting' art and culture because they challenged a social order based on the separation of beauty (static, contained) and desire (infinite, out of control)" (Spiro 2012: 151).

The same insidious logic influenced how Americans perceived their Jewish citizens. For example, in his travel book *The American Scene* (1905), Henry James expresses a deep anxiety regarding the mass-influx of Jewish immigrants present in New York. James observes that it "was as if we had been thus, in the crowded, hustled roadways, multiplication, multiplication of everything, was the dominant note, at the bottom of some vast sallow aquarium in which innumerable fish, of over-developed proboscis, were to bump together, for ever, amid heaped spoils of the sea" ([1907] 1987: 94). James strings together an impressive number of antisemitic stereotypes to bemoan the excessive and overwhelming presence of Jews in New York. James plays on the stereotype of

---

[14] William D. Rubinstein and Hilary L. Rubinstein define philosemitism as "support or admiration for the Jewish people by non-Jews, and which can reasonably be regarded as the reverse of antisemitism, hostility to or dislike of Jews" (1999: ix). This admiration is based on the same pernicious stereotyping of Jews found in antisemitic prejudices.

14 *Philip Roth and the Body*

the Jew's nose and greed for money, but most insidiously positions the Jew as a threat to America in their ceaseless multiplicities. As Larzer Ziff observes, the imagery used conveys "James's consciousness of the New York Jews as not just massed but proliferating uncontrollably. America is being drowned" (2000: 271).

The anxiety regarding Jewish presences in America's public spaces can be seen in terms of how higher educational institutions discriminated against Jews. In 1922, Harvard proclaimed there to be a "Jewish Problem" as 20 percent of their students were believed to be Jewish (Marcus 2008: 139). Consequently, Lisa Marcus writes, "the university instituted new admission criteria, including photographic identification (as Columbia had done) in order to stem the 'flood' of Jewish students" (2008: 139–40). The notion that Jews will "flood" America ties back to James's consternation regarding the seemingly out-of-control densities of Jewish populations in America's cities.

This porous influx of Jewish immigrants into America was also regarded as threatening to the nation's most beloved sport, baseball. In 1919, it was discovered that the World Series match between the Chicago White Sox and the Cincinnati Reds had been fixed, and the scandal involved the Jewish gangster Arnold Rothstein. Subsequently, Steven A. Riess writes, the scandal "provided fodder to Jew-haters like Henry Ford, who fanned the growing flames of anti-Semitism by blaming underworld Jews for the Black Sox scandal" (2002: 124). Henry Ford, founder of the Ford Motor Company, was a relentless antisemite and his newspaper, the *Dearborn Independent*, demonized Jewish bankers, lawyers, and public service workers. In *Henry Ford's War on Jews and the Legal Battle Against Hate Speech* (2012), Victoria Saker Woeste highlights how Ford's newspaper "carried on the ignoble tradition, developed in nineteenth century, of demonizing Jews in an effort to pressure the state to disavow its relationship with them" (2012: 50). Between 1919 and 1927 (when the paper was forced to close because of its anti-Jewish propaganda), Ford's readership had peaked at nearly seven hundred thousand readers (Woeste 2012: 3). His paper tirelessly promulgated the idea that the Jew was a devious degenerate.

Despite the Declaration of Independence's proclamation "all men are created equal," Jews, along with many other racial and ethnic minorities, faced social restrictions based on their religious and ethnic difference. Depending on the geopolitical space, Jews were barred from entering certain hotels, clubs, and even townships until the end of the Second World War. Christina Jarvis usefully connects America's antisemitism with American anti-Black discriminatory laws but notes that although anti-Jewish discriminations were "not nearly as pervasive

Introduction: The Word as Flesh

as the Jim Crow system of segregation against African-Americans, anti-Semitic policies positioned Jews as outsiders to American mainstream white culture" (2010: 137–8).[15]

Yet in the aftermath of the Second World War, anti-Jewish legal barriers were lifted, and Jews "reshaped their identities after World War II in a social milieu full of crosscurrents" (Brodkin 1998: 140). No longer delimited by quotas, Jews entered universities and businesses, blossoming into one of the "most affluent ethnoreligious group in the country" (Lipset & Raab 1995: 27). Consequently, this had a knock-on effect in terms of how Jews were identified within America. Joost Krinjen contends that there was a "[g]reater acceptance by American society and the simultaneous decline of anti-Semitism went hand in hand with increasing degrees of assimilation, accompanied by steeply rising rates of intermarriage" (2016: 87). Yet there were two particularly distinct developments in recent Jewish histories that ensured Jewish lives in America were, in some abstract sense, detached from the non-hyphenated "American" experience: the Holocaust, and the establishment of the state of Israel. As Karen Brodkin observes, "Jews could become Americans and Americans could be like Jews, but Israel and the Holocaust sets limits to assimilation" (1998: 140). Both the Holocaust and the establishment of the Jewish nation-state brought American Jewry's difference to the fore, reminding both non-Jewish and Jewish Americans that Jews possessed unique cultures, religions, and ethnic identities that set them apart from their white neighbors.

Jewishness retains, even in the most abstract way, a difference, an otherness. Indeed, this intangible Jewish difference became a source of anxiety for American Jews, which they came to articulate through artistic mediums (such as literature and film). Brodkin highlights how American Jews were wary about how white America would receive them, but also notes that Jews "were ambivalent about Jewishness itself, about being too Jewish" (1998: 139).

The fear of being "too Jewish" is a profoundly important anxiety that courses throughout the fiction of Roth. So many of his characters exhibit this exact concern that their Jewish difference becomes visible in America. As Gilman observes, the "Jew who sounds Jewish, for some American Jews, represents the hidden Jew within, the corrupt Jew of the gospel, the mark of difference which

---

[15] Likewise, Eric J. Sundquist highlights that although Jews faced "punitive immigration laws … anti-Semitism was [never] formalized as a practice of the state, even if it was sometimes expressed by government institutions and legal constraints" (2005: 20). Conversely, anti-Black racism was legally encoded in America's judicial system.

16 *Philip Roth and the Body*

offends even after the Jew is integrated into the mainstream of American culture" (1991: 28). The Jew's difference is identified through the body, meaning that the mark of Jewish difference cannot be transcended or escaped.

Yet Jewishness is not racial or biological; it is an identity that does not easily fit within the common rubrics used to define identities. As Laura Levitt points out, categories such as race, class, gender, sexuality, and religion fail to adequately encapsulate what it means to "claim a Jewish position" (Levitt 2007: 810). Jewishness is a symbolically unstable and slippery modality that lacks a distinguishable set of characteristics that enables Jewish difference to be clearly defined. Subsequently, Daniel Itzkovitz contends, "Jewish difference is a difference with no context, or more exactly, with a fluid and ever-shifting content that cannot mark Jewishness as distinct" (1997: 179).

In post–Second World War America, Jews became virtually indistinguishable from white Americans, but this sameness was threatening precisely because the lack of essential details distinguishing Jew from white Americans threatened the concept of national identity entirely. The tension created here becomes a vital focal point for Roth's novels, whose literature focuses on what Levitt terms as American Jewry's "complicated legacy of impossible assimilation" (2007: 808) that continues to revolve around the Jewish body.

Abjection, Antisemitism, and Roth

The above account has—I hope—illuminated the multifarious ways Jews have been perceived as threatening because of their alleged racial, ethnic, and gendered indistinctiveness. The conceptual Jew (in the context of post–Second World War America) signifies an inassimilable difference, a symbolically excessive figure, one whose entry into white American society blurs the borders used to establish racial divisions. Julia Kristeva's theory of abjection, outlined in her seminal work *Powers of Horror: An Essay on Abjection* (1982), has been an enormously useful tool I employ throughout this book in exploring antisemitic anxieties pertaining to Jewish difference, and Roth's literary response to such prejudice.

The abject is that which has been "ejected beyond the scope of the possible, the tolerable, the thinkable. It lies there, quite close, but cannot be assimilated. … The abject has only one quality of the object—that of being opposed to *I*" (Kristeva 1982: 1). Quite simply, abjection is the recognition of a threat to the subject's sense of self, resulting in the repulsion and expulsion of that deemed inassimilable. Eyo Ewara highlights how abjection "initially pertains to the relationship between the body of the child and the body of the mother from which it distances itself in becoming an individual but, even beyond this interpersonal sense of abjection, there is a wider, group-based, social sense of abjection" (2021: 33). Though my book begins by exploring the abjection of mothers, I am far more interested in the group-based abjection Awara highlights and the racial politic underpinning abjection. As Jennifer Purvis highlights, abjection "casts out from the ranks of public consideration the homeless, the fat, the infected, those with disabilities, sex workers and others deemed perverts or criminals, and the poor; it supports the construction and maintenance of national boundaries and identities … that may emanate from place of origin or social status" (2019: 52). The expulsion (literally and metaphorically) of the Jews across America and Europe has meant that there has been a repeated abjection of Jewry in the conceptualization of Jewish difference, one that has had violent and devastating consequences.[16]

Roth's fiction explores how the abject history of transatlantic Jewry seeps into the consciences of post–Second World War American Jewry; essential to this investigation, of course, is the body. As Yael Maurer notes, "Philip Roth's political imagination has long centered on the Jewish male body as a site of anxiety and possible liberation" (2017: 172). This notion of liberty, however, was predicated on an elision of Jewish difference, a collective surrendering to whiteness. Roth's short story, "Eli the Fanatic," exemplifies this concern well.

Set in the fictional suburb of Woodenton during the 1950s, "Eli the Fanatic" examines the ways in which American nouveau-riche Jews sublimated into whiteness by rejecting their "blackly" inflected Judaic past. Eli Peck is the protagonist of this parable-styled tale, who is set the task of closing a Yeshiva school that has established itself in the suburb. Eli finds himself embroiled in a battle of wills against the school's headmaster, Leo Tzuref, and his associate, known only as the Greenie, both of whom refuse to sublimate into America.

16 It is worth noting that Kristeva's use of the term "abject" follows from George Bataille, whose essay, "Abjection and Miserable Forms" explored the uprise of fascism and to counter "'sublimating' tendencies at work among the French cultural avant-garde" (Lotringer 2020: 33). Bataille notes how the "human abjection results from the material impossibility of avoiding contact with abject *things*: it is but the abjection of *things* passed on to those who are exposed to them" ([1934] 1999: 11). For Bataille, abjection is fundamentally tied to the establishment of authority, "a founding exclusion which constitutes a part of the population as moral outcasts" (Tyler 2013: 19). The Jews, of course, were determined as moral outcasts across much of Europe and America.

18 *Philip Roth and the Body*

Woodenton Jewry's anxiety is rooted in the fear of being recognized as Jewish rather than as white. As Victoria Aarons points out, the orthodox Jew's "presence in the town is a measure and felt reminder of what suburban Jews have feared all along: that they will never be accepted, never made members of the club, so to speak" (2000: 14). The body operates as a site for them to perform their adapted whiteness by dressing and appearing "American." In other words, they repress and reject anything they consider Jewish looking. Eli demands that the religious activities of the Yeshiva school remain confined to the Yeshiva grounds, and that the Yeshiva staff "are attired in clothing usually associated with American life in the 20th century" (EF 196). To this, Tzuref concisely replies, "[t]he suit the gentleman wears is all he's got" (EF 196). The suit becomes a metonym for Jewishness itself; the religious garbs symbolize a lost culture and heritage, precariously existing in a country where antisemitism remains committed to extinguishing Judaism's cultural heritage.

Through the character of Eli, Roth examines what happens to those American Jews who refuse to exist in this sublimated white suburbia: What becomes of the Jew who returns to Judaism in 1950s America? In the Rothian universe, they are committed to a mental asylum. The story dramatically unfurls when Eli, to appease both the suburban Jews and Tzuref, sends one of his green suits to the Greenie. Much to Woodenton Jewry's delight, he dons the uniform and strolls through the streets, but in exchange sends his orthodox garbs to Eli. "Inside the box was an eclipse" (EF 212), and this imagery signifies the obscuration of Eli's subjectivity; the division between himself and the Greenie is occulted in an almost mystical moment in which the two's bodies yoke together.

Eli's transformative return to Jewishness is symbolically realized when he puts on the Greenie's outfit. Eli lays the contents of the box onto the dining room table, noting how the jacket, trousers, and vest "smelled deeper than blackness" (EF 212). Seemingly overcome by the religious apparel he has been given, Eli dons the costume and heads to the hospital to be with his newly born son and feels "those black clothes as if they were the skin of his skin—the give and pull as they got used to where he bulged and buckled" (EF 217). Though Eli imagines the clothes to have synthesized with his flesh, the religious garbs remain separate from him. The clothes can be shed from Eli's body, which signifies a gap between Judaism's past and white American Jewry's suburban present. As Aarons points out, "[d]onning the clothes becomes an allegory for the impossibility of embracing the past in any simple or single way" (2000: 17). The spuriousness of Eli's embrace of the past is further complicated by his mental health: Eli has had two nervous breakdowns, and when he dons the Greenie's suit, his family and friends presume him to be having yet another mental collapse.

The story ends with Eli being castigated by the community, stripped of his clothing, and sedated by two interns in white suits (EF 220): "In a moment they tore off his jacket—it gave so easily, in one yank. Then a needle slid under his skin. The drug calmed his soul, but did not touch it down where the blackness had reached" (EF 221). Eli's jacket is torn from him in a flash, showing the abrupt easiness in which Jewish religious culture has been stripped and destroyed by white racism. Eli's religious turn is positioned by his family as a medical matter, meaning his agency and autonomy are manipulatively denied from him.

Judaism is transformed into the abject, the blackness signifying that which cannot be assimilated within the symbolic order. The needle's imprint on the skin establishes that which is abject; as Sara Ahmed explains, "it is through affective encounters that objects and others are seen as having attributes, or certain characteristics, a perception and reading that may give the subject an identity that seems apart from some others" (2005: 104). The mark signifies the border and boundary between Eli and the others, abjecting him into the other, the inassimilable Jew demarcated as insane. Yet Roth's final sentence stresses that Jewish difference—ethereal and murkily defined as a "blackness"—reflects how the abject lingers in the psyche. "It is the 'other' that comes from within (so it is part of ourselves) that we have to reject and expel in order to protect our boundaries. We are unable to rid of ourselves of it completely and it continues to haunt our being" (Arya 2016: 4). The Jewishness expelled by the suburban community of Woodenton remains, and this ghostly sense of haunting is a recurrent trope in Roth's fiction.

The above example demonstrates Roth's fascination with the racial politic underpinning the abjection of certain Jewish identities, but the author's excavation of the abject leans, too, on scatological imagery. According to Kristeva, corporeal waste, menstrual blood, and excrement represent the "objective frailty of symbolic order" (1982: 70); Menstrual blood is noted because it "represents the relationship between the sexes within a social aggregate" (1982: 71). As I hope to demonstrate, Roth's fiction abounds in the abject: menstrual blood, scat, and excrement are symbolically significant features of his work, exploding and unravelling the solidity of the self his male characters attempt to construct.

The scrambling of the self that plays out in Roth's fiction, vis-à-vis the transformation and collapse of the body, recalls Mikhail Bakhtin's theorem of the carnivalesque and the grotesque, as Susan Pickard explains: "the grotesque

20   *Philip Roth and the Body*

body is everything the modern ideal rejects: open, joined to other bodies and life stages in a unity of birth, life, and death (as opposed to separate, closed, and individualized)" (2021: 115). Such openness and porosity are either embraced or rejected by Roth's protagonists, but in *Patrimony: A True Story*, the novelist transforms the abject so that "rather than removal *from*, a *closeness to* is achieved" (Pickard 2021: 124, italics in original).

Roth's non-fictional account of his father's illness and passing features an especially poignant story that is well known to Roth scholars. Shortly after Herman reveals he has soiled himself ("'I beshat myself', he said" [*P* 120]), Roth sets out to clean his father's shit: "'It's like writing a book,' I thought—'I have no idea where to begin'" (*P* 122). Thereafter, Roth provides a deeply detailed and descriptive account of cleaning every crook and cranny of his father's waste, as he realizes "*that* was the patrimony. And not because cleaning it up was symbolic of something else but because it wasn't, because it was nothing less or more than the lived reality that it was" (*P* 123). The abject assumes the most significant symbolic role in the text: "There was my patrimony: not the money, not the tefillin, not the shaving mug, but the shit" (*P* 124). That which we expel, exclude, and eject becomes a symbolic site shared between father and son, one that bridges the gap between the two men.

Shit, piss, semen, and blood are all important symbols in Roth. By highlighting the ways in which the body operates as a signifier within Roth's writing, I weave several theoretical approaches together that orbit around the body and the abject. I focus on Roth's representation of Jewish mothers in Chapter 1 and the ways Roth depicts the Jewish mother's body. I look at *Portnoy's Complaint* and *The Anatomy Lesson*, stressing how Judaism's matrilineal tradition becomes emblematic of a Jewish gender and racial difference that is considered undesirable in post–Second World War American society. In Chapter 2, I examine Roth's representation of antisemitism and the way Jews internalize antisemitic conceptions of Jewish difference oriented around the body. I focus on *The Counterlife*, *Deception*, and *The Plot against America*, highlighting the way all three novels speak to one another in their portrayal of antisemitism, and consider to what extent Jews are made into abject figures. Chapter 3 returns to the American scene, focusing on the pastoral in both *Sabbath's Theater* and *American Pastoral*. In the former, I explore the role of the naked, abject body, while in the latter I explicate how Roth links the abject to women's bodies, and how the women in *American Pastoral* undermine the pastoral fantasy of its protagonist, Seymour "Swede" Levov. Finally, Chapter 4 analyzes the ways the Jewish body was constructed as "black" in Europe, and how this racial difference transnationally appeared in American antisemitism. By doing so I bring to focus the racial body politics of *The Human Stain* (2000), examining how the Jewish and Black body is racially codified in American society, and the racial abjection of African Americans.

Ultimately, the book explores how Roth's works are animated by an endless fascination by the abject. Roth transforms the body's ejaculations, excretions, secretions, and expulsions into symbolic tools that represent the porosity and fluidity of the Jewish self. By doing so, Roth undermines and deconstructs antisemitism's racist endeavors to create bodily distinctions between Jews and non-Jews. Roth weaponizes the corporeality of bodies to create a fiction that celebrates Jewish embodied presences in America and throws categories of identity into crisis.

1

Reading Roth's (M)Others

Maternal Matter

"But where, by the way, is the mother?" (*TF* 168)? Nathan Zuckerman asks this question of his author and creator toward the end of the spuriously titled *The Facts: A Novelist's Biography* (1988). What I ask in this chapter echoes and responds to Zuckerman's inquiry, tracing the ways in which Roth depicts Jewish mothers in *Portnoy's Complaint* and (1969) and *The Anatomy Lesson* (1983). My discussion of mothers invariably brings up fathers (Roth's families are always heterosexual), and by doing so, I examine how Roth satirizes and parodies antisemitic stereotypes surrounding Jewish gender roles. Roth's fiction subversively employs antisemitic stereotypes in his depiction of mothers and fathers as a way of highlighting the sexist imbalances of Jewish assimilation into American society.

I begin with a close reading of *The Facts* as a way of establishing how Roth's fiction has been influenced by psychoanalytic conceptualizations of mothers. My interest here is to focus on how the maternal characters of Roth's fiction are constructed as representative embodiments of Jewish gender and racial difference. Roth, I show, is attentive in how the matrilineal traditions of Judaism are rejected by his Jewish male protagonists in favor of the fantastical white American identity.

By examining Roth's portrayal of bodies in terms of Jewish difference, I consider to what extent he replicates, rather than subverts, sexist and racist stereotypes of Jews. Roth's attempt to satirize antisemitism risks reproducing, rather than undermining, certain facets of antisemitism, namely the exclusion and erasure of Jewish women. Antisemitism has frequently delineated Jewish

---

I would like to gratefully acknowledge the permission to reproduce in altered form portions of 'Jews that Matter: Philip Roth and the Body' published by Bloomsbury Academic in *The Bloomsbury Handbook to Philip Roth* (2024), edited by Aimee Pozorski and Maren Scheurer.

men as effeminate and "the collapse of Jewish masculinity into an abject femininity appears to 'disappear' Jewish women" (Pellegrini 1997: 51). Given Roth's willingness to satirize antisemitism, it is important to consider to what extent Roth "disappears" Jewish women from inhabiting a meaningful place within his literature. If the mother exists as a marginal but symbolically key figure in Roth's fiction, it is worth considering why, and what is at stake in the author's portrayal of Jewish mothers.

The Facts is a useful way of beginning this chapter's discussion of the Jewish mother because it features a poignant description in which Roth recalls his intimate and profound connection with his mother, Bess:

> the link to my father was never so voluptuously tangible as the colossal bond to my mother's flesh, whose metamorphosed incarnation was a sleek black sealskin coat in which I ... the pampered papoose, blissfully wormed myself whenever my father chauffeured us home to New Jersey ... the unnameable animal-me bearing her dead father's name, the protoplasm me, boy-baby, and body-burrower-in-training, joined by every nerve ending to her smile and her sealskin coat, while *his* resolute dutifulness, *his* relentless industriousness, *his* unreasoning obstinacy and harsh resentments, *his* illusions, *his* innocence, *his* allegiances, *his* fears were to constitute the original mold for the American, Jew, citizen, man, even for the writer, I would become. To be at all is to be her Philip, but in the embroilment with the buffeting world, my history still takes its spin from beginning as his Roth.
>
> (*TF* 18–19, emphasis added)

The physical bond to Bess is codified through the external object of the "sleek black sealskin coat" (*TF* 18) that paradoxically emphasizes a separation between mother and son. Philip suggests he is "joined by every nerve ending to her smile and her sealskin coat" (*TF* 18), but this conjoining is unsettled by the conjunction "and," as Roth reiterates that the bond to his mother is constructed through the coat. The mother's jacket represents a protective, warm, and insular space; it operates as an external, makeshift womb for the doting son. Nevertheless, the emphasis on the object displaces the unity the writer posits, as Philip's connection to his mother is only identifiable and expressed through two externalities: Bess's smile (a symbolically unstable and indeterminate pose), and a coat, the warmth of which covers, hides, and makes invisible the mother's body. Yet as Tony Fong points out, "Bessie's power over him is tangible and absolute: her body's plenitude asserts a protective presence over her young son" (2012: 66).

While the mother's relationship to the son is positioned as corporeally coalesced, the father is framed solely as a figure of externality. Philip claims to emerge from his mother as an "unnameable animal-me" (*TF* 18) in a pre-oedipal, pre-symbolic ecstasy of homogenized unity, and identifies the father's presence as a disruption between mother and son. The mother embodies an unblemished purity; the narrator is "her Philip" (named after *her* father). The forename precedes the father's surname, symbolically positioning the mother as prior-to the father. Herman, the figure of "history," marks him out as *his* Roth after Bess imprints or expels herself out/onto him. Herman marks himself upon "her Philip" with his dutifulness, industriousness, stubbornness, resentfulness, illusions, innocence, and allegiances. The seven iterations of the word "his" position Herman Roth as God in Genesis, molding Philip in his image through his seven idiosyncrasies.

Despite the protoplasmic connection Philip feels between himself and his mother, the patriarchal voice dominates and overwhelms the matriarchal body, diminishing Bess into a symbolic void, a mere coat. The lack of detail describing Bess's personality or character is stark when contrasted with the overwhelming figure of Philip's father, who assumes a biblical presence. As Nathan Zuckerman tells his creator, "aside from that sealskin coat, there is no mother ... the fact remains that your mother has no developed role in either your life or in your father's" (*TF* 168). Through Nathan, Roth self-deprecatingly addresses his text's failure to grant the mother a voice within the book, yet despite the mockery, the mother remains a mute figure of otherness.

Bess's absence from *The Facts* reflects how the mother is excluded from the symbolic order Roth identifies as his father's "spin" (*TF* 19). Roth's depiction of his severance from Bess seems to satirize (and reproduce) Sigmund Freud's Oedipal complex. Freud famously hypothesized that every young boy possessed sexual wishes for the mother and a desire to kill the rival father. "To punish the boy for these wishes ... he is threatened with castration, either by the father or by others invoking the father's name" (Stone 2016: 2–3). The mother must be abandoned so that the child can assume subjectivity. For Freud, the (female) mother represents the castrated body, meaning they cannot possess the phallus because they literally lack a penis. Thus, the mother occupies a paradoxical symbolic status within Freudian psychoanalysis: she is an object of desire and love but is simultaneously to be repudiated and rejected. For psychoanalyst and literary theorist Julia Kristeva, the mother's body must be spurned by the child so that they can assume their own identity. "For man and for woman, the loss of the mother is a biological and psychic necessity, the first step on the way to autonomy. Matricide is our vital necessity, the *sine qua non* of our individuation" (Kristeva 1989: 38). For the individual to become an autonomous subject, the mother must be figuratively murdered (i.e., excluded) from the symbolic order psychoanalysis has historically identified as belonging to the symbolic and literal father (i.e., the patriarch).

The mother's exclusion from the symbolic means she is denied or delimited a subjectivity. The mother is "the impossible subject caught in an ever increasing split between her idealization and her denigration ... The mother is part object and part subject, who stands as the gateway to sanity and becoming a mature adult, according to Western philosophical theory and psychoanalysis, or as the cause, the harbinger of her children's madness and even criminality" (Mayo & Moutsou 2017b: 7). The mother's indeterminacy stems from the maternal body, which the child recognizes as a pre-symbolic site in which subject (i.e., the child) and object (i.e., the mother's breast) are indistinguishable. The maternal body is always positioned as an object that is relational to the child; the mother lacks a subjective presence. This relationality is, as Marianne Hirsch has highlighted in *The Mother/Daughter Plot* (1989), a fundamental component of psychoanalytic theories (1989: 167). The mother, Hirsch contends, only exists "in relation to her child, never as a subject in her own right. And in her maternal function, she remains an object, always distanced, always idealized or denigrated, always mystified ... through the small child's point of view" (1989: 167).

The mother is cast out, transformed into the abject. According to Kristeva, "the maternal body is the place of a splitting" (1980: 238), and the disruption of the subject's unitary solidity is perceived as threatening precisely because it disturbs the illusion of symbolic cohesion. Rachel Sharpe and Sophie Sexon contend that the mother's "reproductive capacity produces substance that bring the internal to the external; birthing, bleeding and breastfeeding. In socio-cultural terms, these traits cast the mother figure as an abject monster: that which dissolves the borders between the flesh and the world" (2018: 3). Though the maternal body itself is not abject, its propensity for symbolically and literally rupturing is threatening because it unsettles the notion of subjective unity. Hence the necessity of the child's rejection of the mother's body. As Christine Bousfield observes, the abject "is impossible to bring into the Symbolic ... because it is the 'precondition' of that order. In identifying with the place of the father, we abject the function of the mother or place of the mother, strictly the mother's body" (2000: 330).

The mother's body repulses and repels because it signifies the symbolic breakdown of the subject's individuation; it represents bodily dissolution. Paradoxically, the maternal body "shapes the body into a *territory* having areas, orifices, points and lines, surfaces and hollows, where the archaic power of mastery and neglect, of this differentiation of proper-clean and improper-dirty, possible and impossible, is impressed and exerted" (Kristeva 1982: 72, italics in original). Judaism is a matrilineal religion; the Jewish mother's body literally shapes the subject into a Jewish territory.

Within Roth's fiction, the mother embodies Jewish heredity, and her body represents an overflowing, boundaryless "site" that threatens Roth's protagonists' efforts to establish themselves as "Americans." Roth's mother represents what Zygmunt Bauman terms as the "conceptual Jew ... a semantically overloaded entity, comprising and blending meanings which ought to be kept apart" (1989: 39). Both Alexander Portnoy and Nathan Zuckerman seek to purify themselves by rejecting the mother (and, thus, Jewishness) as an abjection.

The Unforgettable

Portnoy's Complaint is a sticky affair: it abounds in body fluids, insidious male desire, and fantasies of bodily transformation. It is also a novel about mothers—specifically, Jewish mothers. The book's epigraph contains a fictionalized clinical definition of "Portnoy's Complaint" as a "disorder in which strongly-felt ethical and altruistic impulses are perpetually warring with extreme sexual longings, often of a perverse nature" (*PC* n.p.). According to Dr. Spielvogel, the psychoanalyst in Roth's book, "many of the symptoms can be traced to the bonds obtaining in the mother-child relationship" (*PC* n.p.). Alex Portnoy vents about his overbearing mother, supposedly weak father, and tumultuous relationships with non-Jewish women. As David Brauner has argued, "*Portnoy's Complaint* is not simply a prolonged dirty joke, but rather a comic rebuttal of psychoanalysis and a Freudian analysis of its own comic strategies" (2007: 64). Developing from Brauner, I consider to what extent Roth replicates, rather than rebuts, psychoanalysis's tendency to objectify the mother as an object of the subject's desire. For Alex, Sophie Portnoy (his mother) represents a Jewish past that is inescapable and ties him to a racial and gendered otherness that prohibits him from realizing his fantasy of becoming a non-hyphenated American.

The importance of Sophie, a key figure in this psychoanalytic send-up and *Portnoy*'s mother figure, has been well documented in Roth scholarship. Olga Karasik-Updike has recently highlighted how Sophie Portnoy embodies Judaism and its dietary laws. Elsewhere, Melvin Friedman argues that the mother-son confrontation serves as the text's thematic kernel (1973: 171), while Shaun

28   Philip Roth and the Body

Clarkson identifies the ways in which Sophie controls and regulates her son's diet, and how this comes to influence the ways in which Alex perceives women. Cultural anthropologist Joyce Antler highlights the ways in which *Portnoy's Complaint* defined and influenced societal conceptions of Jewish mothers. Antler, for example, laments Roth's novel for its "misogynist message that coded unacceptable behavior as female rather than Jewish," arguing that "Roth ... projected onto the Jewish mother the negative features of 'Otherness'—Old World backwardness, loudness, vulgarity, clannishness, ignorance, and materialism" (2007: 143). Though Antler conflates author with narrator here, the analysis is otherwise sound: Portnoy sees in his mother a degenerate form of Jewishness that subverts gender norms, and thus threatens his fantasy of becoming an American by confining him to Judaism, which he views as inherently un-American. I build on and deviate from Antler by considering the corporeality of the mother in Roth's prose, zooming in on how the novelist entwines the abject and Jewishness and what such braiding reveals about how Jewish motherhood has been conceived of in terms of race and gender.

Sophie threatens Alex because she lacks a stable identity the narrator connects to her bodily excess. Sophie is described and remembered by Alex, meaning the mother's lack of symbolic cohesiveness stems from the fact that she exists as an infinity within his psyche. The novel's first chapter is entitled "THE MOST UNFORGETTABLE CHARACTER I'VE EVER MET" and begins with Alex Portnoy recalling his childhood impressions of his indomitable mother. Sophie Portnoy, Alex tells Dr. Spievogel, "is so deeply imbedded in my consciousness that for the first year of school I seem to have believed that each of my teachers was my mother in disguise" (*PC* 3). Alex identifies Sophie as a figure of excess, meaning that she lacks a stable identity within the narrative, spilling out into every facet of his life. He seeks to expose his mother's supernatural capabilities but notes how "it was always a relief not to have caught her between incarnations" (*PC* 3). Alex fears he "might have to be done away with were I to catch sight of her flying in from school through the bedroom window, or make herself emerge, limb by limb, out of an invisible state and into her apron" (*PC* 3–4). The mother has no inherent stable body, but tellingly enters the symbolic order through the apron. Alex's mother is hyper-visible but paradoxically invisible, present yet absent, human but inhuman. Sophie represents a limitlessness that Alex identifies as fatal to his subjectivity. The mother's formless body is central to Alex's childhood anxieties, as Sophie's physical lack within the material world is counteracted by her paranormal excess Alex connects with their Jewish heredity.

While the mother is pitted as a figure of excess, the Jewish father is a symbol of masculine lack. For Roth's narrator, Judaism represents a distortion of sexual and gendered norms that harks back to antisemitic conceptions of Jewish bodily differences. As I discussed in the Introduction, Jewish men were alleged to be endowed with an excessive femininity. Roth satirically subverts this stereotype through his character, Alex, and his recollection of his parents. For Roth's narrator, Judaism represents a distortion of sexual and gendered norms. Alex laments his parents for the "mix-up of sexes in our house!" (*PC* 4), identifying his father, Jack, as the symbolic unmanly Jew. Jack's unmanliness is exemplified by his un-American behavior, which Alex connects with his Jewishness. For example, Alex tells Spielvogel how his father drinks mineral oil and magnesia, "not *whiskey like a goy*" (*PC* 4), stressing how "[h]e suffered ... from his constipation ... my father reading the evening paper with a suppository up his ass" (*PC* 4–5, italics in original). Alcohol, specifically whiskey, is identified reverently with the mythical gentiles, while Jack drinks unmanly medicines and sticks suppositories up his rectum.

Alex notes how his father is constantly constipated, equating him with a bunged-up suffering that links to stereotypes of Jews as victims, which Alex associates with effeminacy, weakness, and un-Americanness. Alex decries Judaism's history of persecution that he laments as feminine: "Jew Jew Jew Jew Jew Jew! It is coming out of my ears already, the saga of the suffering of the Jews! Do me a favor, and stick your suffering heritage up your suffering ass—*I happen also to be a human being!*" (*PC* 76, italics in original). The six iterations of the word "Jew" evoke the haunting memory of the Holocaust and the six million Jews who died. Alex contemptuously identifies Jewishness with victimhood and suffering, two nouns he denigrates as unmanly and un-American. According to Peter Novick, the image of the Holocaust victim "evoked at best the sort of pity mixed with contempt. It was a label actively shunned. The self-reliant cowboy and the victorious war hero were approved (masculine) ideals" (1999: 121). Novick's last sentence underpins the gendered body politic underpinning Alex's anxiety surrounding the suffering he associates with Jewishness, which centers on his father's phallic lack.[1]

---

[1] Prior to the trial of Adolf Eichmann and the publication of Elie Wiesel's *Night* (1960), Holocaust victims were not given any public platform to speak of their experiences. During the 1940s and 1950s, Alvin Rosenfeld writes, "little public attention was paid in [America] to those people who had managed to survive the Nazi assault against European Jewry" (1997: 136).

Jack, like the victims of the Holocaust, is incapable of asserting himself like the American self-reliant cowboy or victorious war hero. As Clarkson points out, Jack cannot "exercise any control over his family, becoming an absence in the house" (2014: 23–4). The father's inability to shit symbolizes his phallic lack; instead, Alex's father is the one who is penetrated vis-à-vis his suppository, and when Alex rages against the Jews and their suffering, he suggests here that Jewishness is a kind of queerness.[2] Therefore, Alex degrades his father's need of a suppository and identity as a Jew because both represent an effeminacy that negates the phallic penetration the patriarchy is supposed to possess.

Jack's inability to release himself on the toilet plays out elsewhere. For example, when Jack takes Alex to play baseball, he exhibits an unfamiliarity with the bat, reflecting his inability to perform as a patriarch:

> "Okay, Big Shot Ballplayer," he says and grasps my new regulation bat somewhere near the middle—and to my astonishment, with his left hand where his right should be. I am suddenly overcome with sadness: I want to tell him, *Hey, your hands are wrong*, but am unable to, for fear I might begin to cry—or he might!
>
> (*PC* 11, italics in original)

The capitalization of "Big Shot Ballplayer" stresses the incongruity between the voice uttering the expression and the speech expressed, highlighting Jack's lack of familiarity with American idioms. Alex's desire to correct his father's handling of the phallic-shaped bat represents a reversal of the father-son family role. In having to educate Jack on how to hold the American baseball bat, Alex mourns the patriarchal absence in his life. The improper body position Jack adopts reveals the father's physical inadequacy in the eyes of the son, as though Jack was incapable of correctly holding or controlling his own penis. Warren Rosenberg explains that Jack "cannot be an *American* hero for his son, give that he's a failure in business, a failure in learning and imagination, and, perhaps most damning for an American boy, totally inept at baseball" (2001: 192, italics in original). The fear of crying further reveals Alex's desire to maintain proper gender divisions; men, in his view, should not cry. The crying man signifies weakness, which is far removed from the idolized self-reliant cowboy Novick identified as so distinct from the victim

---

[2] Harry Brod claims, "[w]hen Jewish men are viewed as powerless, as victims, they are seen as effeminate in our culture. And effeminacy here signals homosexuality" (1996: 150). Though Brod's claim surrounding "our culture" is ambiguous, Brod supports my argument surrounding the ways victimhood was equated with unmanliness.

of the Holocaust. In other words, the cowboy signifies a desirable American masculinity, whilst Jewishness is associatted with effeminacy and weakness.

The interactions between Alex and Jack parody Sigmund Freud's reflections of his father in *The Interpretation of Dreams* ([1899] 1997). Alex sees Jack as a failure because he is not like the American sportsmen he admires, as Roth illuminates in the passage below: "'Come on, Big Shot, throw the ball,' he calls, and so I do—and of course discover that on top of all the other things I am just beginning to suspect about my father, he isn't 'King Kong' Charlie Keller either" (*PC* 11). The scene parallels Sigmund Freud's reflections on his father's failures. In *The Interpretation of Dreams*, Freud's father, Jakob, recalls a moment where a Christian accosted him on the streets, knocking his kippah from his head. Jakob picks up his kippah and carries on walking, which strikes Freud as unheroic conduct on the part of the big, strong man who was holding the little boy by the hand ([1899] 1997: 97). Freud ends this anecdote by contrasting Jakob's actions with the general Hamilcar Barca, observing that "[e]ver since then Hannibal has had a place in my phantasies" ([1899] 1997: 98). Both Freud and Portnoy lament their father's unheroic conduct: Freud's father does not confront or defend himself when faced with antisemitism, while Alex's father cannot engage in American sports. Disillusioned by his father's actions, Freud "turned instead to a Hannibal, to a tough Jewish fantasy" (Breines 1990: 29). Likewise, Alex turns to Charlie Keller, a famous American baseball player, retreating to a tough Jewish fantasy of America centered on a supposed restored gendered norm where men and women behave according to the gendered binary Alex romanticizes.

If Alex's father fails to live up to the masculine myth Roth's narrator fetishizes, Sophie Portnoy is threatening precisely because she is too masculine. Sophie is boundless: she can "accomplish anything" (*PC* 11). Alex's mother possesses an uncanny ability to predict the weather ("[w]hat a radar on that woman!" [*PC* 11]), and Sophie is like a "hawk" when monitoring the butcher to ensure their meat remained kosher (*PC* 11). Alex describes, at length, the invasive medical procedures his mother would administer to keep him healthy:

> For mistakes she checked my sums; for holes, my socks; for dirty, my nails, my neck, every seam and crease of my body ... A medical procedure like this (crackpot though it may be) takes time, of course; it takes effort, to be sure—but where health and cleanliness are concerned, germs and bodily secretions, she will not spare herself and sacrifice others.
>
> (*PC* 12)

For Sophie, keeping Alex clean and healthy is synonymous with keeping him Jewish, as she regulates his ingestions and expulsions to ensure he remains kosher. Alex's resistance to his mother's panoptic domination over his body is reflected in his language: the word "my" is repeated five times, stressing Alex's intention to claim ownership of his own body. Yet Sophie repeatedly lurks over his every move, operating with surgeon-like precision to inspect Alex's body.

Alex rebels against his mother's cleanliness by consuming non-kosher meats such as French-fries and hamburgers. When she discovers her son's betrayal, Sophie chastises him, uttering the word "hamburgers" as bitterly "as she might say *Hitler*" (*PC* 33, italics in original). The allusion to the Nazi leader stresses the hyperbolic severity of the situation for Sophie: her son's consumption of American fast food represents the cultural death of Judaic traditions, signifying the realization of Hitler's "Final Solution." Although Sophie's hysterical outburst is absurd, Brett Ashley Kaplan points out that the reference to Hitler reveals "the proximity of the Holocaust to the consciousness of these characters" (2015: 29–30).

Yet the immediacy of the Shoah is simultaneously marked by its distance from American Jewry's experiences, a distance made more apparent by the literature published during the 1960s and the testimonies given during the Eichmann trial. For America's Jews, the Holocaust could only be consumed through literature, television, film, or art, marking a very significant gap between their European counterparts whose suffering had been commodified into a media production. The Jewish survivor of the Holocaust became an iconic symbol, the ultimate figurehead of victimhood whose varied experiences of trauma overwhelmed America's imaginations. Arthur Hertzberg claims that "the underlying message that Jews were getting from what came to be called the 'Holocaust industry' or 'Shoah business' was that Jewish identity involved suffering" (1997: 382). As discussed earlier, Alex internalizes the synthesis between Jewishness and victimhood, but does not valorize or glamorize their collective suffering. Sophie's hysteria and obsessiveness, combined with his father's physical weakness, represent a Jewish identity that Alex identifies with suffering, which represents a racial otherness and an abject femininity. Alex begs Dr. Speilvogel to "[b]less me with manhood! Make me brave! Make me strong! Make me *whole!*" (*PC* 36-7, italics in original). Bravery, strength, and an ability to penetrate exemplify an American masculinity Alex craves. As Debra Shostak observes, "[t]he goy is manly, consuming, and acting; fearing to act or consume, the Jew is morbid, hysterical, and weak" (2004: 116).

Alex attempts to become "whole" by violating his family's kosher diet, but also uses sex as a means of trying to claim this mythic masculine identity. After being confronted with the Hitlerian hamburger, Alex bolts to the bathroom: "I tear off my pants, furiously I grab that battered battering ram to freedom, my adolescent cock, even as my mother begins to call from the other side of the bathroom door. 'Now this time don't flush. Do you hear me, Alex? I have to see what's in that bowl!'" (*PC* 33). Alex's rage is comic but violent. The words "tear," "furiously," and "battered" express an uncontrollable anger directed at his mother, whom Alex identifies as a barrier prohibiting him from freedom. Alex seeks to reverse Walt Whitman's famous proclamation: "unscrew the locks from the doors! unscrew the doors themselves from their jambs!" ([1855] 2009: 54). For Alex, freedom means keeping the doors screwed in their jambs and the locks secured. Within the solitary confinement of the bathroom, Alex can do what his father cannot: excrete himself—or, to invert yet another Whitman line, celebrate himself ([1855] 2009: 23).

Alex masturbates to re-enforce the borders his mother seeks to violate; that is, by taking hold of his penis and locking out the overbearing feminine figure, Alex seeks to maintain a gendered separateness inherently tied to the negation of his Jewish identity. Alex's semen assumes a symbolically significant role for the disobedient son. As Elizabeth Grosz explains, "[s]eminal fluid is understood primarily as what it makes, what it achieves, a causal agent and thus a thing, a solid: its fluidity, its potential seepage ... is perpetually displaced in discourse onto its properties, its capacity to fertilize, to father, to produce an object" (1994: 199). For Alex, semen represents a solidity that affirms his masculinity, reifying his place within the symbolic order as a man. Ironically, however, Alex's excessive masturbatory sessions replicate another antisemitic myth: the sexually hysterical Jew. In other words, Alex's efforts to separate himself from his Jewish family, whom he laments for confusing gender roles, replicate antisemitic conceptualizations of the male Jew as an overflowing "woman." Furthermore, Sophie's call from outside the bathroom door reminds Alex his body remains bound to a Jewishness symbolized by both his own circumcised penis and his mother's loud, excessive voice.

Scholars such as Dean Franco have read Alex as a defiler of Sophie's ordered cleanliness. Franco describes Sophie as a mother "obsessed with purity and cleanliness, while Portnoy is committed to a defilement, a dialectic internalized and performed in Portnoy's adult social and professional life as well" (2009: 91). This may be accurate, but Alex's defilement also centers on his desire to reinstate and reinscribe gender norms he perceives his parents' Judaism to have exceeded and scrambled. Alex's quest is centered against not only purification but also a masculinist mythology that reinstates self/other binaries and reinforces gender norms. In other words, Alex wants to purify himself of his mother's Judaic rituals and culture.

Sophie threatens Alex's sense of masculinity through her invasiveness. In one of the novel's most iconic scenes, she stands over her son with a breadknife to ensure he eats all his dinner. She asks: "Which do I want to be, weak, or strong, a man or a mouse?" (*PC* 16). Manliness is inherently tied to strength, while the mouse represents weakness, inhumanness, and an animalistic otherness. Shostak points out that for Sophie, "the man/mouse choice exists wholly within the frame of Jewish manhood ... [but] for Alex ... the goy is the man and the Jew is the mouse, where 'Jew' comes to stand for the forces of repression and renunciation" (2004: 86). Sophie's question thus threatens Alex with emasculation that equates Jewishness to abjection. Sophie unknowingly reinforces Alex's internalization of antisemitism: if Alex refuses to eat his meals, he risks becoming the weak, inhuman, and verminous "Jew" Nazi Germany envisaged.

While Alex's ingestions and secretions are the focal point of Roth's novel, there are two episodes in which the Jewish mother's body dominates the text and represents what Kristeva defines as the abject. The first of these scenes occurs in the toilet, an important arena within *Portnoy's Complaint*; it is a site in which the male characters struggle with their masculinities through their bodily expulsions and/or secretions and has received much critical attention in terms of Roth's exploration of Alex's masculinity. I wish here to turn our focus to Roth's portrayal of Sophie's menstruating body and how Alex fears menstruation as a symbol of feminine difference. Alex recalls an incident wherein Sophie frantically calls for her son's help, demanding he run to the drugstore and buy her sanitary products. Returning home, Alex "[b]reathlessly handed the box to the white fingers that extended themselves at me through a narrow crack in the bathroom door ..." (*PC* 43). Alex's panting may well reflect his fatigue at having to run to aid his mother, but it could equally reflect his feelings of anxiety and dread at the possibility of glimpsing his mother's bleeding body. The closed bathroom door once again serves to separate the bodies of mother and son, but the small rupture represents a fragility in the edifice of the framework that threatens to collapse the boundary between Alex and Sophie. The fingers, separately demarcated from the hand, torso, or body itself, are defined as white. The joints' skeletal coloring seems to represent the threat of death itself. If so, does Sophie's menstruating body represent a fatality to Alex's conception of himself as a man? Alex's anxiety is most aptly symbolized in the final moment of the passage, ending in an ellipsis. This suspension point signals an omission or a rupture from speech or language, an unspeakable thought or fear that words cannot articulate.

The ellipsis used here represents Julia Kristeva's abject, as Sophie's menstruating body "disturbs identity, system, order" (Kristeva 1982: 2). The ellipsis signifies the very breakdown of language; confronted by the mother's porous, flowing body, the symbolic order through which Alex constructs himself and his mother fails him. For the briefest of moments, Alex is silenced. Though the color white is referred to here, there is no mention of blood or redness. The mother's body is made invisible, erased from language. The door remains closed, as it were. As Imogen Tyler writes, "when the maternal is no longer recognizable as a body and thus as a subject … it/she becomes abject" (2009: 86). For Alex, menstruation represents a gendered difference that must be excluded.

Sophie's expulsions represent a danger to Alex. Kristeva writes, "[e]xcrements and its equivalents (decay, infection, disease, corpse, etc.) stand for the danger to identity that comes from without: the ego threatened by the non-ego, society threatened by its outside, life by death" (1982: 71). Alex is confronted by his mother's menstrual blood, that which very obviously signifies a feminine outside, and one that is fundamentally tied to the maternal body. Alex's anxiety regarding his mother's menstruations leads him to believe that Sophie should have bled out rather than ask her son for help:

> Better she should have bled herself out on our cold bathroom floor, better *that*, than to have sent an eleven-year-old boy in hot pursuit of sanitary napkins! Where was my sister, for Christ's sake? Where was her own emergency supply? Why was this woman so grossly insensitive to the vulnerability of her own little boy—on the one hand so insensitive to my shame, and yet on the other, so attuned to my deepest desires!
>
> (*PC* 44)

In asking where his sister is, Alex seeks to maintain and preserve sexual binaries through gendered roles; the young man should not be charged with buying goods solely meant for the female body, as such an act threatens Alex's "vulnerable" masculinity. Thus, the menstrual blood exuding from his mother signifies the death of the masculine self. Christine Bousfield writes that the abject is "located wherever there is ambivalence, ambiguity, the improper

36   *Philip Roth and the Body*

or the unclean, the overflowing of boundaries, fusion and confusion" (2000: 331). Sophie's menstrual breakdown signifies a bodily overflow that distorts the gap between the masculine and feminine, as the boundary between mother and son threateningly appears to be in jeopardy of being breached. Alex's narcissism dismisses the mother as a subject: Sophie's body, in its most vulnerable, bare, and human form, is almost made visible to Alex, distorting his entire production of Sophie-as-monster while simultaneously threatening to rupture his masculinist efforts to maintain this fatuitous division between the masculine and feminine.

Yet Alex's final reflection that his mother is attuned to his deepest desires parodically returns to Sigmund Freud's Oedipal complex. After detailing his mother's menstrual sufferings, Portnoy recalls a moment in which "I am so small I hardly know what sex I am" (*PC* 44). This proclamation serves to make central the carnal uncertainties of Roth's narrator, immediately highlighting the ways in which Sophie influences the young boy's sexual self. Basking in the attention of his adoring mother, Alex is "absolutely punchy with delight" as she asks, "[W]ho does Mommy love more than anything in the whole wide world?" (*PC* 45). The narrator is aware his mother "sleeps with a man who lives with us at night and on Sunday afternoons. My father they say he is" (*PC* 45). Alex's father is deferred to with little affection, as he describes how "[t]his man, my father, is off somewhere making money, as best he is able. These two are gone [Alex's father and sister], and who knows, maybe I'll be lucky, maybe they'll never come back" (*PC* 44). Alex's desire for his mother combined with Sophie's flirtatious responses to her son's affections threaten the gendered and familial divisions between mother and son. Roth parodies Freud's famous argument that the son "regards his father as a rival in love" (*PC* 217) for the mother but uses the Oedipal complex to underscore the racial and gendered uncertainties of Jewish identity in postwar America.

Alex perceives Sophie to be overwhelming because of her feminine excessiveness that exceeds and disrupts the gendered borders Roth's narrator fetishizes; this gendered excess closely interlinks with Jewishness. As I discussed in the Introduction, Jewishness was conceptualized as excessive, eluding and or disrupting categories such as religion and race, and Roth's psychoanalytic narrative undoubtedly leans on this stereotype. The book's protagonist and of all its characters are cartoonish exaggerations. Marie Syrkin laments that for "all the broad caricature and abundant visual realism, Portnoy never becomes a human being" (1980: 334). While Alex's inhumanness affronts Syrkin, I find

Sophie Portnoy's representation to be the most problematic element of the text, and Alex's inhumanity a brilliantly effective satire of antisemitism.

Portnoy's Complaint also satirizes Freud's psychoanalysis, and by doing so, Roth hollows out Freud's Oedipal complex into farce. Sophie greets her son on the phone by describing him as "my lover" (*PC* 97), and when the four-year-old Alex is caught admiring his mother's body, Sophie invites him to touch her: "'Feel.' '*What?*'—even as she takes my hand in hers and draws her body—'Mother—' 'I haven't gained five pounds,' she says, 'since you were born. Feel,' she says, and holds my *stiff* fingers against the swell of her hips, which aren't bad ..." (*PC* 46, emphasis my own). The invitation to fondle his mother's body instigates a shock, signified by the dashes, that disturbs the familial relationship between mother and son. Alex attempts to maintain boundaries by iterating the title "Mother" (*PC* 46), seeking to resituate her within a recognizable and familiar position. Yet when she allows him to further explore her body, Alex's fingers are described as "stiff" (*PC* 46), comically hinting at the young boy's erection. Freud's essay "Medusa's Head" is useful here, as the psychoanalyst highlights the ways in which Medusa's head becomes a kind of castration complex. Yet as Freud notes, "becoming stiff means an erection" (1953a: 273), and for Alex, his stiff fingers amplify the sexual imagery Freud's reading of the Medusa head articulates. Sophie's body—like Medusa's head—possesses a transgressive, sexual potentiality that literally and symbolically makes Alex freeze.

Roth explores his protagonist's struggle to maintain the division between man and woman through the mother-son relationship. As Alex learns to separate himself from his mother, he becomes disgusted by Sophie's behavior. Alex complains that after twenty-five years, his mother "still hitches up the stockings ins front of her little boy," pondering whether or not his father would act if "there in the living room their grown-up little boy were to tumble all at once onto the rug with his mommy, what would Daddy do? ... Would he draw *his* knife—or would he go off to the other room and watch television until they were finished?" (*PC* 46, italics in original). The uncertainty aroused by the potential act of incest now enrages and disturbs Alex. In considering what his father would do in the event of the mother and son actualizing their strange sexual parlor game, Alex wishes his father would reinforce his phallic and patriarchal power over the mother. His desire for Jack to unsheathe his italicized knife stresses Alex's desperation to restore a patriarchal and masculinist order, wherein the mother's physical body is made proper through a potentially violent penetrative act. Yet the dash and subsequent consideration of Jack departing should such an act of incest occur reaffirms the masculine absence Alex sees in his father; Jack's lack of masculinity is once again overcompensated by the voraciousness of the Jewish mother.

In satirizing Freud's Oedipal complex, Roth's novel undermines and deconstructs the psychoanalytical framework that conceived of a very bodily and sexual divide between man and woman. Roth invalidates the Freudian projection of the mother as an object of desire and repulsion by highlighting the performative ways gender and "race" are constructed. Through satire, Roth enlarges and re-enacts the castration and Oedipal complex to demean the Freudian therapy model. By doing so, Roth highlights the ways in which psychoanalysis serves to perpetuate patriarchal misogyny that others the mother into an objectified body.

Yet *Portnoy's Complaint* is limited by its satire. Roth's parody reproduces Freud's own failures in his production of the maternal figure as a Jewish literary topic. Sophie's anxieties over her son's physical and spiritual well-being seem to be intimately concerned with the Holocaust and the loss of Jewish religious and ethnic culture. Yet her consternations are brushed off by the repulsive narrator as mere by-products of her monstrousness. In failing to provide a view of Sophie which extends beyond Alex's perspective, the novel ensures the Jewish mother remains as a dehumanized object, a monster of Jewish and thus racial otherness that is endless and inescapable. In sum, *Portnoy's Complaint* fails to find a way in which the mother can speak or take up a subject position; Roth cannot envisage a way in which the mother can be symbolized beyond abjection.

"A breast, then a lap, then a fading voice"

Nathan Zuckerman and Alexander Portnoy both harbor fantasies of self-renewal that orbit around the escape and/or repudiation of the mother. The "Zuckerman Bound" trilogy is primarily concerned with the newfound celebrity status enjoyed/endured by Roth's oft-used narrator, Nathan Zuckerman, and the familial strife his novel-writing induces. *The Ghost Writer*, Roth's opening novel in this triptych, introduces us to the central consternation driving the novel(s): the visibility of Jewish difference in American society post-Second World War. Nathan writes a story based on a "real-life" familial dispute over money, which his father protests because it apparently affirms antisemitic stereotypes that

Jews are avaricious: "your story, as far as Gentiles are concerned, is about one thing and one thing only. ... It is about kikes. Kikes and their love of money" (*GW* 68). As the word "kike" implies, Zuckerman's father's consternation is rooted in antisemitic conceptualities of Jewishness steeped in ancient, hateful libels. Nathan's father enlists the help of Judge Wapter to make his son see the perilousness of his fictive enterprises: "Why in a story with a Jewish background must there be (a) adultery; (b) incessant fighting within a family over money; (c) warped human behavior in general?" (*GW* 74). Wapter's concern surrounding the manner Zuckerman's stories portray Jews implies his fiction should seek to construct them in a more positive manner; Jews, Wapter would have it, should be portrayed as loyal, familial, and moral, in case the imagined non-Jewish reader's rabid Judeophobia is affirmed!

The fear of antisemitism expressed in *The Ghost Writer* is steeped in a combination of post-Shoah anxieties and postwar cultural blossoming for American Jewry. As such, Wapter and Zuckerman's father seek in their son's fictive productions a Jewishness that is agreeable, and thus wish to expel and/ or erase the dirty impurities of Jewish life from the non-Jews' gaze. Nathan sees his father and Wapter as Jews guilty of whitewashing, and points to the recent Broadway production of Anne Frank's diary as evidence of American-Jewry's efforts to sanitize their Jewish identities. Indeed, his mother—in a bid to appease both parties—asks Nathan to tell their father he saw the play, but he drolly replies: "I will not prate in platitudes to please the adults!" (*GW* 78).

The Ghost Writer's reference to Anne Frank's diary is an important thematic concern for Roth, as it represented a sanitized Jewishness the likes of Wapter and Nathan's father would (and do) find agreeable. Essential to such agreeability is the muting of Frank's Jewishness, the repression and squishing of the family's religious identity. Author Meyer Levin had originally secured permission to adapt the diary into a play, but Otto Frank, Anne's father, rejected his version, in part because of how Levin had focused on the family's Judaic differences (it was seen as *too* Jewish). Frank eventually allowed Frances Goodrich and Albert Hackett to turn the diary into a play, and their production centered on universalizing the Frank family's suffering to appeal to the mainstream. Consequently, the play concludes with Frank's infamous proclamation: "I still believe, in spite of everything, that people are truly good at heart" ([1947] 1996: 332). The decision to end the play with Frank's quote, Bruno Bettelheim contends, "explains why millions loved play and movie, because while it confronts us with the fact that Auschwitz existed, it encourages at the same time to ignore any of its implications.

40 *Philip Roth and the Body*

If all men are good at heart, there never really was an Auschwitz; nor is there any possibility that it may recur" (2000: 189).

Roth's fiction, conversely, does not busy itself with didactic acts of remembrance or consolidatory moral platitudes; instead, Roth—like his narrator Zuckerman—writes everything, refusing to "leave anything out" (*GW* 62), including the ugly desires and deviancies that plague Jews and non-Jews alike. Zuckerman—retreating to hideout with his literary idol, E.I. Lonoff—meets and becomes infatuated with Lonoff's assistant, Amy Bellette, and imagines she is Anne Frank. In Nathan's fantasy, he invents Frank discovering that her diary has become an international bestseller and pondering her best course of action: "Her responsibility was to the dead, if to anyone—to her sister, to her mother, to all the slaughtered schoolchildren who had been her friends. There was her diary's purpose, there was her ordained mission: to restore in print their status as flesh and blood" (*GW* 105). Roth's fiction undertakes the same mission: restoring and/or reminding American Jewry of their fleshiness.

The irony of Roth's goal, as exemplified by *The Ghost Writer* and, to a lesser extent, *Zuckerman Unbound*, is that these novels (and most of his fiction) feature Jewish men unable to envisage and/or conceptualize the women in their lives as "flesh and blood" (*GW* 105). Jewish mothers are often dismissed, disregarded, or ignored by Roth's male protagonists. In the first two novels of "Zuckerman Bound," for example, the mother is a marginal figure, a side-character attempting to keep the peace between warring father and son. *The Anatomy Lesson*, however, reflects on the forgotten Zuckerman mother, a paean induced by his bodily collapse: "When he is sick, every man wants his mother; if she's not around, other women must do" (*AL* 297). The joke—such as it is—stresses the relativity of the mother's position in the eyes of the son, pitted as a replaceable, almost disposable, object. Nathan suffers from a mysterious "hot line of pain that ran behind his right ear into his neck, then branched downward beneath the scapula like a menorah held bottom side up" (*AL* 298). The upside-down menorah represents the topsy-turvy connection Nathan feels toward his Jewishness; on the one hand, it is at once essential to his being as a man and as a writer, the spine of his fictive productions. On the other hand, Nathan's Jewishness is the source of the pain and suffering he endured because of his literature.

The pain is very literal, too. Nathan seeks out maternal care from four different women: Jenny, Diana, Gloria, and Jaga, all of whom service Nathan, acting as his stand-in mother whom he, in turn, pleasures. Nathan lies on "a soft red plastic-covered playmat" (*AL* 302), from which he is fed, serviced, and sexually

Reading Roth's (M)Others

pleasured: "On his back he felt like their whore paying in sex for someone to bring him the milk and the paper. They told him their troubles and took off their clothes and lowered the orifices for Zuckerman to fill" (*AL* 303). Nathan is pitted as infant-like, lying on his back seeking the return of the maternal authority as symbolized by the milk and the lowered orifices. Steven Milowitz reads this scene as Nathan attempting to "recapture the Edenic bond of the mother and the child" (2000: 101), and as Nathan sucks away at these women, he strives to escape his bodily present (full of pain), and return to the (past), to the safety and security of his mother's womb.

Nathan's desire to retreat to the metaphoric womb has been read by Kate Wilson as a continuation of "his ceaseless frustration [which] has always been with 'fathers' and their influence on what he writes" (2005: 112). Yet this analysis overlooks the mother as a mere by-product of Nathan's struggle against the father. *The Anatomy Lesson*, I argue, is Roth's most meditative fiction on how the mother is defined through the body. Nathan reflects on how Selma existed in his eyes as a "breast, then a lap, then a fading voice calling after him, 'Be careful.' Then a long gap when there is nothing of her to remember, just the invisible somebody, anxious to please, reporting to him on the phone weather in New Jersey" (*AL* 328). The triptych of images reconstructs Selma through her materiality: the breast provides Nathan with sustenance, growth, and nurturing; the lap is a site where Nathan can sit, observe, play, and learn; and finally, the disappearing voice signifies the blossoming of the boy's independence as he masters walking, playing, and functioning beyond his mother's body. The pubescent years are signified by the gap of nothingness, for as Nathan becomes a man, the mother, in the eyes of the oblivious son, becomes an "invisible somebody" (*AL* 328). The unseen Selma is thus made into a figure of otherness for Nathan, to whom he offers banal platitudes (regarding the weather, for example) as a means of appeasement.

The mother is marked entirely by her bodily function in relation to the son, and when she is no longer required, Selma Zuckerman becomes obsolete and invisible. According to Nathan, Selma did not partake in the political, ideological, or historical discussions that enrapture Nathan's morally outraged father. Instead, it is the father and son who are immersed in a Jewishly inflected historical dialectic: "a first-generation American father possessed by the Jewish demons, a second-generation American son possessed by their exorcism: that was his whole story" (*AL* 324). But what of the mother? Is Selma Zuckerman not also possessed by the same first-generation Jewish demons that plague

42 *Philip Roth and the Body*

Nathan's father? The mother is required only when the son becomes unwell, but in her absence, Nathan realizes his mother has remained an enigmatic figure. Her invisibility starkly contrasts the loud, visible, and overwhelming father for whom Nathan toiled against almost all his adult life.

Roth connects the mother's unknowability with the Holocaust. The year following Nathan's father dies, Zuckerman's mother develops a brain tumor. Asked by the neurologist to write down her name, Selma takes the pen, "and instead of 'Selma' wrote the word 'Holocaust', perfectly spelled" (*AL* 324).[3] Nathan keeps this article, instilling the paper and its contents with an inflated meaning that signifies the mother's unknown alterity. Donald Kartiganer contends this scene "transform[s] her death by brain tumor in a Miami hospital into the mass executions in Europe thirty years earlier" (2007: 48). Selma's identification with the Holocaust represents the searing distance between Nathan, Selma, and indeed Roth from European Jewry's experience of the Holocaust, paralleling the disconnect felt between Nathan and his mother.

Selma's identification with the Holocaust challenges Nathan's prejudiced assumptions regarding his mother's subjectivity. He (wrongly) assumes his mother wrote nothing but "recipes on index cards, several thousand thank-you notes, and a voluminous file of knitting instructions" (*AL* 324), presuming "that before that morning she'd never spoken the word aloud" (*AL* 324). Alex identifies his mother by a kitchen apron, and Nathan recognizes Selma via her cooking recipes and knitting directions; both women's subjectivities are unimaginable to the tyrannical sons. Sophie remains trapped in the Freudian paradigm he has reinvented her through, yet Selma's subjectivity explodes from within; the tumor, Nathan reflects, "forced out everything except the one word. That it couldn't dislodge. It must have been there all the time without their even knowing" (*AL* 324). The cancerous tumor kills Selma but reveals the mother's subjective depth to the son, dislodging (*AL* 324) Nathan's flattened perception of her.

Roth's symbolization of Selma's cancer and the Holocaust immediately fails, both in relation to its depiction of cancer and in its relationship to the Holocaust. In *Illness as Metaphor* ([1978] 2009), Susan Sontag argues that "modern disease metaphor are all cheap shots" ([1978] 2009: 85). By adopting a cancer image in relation to the Holocaust, Roth stresses the impossibility of representing the Holocaust as an American novelist. The Holocaust is not like cancer; it is

---

[3] According to Roth Pierpont, "[t]his inventive little parable was not invented." The story was told to Roth by his lifelong editor and friend Aaron Asher, whose mother, a European Jewish immigrant, had made the very mistake Selma Zuckerman makes (2014: 130).

unimaginable for a Jewish American and cannot be objectified into a concrete form of language. As Michael Rothberg points out, Roth's fiction explores "the unbridgeable distance between the Holocaust and American life—and the inauthenticity of most attempts to lessen that distance" (2007: 53).[4] Judaism's matrilineal tradition has given the mother's body a weighted symbolic function, as Judaism descends from the maternal rather than patriarchal body. Thus, the Jewish mother and her body are symbolically tied to a collective Jewish history that includes the Holocaust.

Both Nathan and Alex seek to escape the mother precisely because they equate the maternal with Jewishness. For Kristeva, the rejection of the mother as abject is central to the self's proclamation of independence from the maternal. As Christine Bousfield explains, when "the child ... feels threatened by the abject, she abjects the maternal body in order to separate, to maintain her clean and proper body from non-difference" (2000: 331). In Roth's fiction, however, the abjection of the mother is intertwined with a rejection of Jewishness to (re)create the male self as an American. Alex seeks to separate himself from his mother to restore gendered divisions and negate the mother's gendered difference inherently connected to recent Jewish suffering. For Nathan, the mother is gone, and the absent body of Selma becomes desirable because Roth's character seeks to escape his present, away from the strife and pain he symbolically and literally suffers. However, the abjected mother, like the Holocaust, cannot enter the symbolic order; both resist any kind of objectification into language, signifying the collapse of meaning.

Therefore, while the father, even in death, is visible, knowable, and identifiable, Selma Zuckerman is indeterminably marked—a spectral figure who haunts the unruly son. Steven Milowitz makes a similar and compelling observation: "The mother resides always within both worlds, shuttling forever and unpredictably between the two, never becoming one or the other. The father is a knowable entity, who rarely contradicts his code while the other is fraught with contradiction" (2000: 98). Thus, Nathan's question, "Mama, where are you?" (*AL* 327), reflects his desire to (re)discover, (re)locate, and (re)materialize the mother from beyond the grave. In other words, Nathan seeks a restoration and return to the mother before abjection.

---

[4]   See Budick (2003: 212–30). Elsewhere, Rachel McLennan discusses the ethical implications of this comparison in *Representations of Anne Frank in American Literature: Stories in New Ways* (2017: 37).

When Nathan discovers Selma's book of knitting instructions, stained with what he suspects is his mother's breast milk, he closes his eyes and "put[s] his tongue on the page" (*AL* 342). Writing on the indeterminacy of women's bodies, Iris Young highlights how "[f]luids, unlike objects, have no definite borders; they are unstable, which does not mean that they are without pattern" (qtd. in Grosz 1994: 205). Nathan seeks to conjure the mother here and make her into a solid, stable object by tonguing the material of her book, as though the milk itself can summon her back to the mourning son. Yet as David Coughlan observes, Selma is "just a step beyond ... so close and yet uncontactable, communicating nothing" (2016: 99).

Selma appears before Nathan in two drink- and drug-induced dreams, symbolizing—in very heavy-handed terms—his wish for her return. In the first dream, Selma is posing on a platform for an art class, "her face obscure, her age indecipherable except for the youthful breasts, grotesquely high and spherical and hard" (*AL* 459). The maternal returns with the promise of life, as signified by the youthful breasts, but remains incomprehensible (note her agelessness and facial obscurity). The setting is noteworthy, too, as the artist can only conceive of Selma through an aesthetic pedagogical prism; Selma poses, awaiting her son to re-imagine and re-draw her. Her body is grotesque, obscure, and pulses with a phallic power as indicated by the hardness of her spherical breasts, which metaphorically reflects the disconnection Nathan feels for the mother he once knew, and simultaneously underscores the impossibility of Nathan's fantasy of self-recreation. The second dream, too, underpins the disconnect Nathan feels for his mother.

> She flew into his room ... as a dove, a white dove with a large round white disc, toothed like a circular saw, whirling between her wings to keep her aloft. "Strife," she said, and flew out through an open window. He called after her from where he was pinned to his bed. Never had he felt so wretched. He was six and calling, "Mamma, I didn't mean it, please come back."
>
> (*AL* 459)

Like Noah's dove, Selma returns to him here with the promise of life. Yet the innocence of the image is sinisterly reconceived: the circular saw is castrating, and the frantic whirl of the dove's beating wings suggests a struggle, reflecting the familial conflict Nathan's literature induced. Indeed, the dreamlike mother explicitly underpins this with the single utterance of "strife" (*AL* 459). Selma's monosyllabic proclamation is accusatory, but vague and indeterminate. Is Selma speaking of her own suffering at seeing her son and father conflict? Or does the utterance reveal the mother's unspoken and undetailed struggle as a Jewish-American living in the shadow of the Holocaust? The mother does not give us an answer; instead, she exits out the window. The scene calls to mind the opening of *Portnoy's Complaint*, as Sophie enters through the window in Alex's nightmarish construction, yet Nathan does not seek to excommunicate his Selma from his being; rather, he feverishly seeks her return and forgiveness.

The mother assumes a ghostly role that represents the paradoxical position she assumes in his life as an absence/presence. Selma haunts Nathan, as he realizes, "[s]*he's with me here* ... his mother's ghost had tracked him down. He wasn't being poetic or mad. Some power of his mother's spirit had survived her body" (*AL* 459, italics in original). The identification of the mother as a ghost signifies a disruption; as Andrew Bennett and Nicholas Royle observe, "[g]hosts disturb our sense of the separation of the living from the dead" (2009: 133). The splitting between spirit and body ruptures a unitary whole Nathan understood his mother as. The ghost, Karin De Boer writes, "intimates a possibility that cannot be reduced to either presence or absence, while we ... recoil from the summons of the ghost to let this possibility occur, and seek refuge in an ontological domain informed by fixed oppositions" (2002: 30). Nathan flees toward "a second life" (*AL* 435), signaling his refusal of the ghost and the haunting presence-past of Jewishness and all the strife this identity has brought him. Nathan seeks an ontology rooted in rigidified oppositions, one that rejects the distortions between the living and the dead the ghost represents; in other words, Zuckerman seeks escape from his ghost-riddled Jewishness.

Nathan flees by disavowing fiction. "I'm sick of raiding my memory and feeding on the past ... I'm sick of channeling everything into writing. I want the real thing, the thing in *the raw*, and not for the writing but for itself. Too long living out of the suitcase of myself" (*AL* 442, italics in original).[5] Nathan separates writing from reality, creating an arbitrary division between the past, present, and future. Fiction, Zuckerman has it, is not raw or real, but artificial and empty; it is too fluid and formless; its leakiness induces breakdowns, arguments, literal and symbolic collapse. The image of Nathan living out of the suitcase of himself reflects the narcissistic dislocation Nathan feels fiction has induced in his life.

---

[5] Posnock observes how Zuckerman's desire for the real aligns him with a "long line of American authors who find the single-minded pursuit of art an estrangement from life" (2006a: 127); it is ironic then that Nathan seeks to flee the art of writing but finds himself enacting the same patterns of behavior that have dominated American literature.

Nathan chooses to become an obstetrician because there is nothing but "bilge, the ooze, the gooey drip. The stuff. No words, just stuff ... No more words!" (*AL* 369). The surgeon's life represents a rigidity that cannot allow for abstractions; for Nathan, being a doctor signifies a life of absolutisms, removing him from the porous instabilities of novel-writing. The return to the womb here is made very literal: it signifies the death of language, a return to the self-prior to speech or text—the raw existence Nathan craves. Wilson reads Zuckerman's decision as the author's attempt to atone for the symbolic murder of his father and to "bring forth life, rather than putting an end to it" (112).[6] Yet Nathan's actions reflect his craving to return to the maternal body, wherein he can literally re-enter into the mother's womb.

This fantasy represents a will toward self-annihilation that resists the specter(s) of his mother; Nathan does not seek unification with the haunting memory of his mother but wants to escape the ghostly multiplicities that torment him. Bobby's life represents an existence of absolutism: "Life vs. Death. Health vs. Disease. Anesthesia vs. Pain" (*AL* 440)—a life free of moral obscurities, a world without the complexity language produces.[7] In the surgeon's world, the ghost cannot exist; there is only life and death, with nothing in-between.

The second life Nathan envisages (i.e., the return to the womb) wills toward the death of his mother's ghost; Zuckerman seeks to extinguish the disruptive absence-presence of the ghost and restore order. "Time is out of joint" for Nathan, and like Hamlet, he seeks to set it right. Unlike Shakespeare's hero, however, Nathan flees from the ghost, meaning the mother remains voiceless and invisible. The novel ends with Zuckerman, fueled by Percodan and alcohol, breaking his jaw in a calamitous and raucous episode in which he attacks his former roommate's father. Nathan escorts Bobby's father to his wife's grave, symbolizing the displacement of Nathan's mother and the son's abjection of the mother. Despite Nathan's good intentions, Mr. Freytag's remonstrations regarding Bobby's son remind Zuckerman of his own father: "Everything we gave him, trapped like that in Bobby's genes, while everything we are *not*, everything we are *against*—How can all of this end with Gregory? Eat shit? To his *father*?—I'll break his neck for what he's done to this family! I'll kill that little

---

[6] Brauner highlights how Zuckerman's unhinged state "reveals the extent to which he has accepted the legitimacy of the charge [of murder] and internalised the guilt of the crime" (2007: 38).

[7] Laura Muresan writes that for Zuckerman, "being a writer means being continually faced with one's own limits, as writing is always open to interpretation. Medicine is an exact science, or so he thinks, that will allow him to exert control over events and make decisions that will not necessarily concern his own person" (2015: 85).

bastard! I *will*!" (*AL* 483, italics in original). Mr. Freytag's consternations echo the same patriarchal troubles Nathan has with his own father; Jewish identity is loftily heralded as a prestigious and proper identity that is being desecrated by the unruly grandson. Mr. Freytag's accusations echo the charges of antisemitism Nathan faced following his publications. Incensed by the memories of his supposed treachery, Nathan lashes out against Mr. Freytag, and attempts to strangle him. As Brauner observes, Nathan's attack against Mr. Freytag echoes "his murderous feelings toward his own father" (2007: 39). His attempts to strangle and suffocate the Jewish father signal a desire to silence the Jewish patriarchy, reversing Mr. Freytag's threats against his grandson. Yet the violent attack subtly underscores the physical presence of the father. Bobby's mother is in the grave, while Selma Zuckerman is a specter from whom Nathan flees. Both mothers remain invisible and physically absent, while the patriarchal father is materially present and embodied. For Nathan, the father is definable and thus attackable, while the mother represents an alterity that cannot be reconciled or symbolized.

Nathan's attack against Mr. Freytag ends in farce: he falls onto a tombstone and breaks his jaw. Consequently, Nathan is hospitalized, his mouth is wired shut, and he is trapped within his body, becoming infant-like yet again. Zuckerman, as he does in the novel's beginning, seeks his mother's care. Ironically, Nathan can only communicate this desire through writing: "WHEN HE IS SICK EVERY MAN NEEDS A MOTHER" (*AL* 489). The novel ends with Nathan still determined to submit himself to medical school; even after all he has endured, the fantasy of self-reinvention continues to compel the beleaguered author. The novel ends with Nathan roaming "the busy corridors of the university hospital, patrolling and planning on his own by day, then out on the quiet floor with the interns at night, as though he still believed that he could unchain himself from a future as a man apart and escape the corpus that was his" (*AL* 505). Zuckerman seeks to continue with the fantasy of self-reinvention centered on the negation of the mother. His corpus is tied to his mother's; the two are inescapably entwined, even as Nathan seeks to escape his own bodily presence. Roth's Jewish mother represents a suppressed Jewishness that has no voice, no visibility, and no presence. The mother symbolizes an unrecognizable rupture Nathan cannot contend with; thus, Selma Zuckerman remains locked in the margins of "Zuckerman Bound," haunting all three novels in her absence/presence.

Nathan may never speak or write his mother's ghost, but Roth's fiction repeatedly resummons the specter of the Jewish mother. For the most part, the maternal signifies a loss symbolized through bodily absence. The Jewish son seldom gazes upon the Jewish mother; rather, the male gaze looks away toward the American woman's body. The Jewish mother becomes synonymous with a past full of strife, while the white woman's body is heralded as the raw, real thing, representing a fantastical future free from strife and struggle. Yet as I discuss in the next chapter, the dream of assimilation in America is complicated by the newly established nation-state, Israel, and the specter of antisemitism.

2

The Jewish Stain

Roth and Antisemitism

This chapter discusses antisemitism and the Jewish body in *The Counterlife* (1986), *Deception* (1990), and *The Plot against America* (2004). These three novels have an entwined interest in how Jews are physically marked and influenced by antisemitic ideas of Jewishness, concepts rooted in physiognomic stereotypes. My intention here is to probe how Roth presents Jewish bodies under the gaze of the antisemite, and how his abject imagery undermines/troubles antisemitic fantasies of Jewish difference.

Roth dismissed suggestions his fiction resists antisemitism. As he points out in an interview with Alain Finkielkraut, "however much I may loathe anti-Semitism … my job in a work of fiction is not to offer consolation to Jewish sufferers or to mount an attack upon their persecutors to make the Jewish case to the undecided" (*WW* 132). Yet his work *does* interrogate the impact antisemitism has on Jewish lives in America, England, and Israel, so although I agree with Brauner that Roth "has no more sought to combat anti-Semitism in his fiction than to fuel it" (2007: 199), his gnawing, gnarly portrayal of Jewishness does—despite the author's repudiation—undermine antisemitic narratives that dehumanize Jews. Roth's fiction is overwhelmingly *alive* with Jews: Jews who fuck, Jews who shit, Jews who are prodigiously embodied. For Roth, Jews are not merely people of the book; they are people of the body, too.

Portnoy's Complaint (1995 [1969]) responded, in part, to his contemporaries' portrayal of Jews who, as Roth saw it, were devoid of bodily presence. In *Reading Myself and Others* (1975), Roth accuses Bellow of creating a binary between his Jewish and non-Jewish characters (*WW* 88-9). Bellow's heroes struggle with the ethics of "Jewhood," while the gentile characters are granted a "release of appetite and aggression" (*WW* 89). Roth goes even further when discussing Malamud: "For Malamud, generally speaking, the Jew is innocent, passive, virtuous … the

50   *Philip Roth and the Body*

Gentile, on the other hand, is characteristically corrupt, violent, and lustful" (*WW* 90). He arrives at a similar conclusion when discussing Mailer, noting how the lusting Jew is "an odd type, as it turns out, in recent Jewish fiction, where it is usually the goy who does the sexual defiling; also, it has been alleged, one of the 'crudest and most venerable stereotypes of anti-Semitic lore'" (*WW* 90). Roth, it is safe to say, remedied this gap, effectively reclaiming the sexually lustful Jew from the antisemite's hands, sculpting sexual deviancy into the skin of his Jewish protagonists. Roth's hyper-embodied Jew was an indirect response to antisemitism and the cautious portrayal of benevolent Jews emanating from Bellow and Malamud.

The Ghost Writer (1979) signaled Roth's intention to explore antisemitism more directly. Zuckerman's novel *Carnovsky*, a mirror of *Portnoy's Complaint*, garners the beguiled narrator a similarly raucous reception that Roth himself endured. Significantly, of course, the anger—in both fiction and reality— stemmed from the Jewish community, rather than an antisemitic mob. "I had informed on the Jews. I had told the Gentiles what apparently it would otherwise have been possible to keep secret from them: the perils of human nature afflict the members of our minority" (*WW* 59). Roth's early career was defined by Jewish outrage and anxiety stemming from the *possible* misuses of his fiction by antisemites, rather than *actual* experiences of anti-Jewish violence.

The Counterlife was a turning point in Roth's oeuvre, however, as he explored Jewishness beyond the American scene that detailed direct encounters with antisemitism. Specifically, he grew interested in Jewish identities in Israel and England. The former, a place where Jews are ubiquitous, is complicated by the ongoing conflict and colonial territorialization undertaken by the Israeli government and the shadow of the Holocaust. England, conversely, is a country where Jews make up a tiny minority and has been mired by a history of violent antisemitism and anti-Jewish prejudice. Both were fertile sites for *The Counterlife* and *Operation Shylock: A Confession* (1993), while England dominates *Deception*. Conversely, the setting of *The Plot against America* is indicated by its title, yet unlike Roth's other American novels, he constructs a counter-America, an alternative-history where American Jewry faces institutional antisemitism. *Plot's* frame links it to the two other novels featured here, as all three texts employ meta-narrative structures that probe the performativity of racial, gendered, and national identities.

As the scope of Roth's fiction grew, his novels retained a repeated interest in the way Jewishness was conceived of, both through Jewish and non-Jewish perspectives. The body was essential to such inventions and was an integral feature of Roth's examinations regarding how Jews were (re)imagined. Likewise, abject imagery continues to be an integral motif in each of these novels, and I probe how Roth explores the racial abjection of Jewry in American, British, and Israeli contexts.

Jewish Shadows

The subject of antisemitism has been a recurrent topic of interest in Roth studies.[1] Kaplan argues Roth's use of doubling expresses "the doubled anxiety of the Jewish character who fears *both* becoming victim *and* becoming perpetrator of anti-Arab violence and/or American racism" (2015: 54, italics in original). I have found Kaplan's argument immensely fruitful in reconsidering Roth's portrayal of Jewishness, particularly in the two novels she discusses. Both *The Counterlife* and *Operation Shylock: A Confession* are haunted by what Zygmunt Bauman terms the "conceptual Jew—a semantically overloaded entity, comprising and blending means which ought to be kept apart" (1989: 39). Roth explores how Jews are caught up in a double consciousness in which the antisemite's conceptual Jew always influences how Jews are perceived. There are multifarious homilies scattered throughout the novel regarding Jewishness and antisemitism that illuminate the conceptual Jews' presence.

In the third chapter, "Aloft," for example, there is a passage that underscores the presence of the conceptual Jew: "I always think of England as one of those places where every Jew's shadow has an enormous hooked nose ... Sure, no Jew exists *anywhere* without his shadow, but there it's always seemed to me worse" (*CL* 174, italics in original). The nose symbolizes the history of antisemitism that has been inscribed on the Jewish body, one that lingers within the Jewish conscience. The nefarious impressions of the Jew emerge in *Operation Shylock: A Confession* (1994) too. As the title indicates, Roth's novel is interested in the history of antisemitism and the Jewish people. The premise is outrageously postmodern: Philip Roth—hopped up on Halcion (briefly, I might add)— discovers during his ailment that a man called Philip Roth has been touring

---

[1] See for example Alan Cooper's *Philip Roth and the Jews* (1996), the second chapter of Brauner's *Philip Roth* (2007: 21–46), and Gustavo Sánchez Canales's "Antisemitism" in *Philip Roth in Context* (2021: 241–51).

Israel promoting a radical new movement called Diasporism that aims to bring the Jews back to Europe and out of the Middle East.

Shenanigans ensue, as Philip sets out to the Holy Land to find his doppelganger, all while the trial of the alleged Nazi war criminal John Demjanjuk takes place. The novel contains what I consider to be Roth's finest prose (his awful description of Demjanjuk is just jaw-dropping in its vivacity) but takes a massive tumble thereafter as Roth gets lost in his fun house. Still, it features a wonderful rant from a character called Supposnik, who claims: "Jewish people have lived in the shadow of this Shylock. In the modern world, the Jew has been perpetually on trial; still *today* the Jew is on trial, in the person of the Israeli—and this trial of the Jew, this trial which never ends, begins with the trial of Shylock" (OS 274, italics in original). Paule Levy astutely points out that in both these novels, Roth's relief—the power of language—is also the source of distortion, the medium in which reality and fantasy blur and melt (Levy 2002: 68). The individual Roth grants these lines to is a spurious figure, one whom the reader is invited to treat with the utmost suspicion and doubt. Such is the case with *The Counterlife*, as Roth provides his shadowy nose comment to the character of Jimmy, who threatens to hijack the plane he and Zuckerman are on. Jimmy is deranged, as he decrees Jews must "FORGET REMEMBERING" (CL 169), writing a manifesto that demands the closure of Yad Vashem, Jerusalem's Museum, and the Remembrance Hall of the Holocaust (CL 169). In other words, the double consciousness of the Jew in both novels are presented by specious characters whom the reader cannot take too seriously. The shadows of antisemitism are indeed looming in Roth, but so too are the Jewish miscreants seeking to use and abuse Jewry's history of suffering for their own gain.

Roth delights in such underhanded tactics, as *The Counterlife* repeatedly pulls the rug from the reader's feet. The tricksy duplicitousness is a recurrent strategy in this postmodern novel, where the actions and events of each chapter are followed by a contradictory variation.[2] That being said, *The Counterlife* maintains a consistent interest in the impotent male body and Jewish identity, both of which form the novel's spine, as Henry and Nathan Zuckerman's entwining narratives orbit around mutually informing fantasies of self-renewal.

We begin with a ten-page account of Henry's heart condition and subsequent treatment, which leaves him sexually impotent. Much to Henry's chagrin, he is unable to continue his affair with his dental nurse, Wendy. "*He was plagued by*

---

[2] See Newlin (2012: 161–77) and Pinsker (1990: 137–53).

mental images of outlandish cocks and by the fantasies of Wendy with all those other men ... He began to secretly idolize all the potent men as though he no longer mattered as a man himself" (*CL* 11, italics in original). Henry's admonishment regarding his own materiality stems from how he perceives himself as a man. He ties his value to his penis and ability to maintain an erection. Masculine materiality is a recurrent concern here, as the question of his prowess (or lack thereof) returns in the following chapter. It is worth noting, however, that the italicized opening is a three-thousand-word eulogy Nathan tries and fails to write for his brother, who—obsessed with regaining his sexual potency—undergoes surgery and subsequently dies.

Or does he? In Chapter 2, "Judea," Henry is alive and well! His surgery is successful, but instead of continuing his affair, he absconds to Israel, takes on a new identity as "Hanoch," and lives in a kibbutz in the West Bank with his newfound mentor, Mordecai Lippman, a right-wing Zionist. This time, then, Nathan does not attend his brother's funeral; instead, he flies to Jerusalem at the behest of Henry's wife, Carol, and assesses the situation. Initially, Nathan surmises his brother "appears to have left his wife, his kids, and his mistress to come to Israel to become an authentic Jew" (*CL* 78). The quest for authenticity is tied to two merging concerns: Henry's desire to affirm his masculinity and his determination to live a serious life. "I am nothing, I have never been *anything*, the way that I am this Jew," he tells Nathan, "I am not *just* a Jew, I'm not *also* a Jew—*I'm a Jew as deep as those Jews*. Everything else *is* nothing. And it's that, *that* all these months has been staring me right in the face! The fact that that is the root of my life!" (*CL* 65, italics in original). Henry's fixation on being a singularized "Jew" and the rejection of "everything else" symbolically link to the Henry of Chapter 1, as both fetishize a phallic power that is predicated on a mythical wholeness.

Henry's journey to Israel seems predicated on a desire to return to the metaphoric womb, the ultimate escape free from what he calls "the Oedipal swamp" (*CL* 144), echoing Nathan's desire to go back to "the bilge, the ooze ... the stuff. No words, just stuff. ... No more words!" (*AL* 369). For Henry, Judea is where Judaism began: "It's no accident, you know, that we're called Jews and this place is called Judea ... this is where the Jews *began* ... *This* is Judaism, *this* is Zionism, *right here*" (*CL* 113, italics in original).

Henry's transition into Hanoch represents the reproducibility and instability of the nation as a performative construction. Henry's actions (including his adoption of the name, Hanoch) reflect the "double-time" of nationality Homi

K. Bhabha describes in *The Location of Culture* (1994). As Bhabha observes, "the people are the historical 'objects' of a nationalist pedagogy, giving the discourse an authority that is based on the pre-given or constituted historical origin *in the past*" ([1994] 2008: 145, italics in original). Henry's Zionist turn is based on the pre-given constituted origins the Jewish people claim over the land in Palestine/Israel. However, as Bhabha also points out, "the people are also the 'subjects' of a process of signification that must erase any prior or originary presence of the nation-people to demonstrate the prodigious, living principles of the people as contemporaneity: as that sign of the *present* through which national life is redeemed" ([1994] 2008: 145, italics in original). The historical landmarks that affirm the subject's belonging to the nation must be performed in the present. Their lives, customs, rituals, and culture thus come to represent the nation itself, which has been established and defined in another epoch, beyond the present through which the "nation" is articulated.

Henry's performance, however, is unconvincing, uncertain, and riddled with an anxious defensiveness. There's a childishness to Henry's Hanoch that is noted by Nathan when watching him interact with Mordecai's son: "they grinned at each other while they sang, as though between them there were some joke about the song, the occasion, or even about my presence at the table. Many years back I exchanged just such grins with Henry myself" (*CL* 122). Henry's infantile playfulness illuminates his naiveté; indeed, his adoption of Israeli culture and language requires him to return to school where he and his fellow students sit "in a half-circle around their teacher's chair" (*CL* 101). Henry is reduced to a child: powerless, clueless, and extremely impressionable, he seems spellbound by the powerhouse that is Lippmann.

The teacher's oration does not disappoint. Lippmann predicts an American Holocaust in which the goyim will "permit the resentful blacks to take all their hatred out on the Jews" (*CL* 128). The absurdity of this prophecy ironically conflicts with Nathan's earlier statement that "America simply did not boil down to Jew and Gentile, nor were anti-Semite's the American Jew's biggest problem" (*CL* 58). Nevertheless, Lippmann does make the occasional credible observation. For example, he claims, "first it was Jewish passivity that was disgusting, the meek Jew, the accommodating Jew, the Jew who walked like a sheep to his own slaughter—now what is worse than disgusting, outright *wicked*, is Jewish strength and militancy" (*CL* 133, italics in original). Lippmann's solution, however, centers on Jewish strength and militancy that hinges on an absolutist logic of us and them. When discussing the media's portrayal of the Israel-Palestine conflict, Lippmann claims, "They [the media] prefer now the greedy, grasping Jew who oversteps his bounds—the Arab as Noble Savage versus the degenerate, colonialist, capitalist Jew" (*CL* 132). Lippmann's description underpins the warring ideology driving his nationalism; Israel's nationhood, in his view, hinges on a one-state solution. "He [the Palestinians] can have any experience he likes, live here however he chooses and have everything he desires—except for the experience of statehood" (*CL* 133). In Lippman's absolutist view, for Israel to maintain its nationhood, the country must expel the Palestinian state (abjection).

Nathan compares Mordecai's bombastic performance to their father's speeches they grew up with in America: "strip away the hambone actor and the compulsive talker, and we could have been back at the kitchen table in Newark, with Dad lecturing us on the historical struggle between the goy and the Jew" (*CL* 142). The maleness of Lippmann is likewise noted—"The man is the embodiment of potency" (*CL* 141)—underscoring—in Nathan's view at least—the rationale behind Henry's childlike admiration for Mordecai. He represents phallic male power, precisely the kind Henry was both lacking and desirous of in America. Nathan's psychoanalytical breakdown of his sojourn irks Henry, who sees his brother's preoccupation with the familial to be frivolous and immaterial: "What matters isn't Momma and Poppa and the kitchen table, it isn't *any* of that crap you write about—*it's who runs Judea!*" (*CL* 144, italics in original). Henry tries to cast out the excesses of his life and dedicate himself to the singular cause of Lippmann's Zionism, comparing the familial, Freudian formulations that drive his brother's fiction as "crap," shit that can be wiped away.

The problem for Henry—at least in Nathan's view (although Roth's voice courses through him here)—is that the Zionist project as envisaged by Lippmann is not as absolute as Henry would have it.

> Zionism, as I understand it, originated not only in the deep Jewish dream of escaping the danger of insularity ... but out of a highly conscious desire to be divested of virtually everything that come to seem, the Zionists as much as to the Christian Europeans, distinctively Jewish behavior—to reverse the very form of Jewish existence. The construction of a counterlife that is one's own antimyth was at its very core.
>
> (*CL* 151)

Nathan's summary of Zionism echoes Daniel Boyarin's view that the "Jews, as Zionists, constitute themselves both as natives and as colonizers. Indeed, it is through mimicry of colonization that the Zionists seek to escape the stigma of

56   *Philip Roth and the Body*

Jewish difference" (1997: 303). For Roth, the stigma of Jewish difference can be "reversed"; Jewishness can be reconstructed and made anew, but only if it allows for the contradictory instabilities that *being* induces.

The reconceptualization of an identity hinges on the reactive recognition of others. As Nathan notes in an oft-quoted passage: "The treacherous imagination is everybody's maker—we are all the invention of each other, everybody a conjuration conjuring up everyone else. We are all each other's authors" (*CL* 149). While Nathan finds this mutuality liberating, there is a subtle suggestion of precarity. The imagination here is pitted as treacherous, implying the co-authorial state of selfhood is rife with potential for betrayal and deception. Likewise, "conjuration" has connotations of ghosts and spirits, implicitly returning us to the shadow of the hooked nose poor Jimmy refers to. In other words, if we are the authors of one another, this writerly process of inscribing identities onto each other remains fraught with potential for both real and figurative violence, the latter of which comes to fruition, as Zuckerman is confronted with English antisemitism in the final chapter of *The Counterlife*.

"I am that stink"

During Jimmy's tête-à-tête with Zuckerman, he asks, "Can I … just ease myself in with the British upper claahhses and wash away the Jewish stain?" (*CL* 174). Although this is not the intended purpose of Nathan's relocation to England, the question retains a relevancy throughout *The Counterlife*, particularly in the final chapter, "Christendom," as the author's Jewishness, rather than Henry's, is thrust under the microscope. Indeed, there is a prophetic quality to Jimmy's inquiry, as the mythology of the "dirty Jew" rears its antisemitic head in Nathan's England, shattering the author's pastoral fantasy.

Although neither Henry nor Nathan overtly intends to "wash away the Jewish stain" of their identities, both men's wives exhibit an uneasiness regarding their religious backgrounds. Carol can be forgiven for such discomfort given the circumstances, but she makes a particularly pointed remark regarding Orthodox Jews that is worth highlighting. On the phone to Nathan, she refuses to let her children visit without her: "If he [Henry] was crazy enough to do what he's done to himself, he's crazy enough to keep them there and try to turn Leslie into a little *thing* with squiggle curls and a dead-white face, a little monstrous religious *creature*" (*CL* 155, emphasis my own). Orthodox Jews are conceived of here as nonhuman cadaverous objects, monsters signifying a form of Jewishness that is abject. The scene exemplifies how certain forms of Jewishness are maligned as improper, inhuman, and incompatible if American-Jewry are to remain assimilated.

Likewise, Maria, or more specifically, her family, perceives Nathan's Jewishness as abject and ugly. Roth's description of English antisemitism feels grossly exaggerative, hyperbolic to the degree of unreal. This accusation is levelled at Nathan's fiction by Henry, who—in a complete upturning of the novel's preceding events—is now the one attending his brother's funeral, as it is Nathan, not Henry, who dies from heart surgery. Henry discovers the opening two chapters of *The Counterlife*, which he reads through, discarding as "Exaggeration. Exaggeration, falsification, rampant caricature" (*CL* 239), a criticism Nathan's Maria echoes in her interview with an unnamed interviewer, where she argues his prejudice motivates the portrayal of non-Jewish women: "his Jewish feelings about Christian women turned into a Christian woman's feelings about a Jewish man. I thought that the great verbal violence, that 'hymn of hate' he ascribed to Sarah, was in *him*" (*CL* 247, italics in original). For Nathan, however, the imaginative act itself is what counts; the question of right and wrong is a superfluous one, as he would later contend in *American Pastoral* (1997): "The fact remains that getting people right is not what living is all about anyway. It's getting them wrong that is living ... That's how we know we're alive: we're wrong" (*AP* 35).

In Roth, there is no inherent self; instead, the self is "a variety of impersonations" reliant on "a permanent company of actors"; as Nathan surmises to Maria, "I am a theater and nothing more than a theater" (*CL* 325). The self is an endless assemblage of roles the individual performs, liberating us from the fantasy of a core, whole self, the antithesis to Henry's Israeli counterself. There is, however, an implicit vulnerability in our act, as the playfulness of our self-performance requires recognition from our would-be audience. Like Prospero in the Epilogue of *The Tempest*, Zuckerman needs "the help of your good hands ... or else [his] project fails" (Shakespeare 2006: 134). In England, it is fair to say, his "ending is despair" (Shakespeare 2006: 136), as he is confronted by an ideological viewpoint that essentializes Nathan's difference into a singular role: the dirty Jew (a role Roth reprises with relish in *Sabbath's Theater*).

The idyllic bliss Nathan enjoys is rudely interrupted following an unpleasant encounter with Maria's sister, Sarah, who informs Nathan that their mother, Mrs. Freshfield, is an antisemite.[3] The religious, cultural, and supposed racial differences between Nathan and Maria become problematic when the former accuses a woman of antisemitism after she repeatedly complains of a smell in the restaurant. The woman stares at Zuckerman, leading Nathan to surmise, "I am that stink" (*CL* 295).

Zuckerman believes the woman is recycling an old antisemitic stereotype in which the Jew possesses a unique stench. The Jew's smell, otherwise known as the *foetor Judaicus*, has a long and complex history in anti-Jewish imaginations that historians have traced as far back to Marcus Aurelius.[4] The *foetor Judaicus* was particularly significant for modern antisemitism's racialization of the Jew. As Sander Gilman explains, "the smell of the Jew acquired importance as a marker of the sexual difference of the Jew ... thus the Jew's smell is a sign of the measurable, observable difference attributed to the Jew" (1995: 152, 153). The Jew's smell was rooted in an animalistic primitivism that marked them as racially inferior, driven by (sexual) instinct rather than intellect.

By invoking the *foetor Judaicus*, Zuckerman's Jewishness is redefined in England as abject; Nathan's otherness is heightened outside of the comfortable familiarity of Newark, where Jewishness and Americanness have hybridized. Nathan's Jewishness separates him from England and, thus, from Maria. As he explains at the novel's end, "England's made a Jew of me in only eight weeks" (*CL* 328). In Nathan's eyes, the woman's incredulity regarding the alleged stench is antisemitic, reducing Nathan's Jewishness to a conceptualization which strips him of his humanity. Maria, perplexed and befuddled by the scene Nathan makes, demands to know, "*Where* is the insult?" (*CL* 295, italics in original). Maria cannot see how or why Nathan understands the intoxicated woman's comments as racially charged, and Roth is careful to give credence to Maria's composed suggestion that "She is just a ridiculous woman who thinks someone has on too much scent" (*CL* 295).

Maria protests that Nathan is obsessed with his identity as a Jew and rashly posits a deeply unsettling distinction between American and English Jewry: "English

---

[3] According to Claudia Roth-Pierpont, "Roth lifted the name 'Freshfield' from Milton's "Lycidas"" (2014: 154), which he misquoted, as the line reads: "fresh woods." Nevertheless, the point remains: Mrs. Freshfield is an exaggerated reflection of bourgeoisie Englishness, with a particularly "old school" form of antisemitism that is thinly veiled.

[4] See Geller (2007: 72–80).

Jews are beleaguered, there are so few of them. On the whole they find the thing rather an embarrassment. But in the U.S. they speak up, they speak out, they're visible everywhere—and the consequence, I can assure you, is that some people don't like it, and say as much when Jews aren't around" (*CL* 303). Any sympathy the reader feels toward Maria during the restaurant episode erodes quickly. In Maria's eyes, American Jews are too loud because they sound too Jewish, and thus make themselves too visible, which affronts and offends her. In England, the Jew is quiet, submissive, and embarrassed by their Jewishness. American Jewry, in Maria's view, has assimilated improperly, having failed to recognize that their Jewishness should be quietly (and thus, privately) articulated, if spoken of at all. Maria sees Nathan's Jewishness so vividly because Nathan repeatedly articulates himself through his Jewishness, as Henry adroitly quips in the previous chapter: "The poor bastard had Jew on the brain" (*CL* 232).

Nathan's willingness to vocalize his Jewishness makes him stand out as a Jew, which Maria finds disturbing. Roth recycles yet another antisemitic stereotype of the Jew who sounds too Jewish. This trope, Gilman writes, is "a stereotype within the Christian world which represents the Jew as possessing all languages or no language of his or her own ... [who] is unable to truly command the national language of the world in which he/she lives" (1991: 12). Roth uses the improper-sounding Jew to attack the ways Jewish bodies have been marked as impure and dirty in relation to the gentile.

The Counterlife ends in refutation: Nathan will not wash away the stain of his Jewish difference. According to Maria, Nathan cannot accept the English life Maria offers because for him "to live as an innocent is to live as a laughable monster. Your chosen fate, as you see it, is to be innocent of innocence at all costs, [and you cannot] ... let me, with my pastoral origins, cunningly transform you into a pastoralized Jew" (*CL* 322).

Zuckerman discards the pastoral because "at [its] core is the idyllic scenario of redemption through recovery of a sanitized, confusionless life" (*CL* 326). Zuckerman instead embraces his Jewishness because the Jewish act of "Circumcision is everything that the pastoral is not and, to my mind, reinforces what the world is about, which isn't strifeless unity. Quite convincingly, circumcision gives the lie to the womb-dream of life in the beautiful state of innocence prehistory, the appealing idyll of living 'naturally,' unencumbered by man-made ritual. To be born is to lose all that" (*CL* 327). For Nathan, the "womb-dream" (*CL* 327) represents the fantastical unification of man and earth that is essential to the Zionism's nationalist fantasy, both of which hinge on

60 *Philip Roth and the Body*

an abjection, expulsion of the dirty, ugliness of humanness (and Jewishness) Zuckerman celebrates. The marking of the penis, the unethical, immoral, religiously archaic act, is the stain of Jewish difference that Zuckerman avows.

If the pastoral demands a rejection of Jewish identity, then Zuckerman's celebration of circumcision reaffirms his commitment to Jewish histories and his identity. As Matthew Wilson observes, the act of circumcision enables Nathan to unite "the narratives of family and of history, the narrative of family and continuity and the narrative of Jews in history symbolized by the same letting of blood" (1991: 53–4). Nathan "find[s] inspiration in a conscience that has been created and undone a hundred times over in this century alone" (*WW* 103).

For Roth, Jewishness is a performance, but this does not diminish or delimit what it means to be a Jew. As Zuckerman surmises, he is a "Jew without Jews, without Judaism, without Zionism, without Jewishness … just the object itself, like a glass or an apple" (*CL* 328). Yet the Jewishness Nathan celebrates is gendered as male, upholding the circumcised penis as a rejection against the Christian pastoral tradition tied to purity. Zuckerman's erect penis represents rejuvenation and hope for the father-to-be; it represents an affirmation of Jewishness that is nascent and blossoming. Yet this is Philip Roth: Nathan's buoyant optimism in these final moments reads hollow and false. In choosing to end on the erect, circumcised penis of Nathan, Roth undermines the narrator's commitment to his Judaism. It is hopefully and hopelessly centered on the male body; Roth's fiction has dogmatically shown the body itself is chaotic and unstable, implying that Zuckerman's rhapsodic sermonizing of Jewishness will inevitably fall apart.

Deceptive Bodies

Deception, as the title indicates, is concerned with lies, falseness, and trickery, linking it with *The Counterlife* in that both are invested in the treachery of humanness and narrative form. The novel's slipperiness is evident from the off, as the book details Philip's affair with Maria, the former of whom—rather conspicuously—is an author, bearing an uncanny alikeness to one Philip Roth. The book is structured as a two-person dialogue, purposefully devoid of the usual idiosyncrasies we might expect of a Roth novel.

There has been, relatively speaking, limited scholarship dedicated to this short novel, which is understandable; it is a meager work of fiction that lacks tension, character, or plot, particularly when compared with the other books

The Jewish Stain

Roth produced during this time (*Deception* was written after *The Counterlife* and before *Patrimony: A True Story*). However, *Deception*'s sparseness is by design, and what it lacks in plot, it makes up for in introspectively questioning the categorical distinctions we impose between fact and fiction. As Roth's narrator dismissively contends, "I write fiction and I'm told it's autobiography, I wrote autobiography and I'm told it's fiction, so since I'm so dim and they're so smart, let *them* decide what it is or isn't" (*D* 190). It's a pouty proclamation, a sulky rebuttal against readings of Roth's work that garnered him celebrity status and extraordinary wealth, which arguably inspired the entirety of the Zuckerman Unbound trilogy.

The incomprehensibility of categorical distinctions is also explored in terms of Jewishness and race. This interest arises, albeit problematically, in an encounter between Philip and a Czech writer named Ivan, the latter of whom is convinced that his wife is having an affair with Andrew, his Black neighbor. Ivan denigrates Andrew in an extremely racist fashion, accusing him of being illiterate, "primitive," and sexually promiscuous. As Berlinerblau has noted, Philip listens passively and fails to challenge Ivan's unhinged racist diatribe.[5] Ivan then accuses Philip of having slept with his wife and surmises that "With the nigger it's his prick and with the Jew it's his questions. You are a treacherous bastard" (*D* 89). He threatens to shoot Andrew "in the middle of the trousers" with a shotgun and tells Philip, "I'll shoot you into the ears" (*D* 86, 92).

Ivan's intention to inflict an explosive, splattered violence on Andrew's genitals (as suggested by the reference to the shotgun) reflects his desire to maintain his own phallic power over the Black male body, which ties to transatlantic racism that is ensconced in racial and sexual violence. Hortense J. Spillers's work is instructive in elaborating on this matter: Spillers highlights how Black bodies have been captured and objectified, which "translates into a potential for pornotroping and embodies sheer physical powerlessness that slides into a more general 'powerlessness'" (1987: 67). Black bodies were stolen, and "Black subjectification equals objectification, and the process through which Blacks enter subjectivity is rife with sexual violence" (Davis 2023: 151). This viciousness is evident in the encounter Roth details, but it also stresses both what binds

---

[5] Berlinerblau, as I noted in the Introduction, claims that "[i]f a researcher were to scrutinize all of these texts [Roth's oeuvre], it would become evident that Roth's representation of African American characters can be neither sympathetic nor thoughtful" (2021: 22). I agree that Roth's representation of African Americans is not as innocent as early scholarship would suggest and concur with him that Roth's corpus presents us with a complex situation regarding Roth and racial representation, one that cannot be dismissed or ignored.

and separates Black people and Jews in terms of how white supremacists have conceptualized each.

Deception brings up two significant stereotypes surrounding Black and Jewish men, both of which are violently coded through the body. As Brandon R. Davis explains, in white sexual mythologies "the Black man has been established as a virulent sexual predator, armed with a large penis and a rabid desire for White female sex" (2023: 153). The Jew, however, is sexually foreboding because they are physically weak but sneaky and cunning. Ivan condemns Philip for all the questions he asks of his wife, implying that he is luring her in through his deceptiveness; he is pretending to be her friend to woo her into bed.

Deception addresses the different ways in which Black and Jewish bodies have been demarcated in the white supremacist schema, albeit lopsidedly. Berlinerblau implies that the narrator—or maybe Roth—should have offered more resistance against the unhinged narrator and that the lack of written and direct opposition on the page undermines or devalues the narrative. Furthermore, Berlinerblau suggests that both narrator and author are more offended and disgusted by antisemitism than racism. I am, to a degree, sympathetic to this reading. There is no doubt Berlinerblau's analysis has some credibility. In reconstructing a racist's viewpoint, writers always risk replicating the voice they seek to undermine. Indeed, it is fair to say that Roth is far more skillful and considered in how he deconstructs antisemitism than racism. However, I am skeptical of Berlinerblau's oblique analysis because of how Ivan is presented. The character is quite clearly an idiot: he is a brutish, vulgar, crass, and reprehensible man whom the reader is encouraged to find as such. The implications surrounding Ivan are easy enough to discern. Furthermore, *Deception*'s portrayal of Ivan stresses how (white) Jews and Black people both face marginalization and discrimination from white supremacy and reads as an affirmation of Frantz Fanon's (2023 [1967]) proclamation that each is a "brother in misfortune" (2023 [1967]: 101). Roth's fiction demands Jews pay attention to transatlantic racism, echoing Fanon's view "that the anti-Semite is inevitably a negrophobe" (2023 [1967]: 101).

Both Roth and Fanon are invested in deconstructing and challenging white supremacist conceptions of Black and Jewish bodies, and the difference each elicits in the racist's imagination.

> The Jewishness of the Jew, however, can go unnoticed. He is not integrally what he is. We can but hope and wait. His acts and behavior are the determining factor. He is a white man, and apart from some debatable features, he can pass undetected. He belongs to the race that has never practiced cannibalism. What

The Jewish Stain 63

a strange idea, to eat one's father! Serves them right; they shouldn't be black. Of course the Jews have been tormented—what am I saying? They have been hunted, exterminated, and cremated, but these are just minor episodes in the family history. The Jew is not liked as soon as he has been detected. But with me things take on a new face. I'm not given a second chance. I am overdetermined from the outside. I am a slave not to the "idea" that others have of me, but to my appearance.

([1967] 2023: 95)

The Jew, in Fanon's estimation, exists in a liminal space that is approximate to whiteness, giving him a distinct advantage in that he can slip from the racist's gaze and go unnoticed; in other words, he can pass as white (and thus is, for all intents and purposes, white).[6] For Fanon, however, *his* identity as a Black man is "overdetermined from the outside" and set by his appearance. The Jew must be detected, while the Black body is already predetermined. Calvin L. Warren's *Ontological Terror: Blackness, Nihilism, and Emancipation* (2018) explicates how "blacks lack being but have existence … they inhabit the world in concealment and non-movement (this is the conditions of objects, despite the word of object-oriented ontologists who project humanism onto objects)" (2018: 13). This is an important observation that has a direct bearing on my reading of the scene outlined in *Deception*, as the conceptual Jew—although tormented and oppressed by the same insidious forces that terrorize Black bodies—is *not* defined by a lack of movement, nor are they ossified into non-being; indeed, what makes the Jew so threatening to white supremacists is the slippery, ooziness of the Jew. The Jew signifies instability, a gendered, racial fluid entity that cannot be contained, neither literally nor metaphorically; the Jew is abject.

The Jews' lubriciousness is outlined in the novel's most arresting episode, when the narrator encounters what he perceives to be an antisemitic Englishman during a walk with fellow novelist, Aharon Appelfeld, and his son, Itzak. As the three men stroll through the streets of London, they are approached by an aggressive individual who chastises the narrator for his appearance:

At first he just glared at me. Then he gestured at his own clothes and he shouted, "You don't even dress right!" I got confused by that. My pullover sweater happened to be dark brown while his was green, but otherwise we were dressed almost exactly alike. […] He was just furious, that's all, the mere sight of me on the quiet, civilized streets of Chelsea had simply driven him up the wall. The fury

---

6 For more on this passage, see Boyarin (2022: 49–51).

was in his stride, on his face, it was in every breath he drew. The whole thing left me very agitated—and a little puzzled. I couldn't understand what he'd meant by telling me that I wasn't even dressed right.

(D 102–3)

The uncanniness of the Jew is what unsettles the antisemite here; the Jews' alikeness enrages him. The presence of Philip in the "quiet, civilized streets of Chelsea" is perceived as threatening, but there is a marked ambiguity in this encounter that signifies a symbolic lack, one that defines both antisemitism and the Jew in the antisemite's imagination. There is, of course, no inherent corporeal distinctiveness between Jew and Gentile, and yet it is precisely the absence of quantifiable difference that so enrages the accoster. Ironically, the body of the antisemite is most discernibly defined in this encounter: the man's face, breath, and gait are noteworthily distended with rage. The antisemite attempts to articulate his disgust by accusing Philip of being inappropriately dressed, yet this accusation is confusing because the two men are similarly clothed. Indeed, what is also significant about this encounter is the lack of direct antisemitic rhetoric deployed here. There is nothing explicitly stated against Philip for being Jewish; instead, the narrator is only able to infer the man's implied meaning.

Philip attempts to make sense of this peculiar encounter and in doing so lays bare the false logic underpinning the antisemitism that he has encountered. Philip concludes that "the reason my clothes just like his were wrong was *because* they were just like his. What with my beard and my looks and my gesticulations, I should have been wearing a caftan and a black hat. I should have been wrapped in a prayer shawl. I shouldn't have been in clothes like his *at all*" (D 104, italics in original). Shostak makes a compelling point regarding this scene, contending that "to the Londoner, his [Philip's] garb is merely a deception, a disguise for his 'real' identity as 'the Jew'" (2004: 69). The Jews' body, specifically Philip's, is arrested in a static textual space that eviscerates his subjectivity, which does not allow for any nuance or complexity to manifest; indeed, the antisemite's repulsion at the sight of him, combined with his inability to articulate the precise nature of his disgust, traps Philip within an imaginary Jewishness that is demarcated (and dehumanized) as other.

The envisaged garments Philip supposes he should be adorned in (caftan, black hat, and prayer shawl) draw us back to stereotype images of Orthodox Jewry. Through this return, Roth reveals how antisemitism annihilates the complex diversity of Jewish lives, relegating Jewishness into a typecast image, one that is constructed through a simplistic binary in which the "hidden Jew" lurks *within*. Antisemitism is thus exposed in *Deception* for the deceitful way it reconstructs and rewrites the Jew into a flattened figure, which Roth—through his prose—challenges, rebukes, and reconceives.

Roth's characters are not passive entities beholden to the antisemite's imagination; rather, the Rothian (male) protagonist is an uproarious, cantankerous, disagreeable individual who—in *Deception* at least—contentiously grates against the English bourgeoisie he encounters. Crucial to Roth's rebuff is the Jewish bodies he writes through. Indeed, *Deception*'s most enriching and nourishing episode, aside from the one detailed above, outlines an almost Rothian mantra that typifies the author's oeuvre: "*Caprice* is at the heart of a writer's nature. Exploration, fixation, isolation, venom, fetishism, austerity, levity, perplexity, childishness, *et cetera*. The nose in the seam of the undergarment—*that's* the writer's nature. *Impurity*" (*D* 99, italics in original). This proclamation encapsulates the spirit of Roth's novels that center on the impurity of human bodies; for Roth, writing serves as an act of resistance against those seeking to establish racially bordered, national identities, and I think this entwines with the antisemitic episode that follows this proclamation. The antisemite Philip encounters is anguished precisely because the puritanical divide between Jew and Gentile is obfuscated by Philip's presence; thus, the racial purity he seeks to uphold is shattered. Roth's fiction shows a repeated interest in exploring and destroying such puritanism, which is ensconced in the maintaining and policing of the sexual, racial, and gendered body politic. While *Deception* describes and resists antisemitism in terms of the individual, *The Plot against America* envisages a far more threatening world wherein America has been engulfed and enveloped by the antisemitic imagination that abjectifies American Jewry.

The Plot against the Jewish Body

"Fear presides over these memories, a perpetual fear. Of course, no childhood is without its terrors, yet I wonder if I would have been a less frightened boy if Lindbergh hadn't been president or if I hadn't been the offspring of Jews" (*PAA* 1). The opening of *The Plot against America* (hereafter referred to as *Plot*) establishes two important entwining strands that define the novel's edifice: first, the narrative is framed as a recollection of childhood memories, lacerating the story with uncertainty, hyperbole, and bias; second, the novel is beset by a terror surrounding the fantastical figure of President Lindbergh and Philip's

Jewish heritage, both of which are inextricably linked. The opening places us in a fictitious world, a reimagined, reconstituted account of the Second World War and American history wherein American Jewry is subjected to and transformed into an abject form of (non) being following the election of the isolationist antisemite and celebrity aviator, Charles Lindbergh. In *Plot*, America does not re-elect President Roosevelt, but instead opts for the anti-war Republican nominee.[7] In this alt-historical work of fiction, Roth—using his own family as the narrative apparatus—questions the socio-racial precarity of American Jewry and the wretched abjection antisemitism inflicts on Jewish bodies. Before delving into the book's treatment of abjection and Jewishness, I will briefly situate my reading in relation to the current (and ever expanding) scholarship on this novel.

Since its publication, *Plot* has benefited from a swell of scholarly and public attention. This, in large part, stems from the novel's political subject matter and the timing of its release. Published in the aftermath of 9/11, many took Roth's novel to be a commentary on George W. Bush's presidency, an interpretation Roth refuted and responded to.[8] Due to a combination of the novel's arresting title, timely arrival, and calculated marketing, the book was a commercial and— for the most part—critical hit (Brauner 2007: 186).

Then came Donald Trump. The election and presidency of the Republican brute brought on a resurgent interest in *Plot*, as scholars and public commentators drew various parallels between the lexically impoverished, racist, misogynistic Trump and the antisemitic Lindbergh. Mark Bresnan, for example, contended that *The Plot against America* "is now impossible to see outside of the shadow of Donald Trump" (2016), while David Simon—author of *The Wire* and the HBO mini-series based on Roth's novel—claimed, "it's startling how allegorical it is to our political moment" (Greene & Rezvvani 2020). Elsewhere, scholars such as Brett Ashley Kaplan, Brittany Hirth, and Maggie Ward have probed the parallels between Trump's and Lindbergh's America. The latter is emphatic, stating, "Roth's counter-factual novel [is] more prophetic than contemporary: it predicts America in the age of Trump" (Ward 2018: 20). Andy Connolly offers a cautious counter-riposte to such readings, arguing that drawing parallels between *Plot* and Trump's America potentially "leaves Roth's novel prey to ideological appropriation, whereby it comes to serve as evidence of the unquestioned

---

[7] Lindbergh was never nominated by the Republicans.
[8] See Roth (2004).

sanity and uncorrupted character of liberalism" (2020: 67). I share Connolly's skepticism but find in Hirth and Kaplan particularly rich analyses which are fruitful rather than reductive.

My intent here is to pivot toward Jewish embodiment, focusing on racial abjection in Roth. This chapter intends to add to and join the conversation established by Debra Shostak, Maren Scheurer, and Patrick Hayes, whose scholarship touches on the abject in *Plot*. I aim to further unpack the abject imagery of Roth's novel, and by doing so, examine *Plot's* representation of Jewish precarity and race, with the aim of bringing a new and more comprehensive account of *Plot's* treatment of Jewishness, antisemitism, and the socio-racial positionality of American Jewry. Such discussions continue and complement present scholarship, as I outline how Roth probes the manifest ways antisemitism impacts American Jewry.

The Death of the Father

The novel begins with Philip describing how the Weequahic community "were no longer observant [Jews] in the outward, recognizable ways … [and that] hardly anyone in the vicinity spoke with an accent" (*PAA* 4). The narrator stresses the absence of visible Jewishness within the community as a means of affirming their Americanness. This is evident when Roth describes a Zionist "stranger" who collects donations for Israel and speaks broken English, whom Philip pities because he "seemed unable to get it through his head that we'd already had a homeland for three generations" (*PAA* 4). Roth establishes a connection between body and nation; Philip associates national belonging with a certain outward appearance that demarcates the stranger as foreign (and thus un-American) because he looks too Jewish. This distinction, however, threatens to collapse when Charles Lindbergh is nominated for president ("Then the Republicans nominated Lindbergh and everything changed" [*PAA* 5]). Philip's secure vision of himself as an American is brought into question through the election of a virulent antisemite who enables anti-Jewish prejudices to emerge in American society. Jewish life in America is revealed to be insecure; specifically, Jewish whiteness, or Jewish approximations to whiteness, which relies on white affirmation and toleration.

The precarity of Jewish lives in America is outlined in a scene that predates the fictitious election of Lindbergh, which is significant as *Plot* begins by underlining the insecurity American Jewry faced in "real-life" American society. Philip details how his father is offered a promotion as an agent with the Newark office of Metropolitan Life in Union (*PAA* 7). While visiting the small town, the family encounter the American Bund, whom Herman decries as "Fascist bastards!" (*PAA* 10). This, coupled with Bess's anxiety of being the only Jewish family in the town ("Ours will be the house 'where the Jews live'" [*PAA* 8]), results in Herman turning down the job offer. This small episode encapsulates the delimiting sociopolitical realities American Jewry faced in pre–Second World War America; antisemitism was not life threatening as it was in Nazi-occupied Europe, but it was real, and it impacted Jews' ability to progress socially and economically. The anxieties surrounding antisemitism are admittedly imaginary (in that both Herman and Beth catastrophize what would happen if they moved to the town), yet the fear of persecution stems from an awareness of their Jewish difference that is articulated and maintained by white American society. The Roth family, as outlined in this scene, *feel* the pressure of American antisemitism and are metaphorically paralyzed as a result.

The paralysis of the family grows in conjunction with Lindbergh's presidency, as the Roths are slowly expelled from American society. This expulsion (an abject term Roth employs throughout the text) alters how Philip perceives himself as an American and as a Jew, and in terms of how he regards his mother and father. Herman's position oscillates quite radically. In the beginning of the novel, he is cast as the prototype liberalist American whose view of the country echoes Seymour "Swede" and Lou Levov of *American Pastoral*: "'Pride of ownership' was a favorite phrase of my father's, embodying an idea real as bread to a man of his background, one having to do not with social competitiveness or conspicuous consumption but with his standing as a manly provider" (*PAA* 8). Herman's masculinity is determined by his ability to earn financially and the ownership he can stake over American land, yet as Philip notes, there is a humbleness to his father's ideations in that his self-identity isn't grounded in hubris. Instead, Herman's pride stems from his ability to provide for his family. Their father's earnestness contrasts the flamboyant Lindbergh. We see this, for example, when Sandy draws him as a "virile hero. A courageous adventurer. A natural person of gigantic strength and rectitude combined with a powerful blandness" (*PAA* 25). Elsewhere, Philip describes Lindbergh as a "lean, tall, handsome hero, a lithe athletic-looking man" (*PAA* 15), further stressing the stark disparity between the humble Herman and the gargantuan Lindbergh.

The divide between the two men is also made apparent in their comparative use of language, which Roth ties to racial conceptualities. Lindbergh is a man of few words; his speeches are sparse and to the point ("straight-talking Lindy, who never had to look or to sound superior, who simply *was* superior" [*PAA* 30]), reflecting—in Herman and the Roth family's' eyes, at least—the cultural vacuity of the president-to-be. Yet as the bracketed quotation indicates, Lindbergh's preciseness was lauded by other corners of the American populace as a symbol of his superiority (over Roosevelt, yes, but perhaps those "loudmouth Jews" whom the author so clearly identifies with). Herman, however, is a loquacious character who adamantly defends American liberal democracy.

In one of the novel's most discussed scenes, the family take a road trip to Washington to visit American landmarks such as the Washington Monument and the Lincoln Memorial. As they enter the capital, Philip notes that "there appeared before us the biggest white thing I had ever seen" (*PAA* 57). The "thing" in question, we presume, is the White House, yet the ambiguity of the noun creates a phallic overtone, alluding to the gendered and racial power-structures that have defined and determined America's governmental structure. During their visit to the Lincoln Memorial, the family are accosted by a couple following Herman's opinionated remarks regarding Lindbergh. Philip notes how the "stranger took a long, gaping look at my father, then my mother, then Sandy, then me. And what did he see?" (*PAA* 64). Philip provides an answer, detailing the physical traits of the Roth family as though he were the stranger looking at them. Herman is called out for being a "loudmouth Jew," which is "followed a moment later by [an] elderly lady declaring, 'I'd give anything to slap his face'" (*PAA* 65). Herman is framed here as a figure of excess, a Jewish man who is too loud and is therefore considered threatening, an alien aberration who needs to be silenced. It is telling here that the Jewish man's body is targeted; the antisemite renders Bess and her children invisible, reflecting antisemitic tendencies to make Jewish women invisible. All the corporeal distinctiveness of the Roth family is obliterated into a three-syllabled insult, reflecting the extinguishing force antisemitism has on Jewish people.

As discussed earlier, Roth has explored the antisemitic trope of the loudmouth Jew before: in *The Counterlife*, for example, Shuki, a friend of Zuckerman's, quips, "Have you ever noticed that Jews shout?" (*CL* 68) and in *Sabbath's Theater* Mickey Sabbath declares, "Shouting is how a Jew *thinks things through!*" (*ST* 95, italics in original). In both novels, however, the observations are made in jest; the humor stems from the absurdity of the claims articulated by Jewish characters. Here, though, Roth—as he does in *The Counterlife* and *Deception*—presents us with a Jew being confronted by a non-Jews' antisemitism. The woman's comment reflects her desire to inflict harm, suggesting the possibility of violence; antisemitism is no laughing matter here, as the democratic right to free speech is implicitly threatened, and as Kaplan notes, it "is not lost on Philip's father, Herman, that this anti-Semitism is uttered literally in the shadow of the engraved words 'All men are created equal'" (2015: 156).

What *is* lost on Herman is the racist power structures that have shaped the American democracy he so proudly cheers. When Mr. Taylor, the tour guide, points to a painting beside the memorial, Roth explicates the father's failure to see the racial-political realities of his country: "Meanwhile, Mr. Taylor, pointing to the painting, said, 'See there? An angel of truth is freeing a slave.' But my father could see nothing" (*PAA* 65). Herman—echoing Seymour's Levov's ironic inability to "see-more" of his country—cannot comprehend or acknowledge the racist oppression of BAME bodies in America; he fails to recognize that the foundational premise of America is rooted in racism, not equality. The soundbite he returns to "All men are created equal" is meaningless because men were not created equally in America.

The Plot against America challenges liberal mythologies of American democracy by subtly underlining how American racial violence and abjection has been at the center of its social structuring. Following the family's encounter with the antisemitic stranger, Philip describes them sat outside the Lincoln Memorial: "It was the most beautiful panorama I'd ever seen, a patriotic paradise, the American Garden of Eden spread before us and we stood huddled together there, the family expelled" (*PAA* 66). The heavy-handed biblical imagery presents the Roth family as though they were Milton's Satan, banished from Heaven, or in this case, national belonging. The illusion of Americanness is entwined with a racial identity that is couched in the unmarked category of whiteness; to exist in the American Garden of Eden, Roth implies, Jewish difference must be erased.

Herman, having been derisorily marked as a Jew, is outed, making his family's Jewishness visible, resulting in their metaphoric expulsion. This ejection becomes literal following an alleged mix-up at their hotel, as the Roth family are removed from the premises. When Philip asks Sandy why, he whispers back to him: antisemitism (*PAA* 69). Crucially, they are moved to another hotel where Philip describes two African American bellhops. Their presence subtly reminds us of the racial power structures that prevail in America, and that Black people have always been "expelled" from the Garden of Eden.

Herman rages against the antisemitism his family endures, and recites the Gettysburg Address once again, but is met with a witheringly mocking reply: "But that doesn't mean all hotel reservations are created equal" (*PAA* 70). This elicits laughter, as Herman is transformed into a *Schlemiel*, a demasculinized loudmouth stripped of any power, who slowly comes to represent—for Sandy especially—a symbol of Jewish foreignness, effeminacy, and benightedness. The antisemitism Roth explores here parallels Nazi Germany's in that it centers around a patricidal impulse. As Rozine Jozef Perelberg argues, "Antisemitism can thus be understood as the wish for patricide—the killing of the Jewish father, the father of the Law" (2022: 865). This patricidal impulse is clear in the novel's opening chapters, as the father's power, authority, and belief in his country gradually diminishes. The obliteration of paternal authority "leads to the creation of the Jews as an abject" (Perelberg 2022: 851).

Clean Americans

The abjection of Herman undermines his authority and status as the patriarchal figure of the Roth family, but also enables Roth to probe the racial history and legacy of America Herman so fervently admires. Herman's authority is questioned by his son, Sandy, and his nephew, Alvin, the former of whom Roth uses to explore America's racist past. The tension between Sandy and Herman increases following the former's participation in the "Just Folks" program, a government scheme ostensibly designed to de-Judaify young Jews and create a disconnect between them and their families.

As insidious and antisemitic as the scheme is, it is far removed from the abject violence undertaken by Nazi Germany against the Jewish people. Indeed, this point is raised in the fourth chapter "Bad Days," where Roth employs a third-person narrator to explicate the political events following Lindbergh's mysterious disappearance. As Roth explains, Lindbergh's Republicans were unable to enforce similar antisemitic measures as the Nazis because "the U.S. constitution, combined with long-standing American democratic traditions, made it impossible for a final solution to the Jewish problem to be executed in America as rapidly or efficiently as on a continent where there was a thousand-year history of anti-Semitism" (*PAA* 324). This section, in which Himmler is dispatched to America and decries Lindbergh as a "Lone Eagle with the chicken heart" (*PAA* 324), raises questions regarding the purpose and intention of the Just Folks program in *Plot*, because Roth does not intend to reimagine the Holocaust in America. Hirth contends that the "Just Folks" storyline "reflects the governmental policies that oppressed minority groups and inhibited social mobility, reminding its readership that this sort of subjugation *did happen* in America" (2018: 76, italics in original). Likewise, Christopher Douglas argues, "Roth's alternate history alludes to the specific mid-century histories of African Americans, Native Americans, and Japanese Americans during and following the war" (2013: 787). The Just Folks program is not a mirror of Nazi Germany's antisemitism nor a comment on America's vulnerability to fascism; rather, it reflects (and condemns) North American racism against Black, Indigenous, and Japanese Americans.

Sandy's body thus becomes a political site in *Plot*, wherein the effects of institutional antisemitism literally play out and manifest. Upon his return from Kentucky, Philip notes the multifarious ways Sandy has physically transformed: he is taller, blonder, tanned, and sounds like a Kentuckian: "he said 'cain't' for 'can't' and 'rimember' for 'remember' and 'fahr' for 'fire' and 'agin' for 'again' and 'awalkin' and 'atalkin' for 'walking' and 'talking,' and whatever you wanted to call that concoction of English, it wasn't what we natives of New Jersey spoke" (*PAA* 93). Sandy's inflected speech and physical change reflect the transformative power white supremacy has on minority subjects, particularly in terms of how they perceive their own identities. Sandy's appearance echoes the fetishized Aryan look lionized by Nazi Germany, mirroring the insidious plot to dislocate Jewish children from their parents and, by extension, their Judaic culture. The language used to distinguish Philip from Sandy is likewise telling, as the narrator defines himself and his family as "natives," which positions himself in alignment with America's Indigenous people, therefore situating Sandy as an invasive, threatening force. This manufactured binary between Sandy and his family is keenly articulated when his mother jokingly welcomes him home as a "stranger" (*PAA* 92), the same word used to describe the man who called Herman a "loudmouth Jew," signifying the growing division festering within the Roth family and the internalization of anti-Jewish sentiments seeping into Sandy's consciousness.

Herman's inadequacy is most starkly presented to the reader when Sandy admiringly describes the Kentucky farm owner whom he stayed with. I shall quote the passage at length, as the extensiveness of the excerpt reflects the gulf in status between the two men as perceived by Sandy.

It went without saying that Mr. Mawhinney was a Christian, fought the Revolution and founded the nation and conquered the wilderness and subjugated the Indian and enslaved the Negro and emancipated the Negro and segregated the Negro, one of the good, clean, hard-working Christian millions who settled the frontier, tilled the farms, built the cities, governed the states, sat in Congress, occupied the White House, amassed the wealth, possessed the land, owned the steel mills and the ball clubs and the railroads and the banks, even owned and oversaw the language, one of those unassailable Nordic and Anglo-Saxon Protestants who ran America and would always run it—generals, dignitaries, magnates, tycoons, the men who laid down the law and called the shots and read the riot act when they chose to—while my father, of course, was only a Jew.

(PAA 93–4)

Roth employs twenty-three verbs in this paragraph, evincing the admiration felt by Sandy for this Kentuckian, who sees in Mawhinney—like Lindbergh—a figure of action, one whose enterprises are interwoven into the very fabric of America itself. The childish mythologizing of Mawhinney skirts over the racism underpinning his American legacy (and American history itself). Indeed, this purification can be seen when Mawhinney is described as "one of the good, clean, hard-working Christian millions" (*PAA* 93), a blatant misrepresentation of an American family entrenched in a history of abject, bloody violence. The term "clean" also subtly alludes to white supremacist beliefs regarding their racial superiority, particularly in contrast to the supposedly dirty, racially impure Jews. Indeed, the division between Mawhinney and Herman is crushingly expressed at the end of this passage, as Herman—once again—is reduced to three syllables ("only a Jew" ([*PAA* 93]), while Mawhinney's history is breathlessly outlined in a tireless, ceaseless paragraph.

The power and allure of Mawhinney's history, the phallic girth of his accomplishments, dazzle the power-lusting Sandy, who sees his family as "ghetto Jews" (*PAA* 193), "living like a bunch of greenhorns in a goddamn ghetto" (*PAA* 270). The twice-repeated insulting reference to "ghetto" highlights how Sandy feels trapped by his parents' Jewishness, which he believes is paranoically tied to self-fulfilling fantasies of victimhood. The term "greenhorn" likewise reflects his view of them as un-American, deculturated Jews lacking any grounding in Americanness. Much like Portnoy and the Swede, Sandy seeks to escape into the fantastical land of white America, which he equates as a historic Eden free from the strife of his family's Judaism.

The Jewish Stump

The narrator of *Plot* is a familiar figure for any Roth reader. He—through tragic circumstances—comes to equate his family's Jewishness with suffering and burden, both of which he ties to his parents' bodies. As the fear of antisemitism dominates Philip's life, the way he perceives his mother gradually changes. For example, the two are sat on a bus when he realizes "my mother looked Jewish. Her hair, her nose, her eyes—my mother looked *unmistakably* Jewish. But then, so must I, who so strongly resembled her. I hadn't known" (*PAA* 134, italics in original). The three physiognomic characteristics Philip zooms in on (hair, nose, and eyes) have all—at one point or another—been used (by Jews and non-Jews) to physically define Jewish difference. As Andrea Levine notes, "Philip comes to see his Jewish body as something he has inherited, something passed on from his parents, regardless of his knowledge or volition" (2011: 44). I would like to complicate Levine's analysis here by suggesting that the linear legacy proposed is a little more diffuse than Levine would have it.

Philip's inheritance of Jewish difference stems not only from his parents but from the society around him; as anti-Jewish discourses blossom, Philip's self-awareness of his Jewish difference is simultaneously heightened. As Stefanie Boese saliently points out, "Philip learns to differentiate only by comparison. For Philip, Jewishness is very much 'an outsider's idea'" (2014: 285). The outsider's gaze affects how Philip perceives his Jewishness; the physiognomic otherness of his identity only emerges when anti-Jewish sentiments fertilize. He externalizes this perceived difference onto his mother (classic Roth!), once again infusing Jewishness with a gendered alterity that is displaced onto the mother's body. The abjection of the mother is, once again, entangled in an intersection of gender and racial body politics.

Inevitably, Roth's narrator seeks to escape the Jewish family drowning in the struggles of Jewishness. The trope of self-renewal plays out in typical farcical fashion, as Philip hatches and executes a plan to flee his family home: "I wanted nothing to do with history. I wanted to be a boy on the smallest scale possible. I wanted to be an orphan" (*PAA* 233). This quote exemplifies Imogen Tyler's point that what "disenfranchised people actively desire is not *flight* but rather anchorage" (2013: 12, italics in original); there is, in Philip's absconding, an urge to be moored in a stable identity marker, one that is not decimated by antisemitism and the traumatic complexities anti-Jewish hatred has inflicted on Jewish bodies.

Instead, Philip dreams of being an ahistorical orphan, a fantastical metonym for Americanness that is yet another metaphor for the white body. Philip abandons his home in the dead of night but is kicked in the head by a horse, losing his beloved stamp collection in the process. He wakes up to discover that he has had eighteen stitches to the head, has no memory of the event itself, but—he repeatedly stresses—"my memory was [otherwise] intact. Luckily. He [the doctor] used that word several times and it sounded like ridicule in my aching head" (*PAA* 234). The cracked skull has been read by Catherine Morley as a reflection of the narrative's indeterminacy, highlighting "Roth's real intention to position the authorial consciousness (both written and unwritten) at the core of the text" (2008: 147), but I am more interested in how the corporeal symbolically grounds Philip to the history he tries to escape. The kick to the head combined with the loss of the stamps destroy Philip's fantasy of self-renewal, literally and figuratively returning him back to his family and the Jewishness he tries to flee from, symbolizing the inescapability of history and the crippling force of antisemitism.

No other character better exemplifies Roth's fascination with the body as a sociopolitical site than Philip's cousin, Alvin, who defiantly flees America to fight the Nazis for Canada. Alvin loses his leg in combat and returns to stay at the Roth household, generating much of the novel's drama. In the fourth chapter, "The Stump," Philip describes his cousin's amputated body: "What I saw extending down from his knee joint was something five or six inches long that resembled the elongated head of a featureless animal" (*PAA* 136). Later, in a similar vein, he repeats the metaphor, comparing Alvin's stump to "a small animal, this time one whose head had to be muzzled extra carefully to prevent it from sinking its razor-sharp teeth into the hand of its captor" (*PAA* 137). In both images, Philip reconceives Alvin's amputated leg as an undefined animal, and in the latter metaphor, he views the stump as castrating, with its acicular teeth eking out, threatening to cut off "the hand of its captor." Philip perceives his cousin's body as a liminal site, one that has transgressed the boundary between human and nonhuman. Indeed, the animality of the stump (subtly) changes, reflecting the fluctuating instability of the amputated leg as a symbolic site. The narrative frame (i.e., writing from the viewpoint of a child) hyperbolizes Alvin's body, which allows "an unabashed confrontation with the negative emotions disability initially elicits in the non-disabled person" (Scheurer 2021: 199).

Alvin's abject body returns Philip to the imaginary level, exposing the ambiguity of the border between self and other. This is comically exemplified when Herman asks if Alvin has luggage, to which Philip's cousin sardonically replies: "Sure I got luggage. Where do you think my leg is?" (*PAA* 129). Alvin's stump throws into question the coherency of the self, "the incompleteness of one's identifications, and can thus contest and even revise one's identifications" (Dohmen 2016: 770). Philip is repulsed by Alvin precisely because he disrupts the signifying chain Philip conceptualizes himself through, confusing almost every bodily order conceivable. For example, Philip notes that Alvin possesses a repulsive smell, as he says: "I thought at first that the smell must be coming from his leg, but it was coming from his mouth. I held my breath and shut my eyes" (*PAA* 127), and Philip later notes that "I'd never before seen anyone so skeletal or so dejected" (*PAA* 128). The misidentification regarding the root of Alvin's stench reflects the abjection of the disabled body; he, like Merry Levov of *American Pastoral*, signifies the "dark revolt of being" that draws toward the place where meaning collapses (Kristeva 1982: 4). The rottenness of Alvin's body has been read by Hayes, Shostak, and Scheurer through Kristeva's theory of abjection. The foremost former argues that "Philip is terrified at the presence of decaying organic matter in the seemingly human because Alvin borders on being a corpse" (Hayes 2014: 211), while Shostak likewise explicates how "Alvin's stump serves as a synecdoche for the body as a corpse" (2016: 25). The corpse, Kristeva contends, "is the utmost abjection. It is death infecting life" (1982: 4), and here—in Philip's view—Alvin's body is abject, blurring the borders between life and death.

Initially, Philip rejects his cousin. "I couldn't bear Alvin because of his missing limb and his empty trouser leg and his awful smell and his wheelchair and his crutches" (*PAA* 134). His repulsion for Alvin stems—in part at least— from the seeming infinity surrounding his cousin's body (as demonstrated by the continuous conjunction "and"); the corporeality of the disabled Alvin is presented as never-ending, a ceaseless flow of "boils, sores, [and] edema" (*PAA* 135). Philip even tries expunging him from his periphery: "I'm unable to describe the rest of his outfit because the fear of gaping merged with the terror of seeing to prevent me from ever looking long enough to register what he wore" (*PAA* 128). Philip looks away from Alvin in a bid to protect and preserve his own sense of self; he is so disgusted by his cousin that he cannot bear to look at him.

Alvin's disabled body reflects the abject condition of the Roth family. As Levine convincingly argues, "Alvin's disabled, repellent body, then, is intimately linked to Philip's own revelation that he himself is visibly, *unmistakably*, Jewish" (2011: 44, italics in original). Alvin's body represents fragmentation and disunity, hence Philip's repulsion toward him, as Alvin reflects the paralysis of the Roth family under the antisemitic Lindbergh regime. Philip seeks to escape his Jewishness because it represents instability, and he desires to become a white American (which he recognises as solid and stable)—thus, his initial disgust at Alvin.

Importantly, Philip exhibits a similarly repellent attitude toward his neighbor and classmate Seldon Wishnow. The Wishnows parallel the lives of the Roth family, except their experiences are more traumatic and violent: Seldon's cancer-ridden father commits suicide; then, his mother agrees to move to Kentucky and is eventually killed in an antisemitic riot, which Philip is partly responsible for as he had the family moved (through his Aunt Evelyn), while Seldon is repeatedly dismissed by the narrator as an embarrassing figure whom he tries to expunge from his life (he actively hides from Seldon, and eventually outright orders him to stay away from him). Philip describes Seldon as "one of those skinny, pallid, gentle-faced boys who embarrass everyone by throwing a ball like a girl but also the smartest kid in our class" (*PAA* 141–2). Seldon is embarrassing because he throws balls like a girl, blurring—in Philip's view, at least—the constructed binary between the masculine and feminine.

Similarly, Seldon's father is perceived in abject terms, as his body—in a strikingly similar fashion to Alvin—is viewed as a living corpse: "his father coughed so frequently and with so much force that there seemed to be not one father but four, five, six fathers in there coughing themselves to death" (*PAA* 142). The cancerous body, like Alvin's stump, is porous, ruptured, and symbolically unstable. When Mr. Wishnow's suicide is discovered, Philip is convinced the corpse is his father, even after his mother reassures him otherwise and Herman appears—alive—at the scene: "I didn't seem to know whether my own father—who'd just headed downstairs with my mother—was really alive or pretending to be alive or being driven around dead in the back of that ambulance" (*PAA* 172). Overwhelmed, Philip becomes ill: "I was vomiting into the dish-towel still in my hand, and when I collapsed it was because my leg had been blown off and my blood was everywhere" (*PAA* 172). In this scene, Philip identifies himself as Alvin, signifying how the boundaries between Alvin and Philip are blurred, as they are with Herman and Mr. Wishnow. In this scene, Roth deftly illuminates the destructiveness of antisemitic persecution, as the individuality of Philip's character is torn apart. Vomiting here becomes a kind of abjection, a

78   *Philip Roth and the Body*

self-preservation, an attempt to exclude the "not-I" (i.e., Alvin, Mr. Wishnow, and Seldon). Philip's sickness—portrayed in a hyperbolically Victorian manner—stresses the fracturing of the collective and individual Jewish body in America, echoing the violent abjection of European Jewry under Nazi rulership.

However, *Plot* ultimately downplays or simply refuses to draw any comparison between European Jewry's experience of the Holocaust and the fictitious antisemitic oppression imagined by Roth. Yes, there are violent pogroms and Jews are murdered in antisemitic riots: "122 American citizens have lost their lives," (*PAA* 313), the unnamed narrator of the fifth chapter tells us. Even in this sentence, however, a searing gap between Nazi Europe and Roth's America is shown; Jews are defined as American, not as Jews, because the antisemitism of Nazi Europe did not occur in Roth's America. The violence is never replicated; the horror is eschewed. As Brauner rightly points out, "the scale of the threat that Roth imagines for American Jews hardly even begins to compare with the magnitude of suffering endured by European Jews" (2007: 199).

Plot concludes ambiguously.[9] Mrs. Wishnow's murder and the violent pogroms point toward dangerous potential violence bubbling underneath America's democracy. As I have alluded to earlier, antisemitic conceptualizations of Jews orbit around the semiotic slipperiness of the Jew, a motif Roth deviously subverts in *The Counterlife*. Here, though, Seldon—when confronted with the abject horror of antisemitism—is crippled by anti-Jewish violence: "He sounds stunned. Stunted. He sounds *stopped*. And yet he was the smartest kid in our class" (*PAA* 279, italics in original). The ossifying, violent, bodily impact of antisemitic oppression—the kind felt by Jews in Nazi Europe—is explored through Seldon, whose body and mind are irreparably altered by the vicious antisemitism he experiences.

Conversely, the Roth family—beaten, bruised as they are—are not stopped by the antisemitism they endure; rather, they rally together against the governmental oppression they face.[10] Sandy simply outgrows his boyish fetishism of Lindbergh, returning to the family fold in a quiet act of reconciliation; Alvin's

---

[9]   Timothy Parrish argues otherwise, claiming "the novel's conclusion is upbeat and effectively negates its originating premise" (2011: 153). Aimee Pozorski views things a little differently, as she highlights how the book ends "with a boy who is a stump, ruined by Lindbergh's America via a process that would allow a Fascist to become a president of the United States" (2011: 130). I find the latter of the two more convincing given the traumatic experience that Seldon endures.

[10] Alex Hobbs reads *Plot* "as the novel most warmly appreciative of the family" (2012: 123). Likewise, Ross Posnock—in his review of the text—notes that "the tender evocation of the strength of parental love and family loyalty ... have been rare, perhaps unprecedented, in his fiction" (2006b: 271).

stump ceases to be a site of horror and Philip becomes a temporary crutch for his cousin. "I couldn't live without you" (*PAA* 145), Alvin tells him, symbolizing the transformation of Alvin's character (in the eyes of Philip) from an abject monster to a morally complex human and the maturation of the narrator. Philip discards his fantasies of abandonment, as Naomi Sokoloff notes, "the protagonist learns to stay put and reconcile himself both to his history and to being a part of his community's past and future" (2006: 308).

Ultimately, though, it is Herman and Bess whom Roth garnishes with the most sympathy and compassion. "[A]ll those blows, insults, and surprises … intent on weakening and frightening the Jews still hadn't managed to shatter my mother's strength" (*PAA* 334–5). Likewise, Herman "regains his position of the symbolic Father, restoring order by his heroic rescue of the wholly traumatized child" (Shostak 2016: 27). Following a brawl between Herman and Alvin, the former, whose "poor human body was black-and-blue and bandaged just about everywhere" (*PAA* 299), emerges somewhat heroically, as he rescues Seldon from Kentucky after his mother is killed in the pogroms. Herman's body here retains its symbolic potency: the bruising symbolizes the pain and agony antisemitism has inflicted on American Jewry, yet it is nowhere near as genocidal or as murderous as the violence of the Holocaust.

To conclude, I want to consider to what extent *Plot* is blinkered by Roth's perception of America. Jennifer Rickel, for example, convincingly argues that the novel "reinforces a revisionist US human rights narrative through the celebration of FDR and New Deal Politics" (2020: 175) that ultimately "retains hope that US ideals may put an end to a corrupt sovereign's state of exception" (2020: 186). Elsewhere, Michaels criticizes the novel for referencing the lynching of Frank Leo, even though "3,500 black people were lynched in America between 1880 and 1930, whilst only four Jews were murdered lynched in the same period; Frank was one of four Jews lynched in the same period" (2006: 290). Both scholars articulate a wariness regarding Roth's vision of America and its racial history.

Roth, however, as I have hopefully demonstrated throughout this chapter, is attuned to the complexities of America's violent, racist history. To end, I want to return to the scene where the family are ousted from the hotel. When the family go to the Evergreen hotel, they meet two African American bellhops, one of whom Sandy draws: "[He was] very dark with strongly African facial features of a kind Sandy had never before gotten to draw from anything other than a photo in a back issue of *National Geographic*" (*PAA* 73). The Black body is commodified into an object that Sandy consumes through *National Geographic* and reconstructs

80 *Philip Roth and the Body*

through his drawings, and both Black men are defined through their physiognomic features. In and of itself, this scene is perhaps insignificant, yet if we pair it with another involving Sandy's drawings, we may better parse Roth's representation of race in America. Both Herman and Sandy travel down to Kentucky to rescue Alvin Wishnow, their former neighbor. During a break, Herman catches Sandy sketching one of the girls and fiercely reprimands him: "You never heard of Leo Frank? You never heard of the Jew they lynched in Georgia because of that little factory girl? Stop *drawing* her, damn it! Stop drawing *any* of them! These people don't *like* being drawn—can't you see that?" (*PAA* 359, italics in original). For Michaels, this only serves to stress the disparate experiences of racial violence in American between (white) Jews and African Americans.[11] Kaplan offers an alternative interpretation, contending that Roth's return "to the Frank case sheds light on the deep imbrication in the white supremacist imaginary of Blacks and Jews and thus helps explain why in moments of danger such as Charlottesville, hatred flows like lava to the two groups" (2020: 52).

Roth is stressing white fragility, poking at the instability of racial monikers that have defined America's social structure. According to Herman, the white southerners fear being reimagined through the gaze of non-white bodies, and this fear—as exemplified by the referral to Frank—can result and has resulted in abject violence. When white bodies are reconceived through the gazes of the mythic "other" there is—Herman implies—a threat of retaliative violence, as the white supremacist will attempt to resituate the symbolic "wholeness" of the white body. I think, however, Roth is being a little tongue-in-cheek here. After all, Roth's fiction generated him ostentatious fame and wealth, a good chunk of which oriented around a Jewish man sexualizing non-Jewish white women.

Roth, a mere thirty years after the events he is writing, penned one of the obscenest novels in American history; he drew white American women in the most unflattering terms possible. Indeed, as Karen Brodkin (and others) have noted, Roth not only benefited from whiteness in America but also actively contributed to post–Second World War conceptualities of what it meant to be white.

So, even though *Plot*'s narrative ends with Philip describing Seldon as "the stump" and himself as "the prosthesis" (*PAA* 362), there is an acute awareness in this novel (and the other works discussed here) that Roth has eluded the white supremacists' clutches; the dirty Jew continues to wander the American scene.

---

[11] See Michaels (2006: 288–302, 290).

3

Jews in the Garden

Sabbath's Theater (1995) signaled Roth's return to America, both in his fiction and in his personal life. The novel—described by Pierpont as his most intense and insanely funny (2014: 191)—is also his most disgusting and abject. The subsequent publication, *American Pastoral* (1997), is—as the title indicates— his most epic, expertly deconstructing the country's pastoral mythologies through the hapless hunk, Seymour "Swede" Levov. On the surface, these novels have little in common. The protagonist of the former, Mickey Sabbath, is a disgraced street puppeteer hell-bent on committing suicide following the death of his beloved mistress, Drenka Balich. *American Pastoral*, conversely, tells the story of Seymour "Swede" Levov, a dreamy American-Jewish idol of Nathan Zuckerman's whose handsomeness and financial success epitomize the American dream, until his daughter Merry turns terrorist, blowing up a post office and shattering the idyllic fantasy surrounding Seymour. Both novels, however, explore the pastoral mythos of post–Second World War America and the transformation of Jewish bodies in this supposedly Edenic space.

What each novel has in common is an invested interest in the land-as-body metaphor that harks back to pastoral mythologies and colonial narratives pertaining to the discovery of the Americas. Indeed, there are echoes of Saul Bellow's *Henderson the Rain King* ([1959] 2007) coursing through both novels. Regarding *Sabbath's Theater*, Ross Posnock highlights the "importance placed on letting go and being the beast marks a notable intersection between Bellow's 1959 novel and Roth's later book" (2006a: 160). Following from Posnock, I am interested in exploring another overlap between Bellow and Roth's novel: namely, the desire both men harbor to *"enter into the green"* ([1959] 2007: 283, italics in original).

Entering into the green is Bellow's metaphor for the pastoral; it represents Henderson's desire to reinvent himself by claiming (and penetrating) a virgin land that has not yet been colonized or discovered. Bellow's Henderson chases what Annette Koldony calls "America's oldest and most cherished fantasy: a daily reality of harmony between men and nature based on an experience of the land as essentially feminine" (1975: 4). Henderson's quest is predicated on a desire to return to what Kolodny terms a "primal harmony with the Mother" (1975: 4). Entering the green thus represents a return to the pre-Oedipal stage in which the subject's body is indistinguishable from the mother's; in other words, entering the green means returning to the pre-symbolic in which subject and object are indivisible.

According to Kolodny, Henderson seeks "redemption through wholehearted and erotic regression, attempting to get back a sense of intimacy he remembers once experiencing" (1975: 145). Kolodny defines this fantasy as the "pastoral impulse" (1975: 8), importantly illuminating how white men perpetually produce American pastoralism to reify and re-impose their dominance and power over the Old and New Worlds (1975: 153). In *Lay of the Land: Metaphor as Experience and History in American Life and Letters* (1975), Kolodny claims Bellow recycles an American literary trope that defines the land as metaphorically female, in which men "[long] both to return to and to master the beautiful and bountiful femininity of the new continent" (1975: 139). For Henderson, Africa represents a prelapsarian space, which enables him to enter "the real past" that he distinguishes from history and "junk like that" (Bellow [1959] 2007: 46).

The desire to escape the present-day tumult of American life is the catalyst for both *Sabbath's Theater* and *American Pastoral*, although both are wildly different in approach and style. Nevertheless, the gooey abject remains at the heart of these two novels, as Roth explodes American fantasies of purity and innocence through his collapsing bodies.

The Monk of Fucking

"Shouting is how a Jew *thinks things through!*" (*ST* 95, italics in original). So bellows Mickey Sabbath, Roth's most uproarious and odious creation, who screams this at his wife, Roseanna, after she meekly observed that "Shouting is *irrational*" (*ST* 95, italics in original). Mickey bristles against her because he rages against rationality, logicality, and reason; instead, Sabbath lives a life committed entirely to sexual pleasure. Mickey is Roth's most beatific product, a standalone figure in the author's oeuvre, embodying what Giles Deleuze and Felix Guattari describe in *Anti-Oedipus: Capitalism and Schizophrenia* (1983) as "non-sense erected as a flow, polyvocity that returns to haunt all relations" (1983: 133).

Mickey unsettles, unnerves, and undermines the rationalism characters like Roseanna rely on. Roseanna—an alcoholic who leans on AA as a crutch—is derided by Mickey because he sees her therapy as an anesthetization of life, an attempt to nullify the ugly cruelty living induces ("Everything at last under control" [*ST* 254]), which for Mickey is an absurd and inane project because "There's nothing on earth that keeps its promise" (*ST* 32). So, when Roseanna—vis-à-vis her therapist Barbara—accuses Mickey of misogyny and blames his mother in a quasi-Freudian fashion ("You hate all women" [*ST* 93]), Mickey rejects Roseanna's hypothesizing regarding his behavioral patterns because "A pattern is what is printed on a piece of cloth. We are not cloth" (*ST* 91). Roseanna's Oedipalizing of Mickey's character represents a sanitizing structuring that threatens to erase the nuances and metaphoric dirt being induces, effectively flattening his actions into a woven (and therefore predictable) pattern. Roth fashions—via Sabbath—a novel oozing with Whitmanic multitudes, creating a runny narrative that slips and slides from the reader's grasp.

Central to this slipperiness is Mickey's body; physically, Sabbath is an anomalous presence in Roth's oeuvre, possessing "one of those chests you don't want to get in the way of, a squat man, a sturdy physical plant, obviously very sexed-up and lawless, who didn't give a damn what anybody thought" (*ST* 123). Mickey is a sex-addled cretin, bearing a strong resemblance to the mariner of Otto Dix's *Sailor and Girl*, which he used as his book cover. Sabbath, like Dix's red-faced, devious-looking sailor, starkly contrasts the cherubic Seymour "Swede" Levov of *American Pastoral* and the buff buffoon, Ira Ringold, of *I Married a Communist* (1998). Indeed, of all Roth's abhorrent creations, Mickey Sabbath is his most powerful and abject, a revolting, disgusting character whose power centers on his sexual hijinks and exploitative, morally dubious relationships and encounters with women.

Sabbath's prick is described in forceful terms, countering antisemitic mythologies regarding Jewish penises; the dick is not "a nub of suffering" (Abrams 2012: 38) as it is in *Portnoy's Complaint*. Instead, there is a phallic force emanating from Mickey's cock, an unparalleled, relentless excess of sexual power surrounding the aged and disgraced street-puppeteer's member. As he derisively tells Roseanna, "Yahweh did not go to the trouble of giving me this big dick to assuage a concern as petty as your sister's!" (*ST* 84). Nevertheless, Mickey's big dick energy is dwindling, as, David Brauner notes, Sabbath's body "is all too

84 *Philip Roth and the Body*

painfully circumscribed by its mortality" (2007: 129). Roth anchors the novel on Sabbath's physical and psychological decline, delving into his usual topics of Jewishness, masculinity, and embodiment through the crumbling psyche and corpus of Mickey Sabbath.

My aim here is to parse the role of the abject in *Sabbath's Theater*, and springboard from Debra Shostak, David Brauner, and Ross Posnock's scholarship. The former observes that "Sabbath speaks in the voice of the abject, the unspeakable, the nonassimilable, the inadmissible" (Shostak 2004: 48), a view I intend to further unpack and expand on by analyzing the abject imagery and Roth's portrayal of American Jewry's assimilation. Elsewhere, Posnock traces how *Sabbath's Theater* entwines with Whitman's *Leaves of Grass* ([1855] 2009), Saul Bellow's *Henderson the Rain King* (1959), and Henry Miller's *Tropic of Cancer* ([1934] 2015), deftly parsing the symbolic significance of nakedness in the novel. This chapter expands from Posnock and Brauner by further exploring the Whitmanic cadences in *Sabbath's Theater* and the entwining manner Roth attacks American heteronormativity through abject imagery pivoted around the Jewish male body, a facet Posnock overlooks.

Scholars have often drawn comparisons between Mickey and Alexander Portnoy, and it's easy to see why: both men are excessively libidinous, sexually devious, and amoral misogynists. The crucial difference between them revolves around the intent and purpose of their sexual sojourns; while Portnoy's sexual exploits orbit around societal and racial status, Mickey's are far more hedonistic and less capitalistic. In fact, Sabbath reneges on all of life's other pursuits to dedicate himself to sex: "Sabbath had simplified his life and fit the other concerns around fucking" (*ST* 60). Mickey's religious devotion is reflected in his renunciation of the sociopolitical realities around him: "For years he had not read a paper or listened to the news if he could avoid it ... Sabbath was reduced the way a sauce is reduced, boiled down by his burners, the better to concentrate his essence and be defiantly himself" (*ST* 126).

Mickey attempts to exist in a metaphorically bare manner, a naked existence devoid of marriage, capital, and material. Sabbath's will toward nakedness is not merely an inherent facet of his street puppeteering but a sort-of manifesto. Mickey's nudity evokes Allen Ginsberg's poetics, whose poetry and performance repeatedly returned to the naked body. As Gregory Woods explains, "his work has involved a systematic rejection of subterfuge and disguise—if not always of pretense—and a refusal of discretion, as if the poem were a body" (1987: 197). Sabbath's rhetoric, too, echoes Ginsberg's meshing of high and low brow

Jews in the Garden

art forms, as both blend the sacred and profane. Mickey, for example, declares himself to be "The Monk of Fucking. The Evangelist of Fornication. *Ad majorem Dei gloriam*" (*ST* 60). Likewise, in Ginsberg's "Footnote to Howl," itself a lowly addendum to the "main" poem, Ginsberg rhapsodically heralds every part of the body: "The nose is holy! The tongue and cock and hand and asshole holy!" ([1956] 1974: 27). Ginsberg's sermonic proclamations of the nose, tongue, cock, and asshole are hardly what we would associate with holiness, just as Sabbath, with his demonic black beard and devious ribaldry, is far removed from what we'd conventionally equate with a monk.

Sabbath's street performance occurs during the mid-1950s, just as Ginsberg's *Howl and Other Poems* was published. Mickey, like Ginsberg, is tried for obscenity because of his art, although the circumstances are markedly different. Sabbath is prosecuted after exposing a woman's breast in public during his puppeteering act. His defenders—echoing the same rhetoric employed in Ginsberg's trial—make grand protestations regarding Sabbath's show, contending his performance blurs the borders between "legitimate" and "street" art: "There is a larger perspective to this case. And the larger perspective is that there is a legitimate street art and what happens in street art is that you can engage people in a way that you can't engage them in a theater … It's the intimacy of street art … that makes it unique" (*ST* 319). Sabbath—retelling the story of his trial—dismisses the "expert" his defense-lawyer brought in ("professors are as full of shit on the stand as the druggist and the cop" [*ST* 318–19]). The academic attempts to sanitize Mickey's art by comparing him with the literary canon's finest writers: "Shakespeare was a great street artist. Proust was a great street artist. And so on. He was going to compare me and my act to Jonathan Swift" (*ST* 319). By turning toward these canonical writers, the defense attempts to tart up Mickey's art, transforming his performance into an ideological tool that simultaneously empties his art of its contents, mirroring the prosecution's effort to redefine his work. The judge is indifferent to the highfalutin rhetoric employed by their expert defendant: "This is absolute nonsense … He touched a breast. What happened is he touched a breast" (*ST* 319). Amusingly, Sabbath concurs ("He was a wonderful man, Mulchrone. I miss him. He knew the score" [*ST* 319]), refusing to impose any kind of seriousness to his art, and thus refuting to imbue (and therefore corrupt) his performance with value.

Both Ginsberg and Roth share an indebtedness to Walt Whitman. Chris Gair highlights how Ginsberg "[draws] on a combination of Walt Whitman's free verse and black bebop jazz idioms, [offering] a hyperbolic indictment of 'respectable' American culture, highlighting many of his own oppositional stance" (2007: 27). Roth, too, implicitly calls on Whitman through Sabbath, as Mickey—symbolically contrasting Portnoy—unlocks the doors of America for his lover, Drenka: "My secret American boyfriend … To have a lover the country which one … it gave me the feeling of having the opening of the door" (*ST* 417). Drenka's speech echoes the romantic sentiment that flows from Whitman's *Leaves of Grass*, where the poet famously implores his readership to "Unscrew the locks from the doors! Unscrew the doors themselves from their jambs!" ([1855] 2009: 54). Mickey and Drenka's relationship symbolically entwines with Whitman's poetics, as their heterodox coupling hinges on a porousness that defies heterosexual norms; through Mickey, Drenka finds America's locks unscrewed, thrusting the doors of selfhood open (pun intended). Notice, too, Drenka's wonderful malapropism: "lover of the country" implies Mickey is a patriot, a descriptor alien to a nihilist that has repeatedly been publicly shamed for obscenity. This solecism echoes Ginsberg's "America," where the poet ironically declares, "I am America/I am talking to myself again" ([1956] 1974: 41). Both Roth and Ginsberg locate Americanness through the male body that exceeds, undermines, and—in Ginsberg's case, especially—resists American puritanism that hinged on heterosexualism.

The pietism Sabbath rails against has several different forms, but all tend to be shaped by the same white middle-class sensibilities. Matthew, for example, Drenka's son, is one such representative of the American puritanism Mickey opposes. A policeman, Matthew finds in his work a liberty that sharply differs from the kinds of sexual liberties Sabbath and Drenka indulge in: "Once you're gone on your shift, you're your own boss out there. Freedom, Ma. Lots of freedom" (*ST* 10). The controllership Matthew describes is predicated on a sense of power over others, which both parallels and juxtaposes with Sabbath. When Matthew recounts his work to his mother, for example, it is described as though he were a spectator watching a theater production: "Matthew had a front seat … at the greatest show on earth—accidents, burglaries, domestic disputes, suicides" (*ST* 11). The metaphor of theater links him to Sabbath, and there is a hint here of relish in the scenes Matthew witnesses (Sabbath, too, greatly enjoys the spectacle of human suffering). Of course, Mickey's theater does not revolve around intervention; instead, he amplifies, exploits, and *exposes* people's vulnerabilities ("The art is being able to get them into the act" [*ST* 318]). Matthew, on the other hand, serves to protect and serve, that is, to prevent what is deemed criminal, delimiting the freedom he reveres. As Matthew's name

Jews in the Garden 87

suggests, he symbolizes an American-Christian heteronormativity that is woven into the fabric of America's foundations, a policing, puritanical force Mickey and Roth rail against.

Much like "Goodbye, Columbus," *Sabbath's Theater* explores the assimilation of American Jewry in post–Second World War America.[1] Gone are the reprehensible Patimkins, and in their stead Roth presents us with Norman Cowan, a well-meaning, solicitous friend and business partner of Mickey's. Norman takes the brunt of Mickey's cruelty, and as his name suggests (Norman = normal man), represents a certain kind of Jewish middle-class normativity. Or as Mickey has it, Norman "emanated the ideals and scruples of humanity's better self" (*ST* 341) who "made himself into that impressive American thing, a nice guy. ... A nice rich guy with some depth, and dynamite on the phone at the office. What more can America ask of its Jews?" (*ST* 342). The explosivity of the stereotypical Jewish voice that alienates Mickey from his wife transfigures Norman into a capitalistic tool, becoming a commodity and an "impressive American thing" (an inhuman object). The comedy of the novel emerges from the disparity between the two men and Mickey's repeated attempt to expose the flaws of Norman's seemingly heavenly, albeit Prozac-fueled life, which "happens not to be a dick-friendly drug" (*ST* 81). Norman's life, impotent and arid, is invaded by the sex-obsessed Sabbath, who attempts to sully and spoil Norman's idyll.

Norman, in contrast to Mickey, appears to have been untarnished by the passing of time, reflecting (in Sabbath's view) the lifelessness of his existence. As Roth notes, the "scope of Sabbath's transformation seemed to astonish him [Norman], in part perhaps because of his own mammoth treasure of satisfied dreams, apparent everywhere Sabbath looked, including into Norman's bright, brow, benevolent eyes ... *nothing* about him seemed changed" (*ST* 139, italics in original). Sabbath, however, looks "like a visitor from Dogpatch, either like a bearded character in a comic strip or somebody at your doorstep in 1900, a wastrel from the Russian pale who is to sleep in the cellar next to the coal bin for the rest of his American life" (*ST* 141). Mickey's appearance ("a wastrel from the Russian pale") implies he represents a pre-assimilatory form of Jewishness linked with the abject wastage, starkly contrasting the immaculately assimilated Norman.

---

[1] The policeman who arrests Sabbath is named Abramowitz, subtly indicating how Jews have entered the social structures of American society.

88   *Philip Roth and the Body*

Norman's impeccability signifies—in Sabbath's view at least—his detachment from living, but there is also a socioeconomic (and racial) demarcation that separates the two men. Norman represents the assimilated, middle-class Jew, while Sabbath is working-class (portrayed as a kind of *Ostjuden*), and this difference creates an imbalanced power dynamism between the two men. Indeed, the narrator notes how "Back in the fifties there was something thrillingly alien about 'Mick'" (*ST* 142). The term "discovered" in conjunction with "alien" implies that Mickey represents an anomalous foreign form of American Jewishness, a brash, abrasive Jewry Norman has seemingly never encountered before. There is also a colonial tinge in the description, as if Norman was a colonist "discovering" Mickey. Though as Sabbath himself notes, "He was just someone who had grown ugly, old, and embittered, one of billions" (*ST* 143), contradicting and/or undermining the holy imagery Sabbath describes himself through previously.

Nevertheless, Sabbath embodies the antisemitic stereotype of the dirty old Jew (antithetical to the immaculate figure of Norman), and refuses to clean up his act; instead, he embraces his "shit-filled life" (*ST* 247), arguing, "it's been a real human life" (*ST* 247). Humanness, for Sabbath and his creator, orbits around the abject, that which we expunge and reject, the very matter Mickey welcomes. "More defeat! More disappointment! More deceit! More loneliness! More arthritis! More missionaries! God willing, more cunt! More disastrous entanglement in everything! For a pure sense of being tumultuously alive, you can't beat the nasty side of existence" (*ST* 247).

The bulk of the novel involves Mickey trying to expose others to the "nasty side of existence," and often his efforts involve the naked body. He either exposes himself and/or undresses others, both literally and symbolically. For example, Sabbath, armed with a stolen picture of Norman's daughter, Deborah, lies in the bathtub with a vaginal cream tube, and attempts to provoke a reaction from Norman by angling his erect dick upward in the water (*ST* 151). "Sabbath's talent for this scene Norman could not hope to equal: the talent of a ruined man for recklessness … to overawe and horrify ordinary people" (*ST* 151). Mickey here embodies the abject, that which is "immoral, sinister, scheming, and shady: a terror that dissembles" (Kristeva 1982: 4). Sabbath laments Norman for seeking defense from the horrors living induces: "Seeking protection against everything. *But there isn't any.* Not even for you. Even you are exposed—what do you make of that? Exposed! Fucking naked, even in that suit! The suit is futile, the monogram is futile—nothing will do it. *We have no idea how it's going to turn out*" (*ST* 344, italics in original). Posnock notes, "Sabbath's Whitmanic tramping and chanting and weeping enact Roth's aesthetic of letting go as undefended openness" (2006b: 176), but Mickey's actions are also predicated on defiling the lives of others, to expose them to the filth, "represent[ing] for the subject the risk to which the very symbolic order is permanently exposed" (Kristeva 1982: 69). Mickey's mission is to bring others into the risk Kristeva describes, to expose them to the instability of the symbolic order their lives are structured through.

Sabbath self-identifies with the abject, as he tells Norman: "I am flowing swiftly along the curbs of life, I am merely debris, in possession of nothing to interfere with an objective reading of the shit" (*ST* 347). The word "debris" is instructive, reflecting the destruction and/or trauma Mickey has experienced in his life, and the damage such horror has inflicted on him. Sabbath's ability to flow "swiftly along the curbs of life," implying a perpetually marginalized status, stems from the loss of his brother, mother, and ex-wife, Nikki; his actions are not triumphant but tragic. So, when Sabbath declares, "To being a human being I've always said, 'Let it come'" (*ST* 152), we ought to read Mickey's flippancy with caution. Life is thus associated with come, both in its verb form as a movement and as a noun, a sexual, viscous fluid tied to orgasmic pleasure. Note, too, Mickey's acquiescence in the statement "Let it," as though he allows life to unfurl before him, without acting or intervening.

There is a trace of Whitman's poem "Respondez" here, in which every line begins with the word "Let," and, in a similar vein to Sabbath, places significance on the naked body. "Let us all, without missing one, be exposed in public,/ naked, monthly, at the peril of / our bodies be freely handled and examined by/ whoever chooses!" (Whitman [1855] 2009: 166). The call toward exposure and nudity, coupled with the directive toward a democratic handling of one another, could well be the manifesto for Mickey and Drenka's relationship. Václav Paris argues that "Whitman's urging of nudity is emblematic of a more general tendency in many of the other lines—a tendency which might aptly be described as the stripping of social norms" (2013: 2), which undoubtedly links to Sabbath, whose will toward nudity registers as an aggressive attempt to desiccate and undermine the social norms of postwar American society. Yet Mickey's nakedness also seems to harken to the losses he has endured; his attempts to strip himself (and others) bare symbolize a yearning to return to a past uninhibited by loss, a return—if you will—to the pre-Oedipal state of innocence.

90   *Philip Roth and the Body*

American Endlessness

Unlike Alexander Portnoy, whose claustrophobic childhood is overwhelmed by his overbearing mother, Mickey Sabbath grows up with a feeling of infinity he credits to the matriarchal figure of his home.

> They'd had endlessness. He'd grown up on endlessness and his mother—in the beginning they were the same thing. His mother, his mother, his mother, his mother, his mother... and then there was his mother, his father, Grandma, Morty, and the Atlantic at the end of the street. The ocean, the beach, the first two streets in America, then the house, and in the house a mother who never stopped whistling until December 1944.
>
> (*ST* 31)

The repetition of "mother" and the ceaseless sound of whistling convey a convivial domestic setting unprecedented in a Roth novel (Herman and Bess Roth of *The Plot against America* are yet to make their appearance). The notion of "endlessness," which eventually comes to signify death rather than life, parallels the fantastical concepts of America as a paradisical site of infinite possibility, echoing colonialist mythologies of the "New World." The list of family members entwining with the streets and ocean suggests wholeness, as though Sabbath's childhood, prior to December 1944, was an American idyll, one he identifies closely with the ocean. "He was from the shore ... There were the jetties, the piers, the boardwalk, the booming, silent, limitless sea. Where he grew up they had the Atlantic. You could touch your toes where America began" (*ST* 30). The Sabbath family dwell in an Edenic site linked to the beginnings of America itself, one that Mickey connects to the "limitless sea."[2] The waves, or rather the porosity of the ocean, are integral motifs in this piss-riddled novel. Death and/ or capitalism in America is often constructed as arid and empty, while life and sex are overwhelmingly wet.

Mickey's paradise is lost following the earth-shattering news that his brother, Morty, is killed in combat. "He enlisted in the Army Air Corps at eighteen, a kid just out of Asbury High, rather than wait to be drafted. He went in at eighteen and he was dead at twenty. Shot down over the Philippines December 12, 1944" (*ST* 15). Initially conceived of as a site of infinite fertility, the sea is now conflated

---

[2]   There's also something rather touching that the sea is "silent." Given my previous discussion of Jews as loud and brash, there is a poignancy in this detail, one that shows Mickey's life was tranquil and calm before the Second World War.

Jews in the Garden

with death as well as life (overlapping, contradictory meanings abound in this headache-inducing novel!). Aimee Pozorski notes, "the language affixed to Morty is direct, practical" (2011: 35), which she contrasts with Drenka's ebbing, abounding paragraphs. The same can be said, however, for Mickey's mother prior to Morty's passing; indeed, the overlap between the two is very much deliberate (more on this later). Roth's prose is loose, fluid, and protracted when describing Sabbath's childhood. Consider this excerpt, for example, which describes his mother:

> A slight woman with a large nose and curly dark hair, she hopped and darted to and fro like a bird in a berry bush, trilling and twittering a series of notes as liquidly bright as a cardinal's song, a tune she exuded no less naturally than she dusted, ironed, mended, polished, and sewed. Folding things, straightening things, arranging things, stacking things, packing things, sorting things, opening things, separating things, bundling things—her agile fingers never stopped nor did the whistling ever cease, all throughout his childhood.
>
> (*ST* 13–14)

The passage begins by noting the colossal size of his mother's nose and hair (two features Mickey [or Roth] focuses on when describing Drenka). Despite her slightness, his mother floats freely around the house, musically flitting "like a bird in a berry bush." The ebb and flow of his mother exemplifies how Sabbath sees her: she is agile, unburdened, and free, utterly happy. There is, of course, a skewered fantasy underpinning this description, one that empties the "realities" of Mickey's childhood, as we are presented with a recollection drenched in exaggeration. Indeed, the idyllic memory is challenged by his mother's ghost who tells him, "Even as a tiny child you were a little stranger in the house ... making everything into a farce" (*ST* 160). The mother's counter-memory of Mickey's upbringing reminds us of his untrustworthiness, yet even this is fraught; after all, it's a ghost that speaks to him, so either Sabbath is literally haunted or he has lost his grip of reality. Nevertheless, the point stands: while Portnoy looked on in horror at his mother's ceaseless productivity (a sign of her supernaturality and phallic power), Mickey remembers his mother's fecundity with reverence.[3]

---

[3] It's worth noting, too, that Sabbath recalls his mother's preparations each spring for Passover: "her memory, her *meaning*, expanded in Sabbath when he recalled the alacrity with which she had prepared each spring for Passover" (*ST* 13, italics in original). I add this as a means of further reinforcing the distinction between *Portnoy's Complaint* and *Sabbath's Theater*; the former is defined by its narrator's Jewish self-loathing and his antisemitic view of Judaism as an intrusion against his assimilatory fantasy; this starkly contrasts with the latter, where Jewishness and Americanness seamlessly entwine.

92 *Philip Roth and the Body*

The syntactical fluidity of the novel is brought to a shuddering halt by Morty's death. "In the house I saw my father. In terrible pain. In terrible pain. My mother hysterical. Her hands. Her fingers. Moaning. Screaming. People already there. A man had come to the door. 'I'm sorry,' he said and gave her the telegram. Missing in action" (*ST* 297). The stuntedness of these sentences and the crippling repetition of "terrible pain," combined with the attentiveness toward the mother's fingers and hands (foreshadowing, perhaps, Mickey's arthritic affliction), exemplify the awful trauma induced by Morty's death. There is a discernible lack of flow in the quoted passage as the abruptness of the constant minor sentences gives weight to every moment described. The passage is cumbersome, filled with pain, confusion, and a new sense of anguish (notice, for example, how Mickey identifies his home as "the house," indicating an estrangement from the place). The telegram, and the faceless, featureless man, brings an end to the endlessness Mickey grew up with. "The family was finished. I was finished" (*ST* 298). Again, the short, sharpness of the sentences and the schematic prose, which so starkly contrasts the breathlessly elongated description of his mother before Morty's passing, exemplify the crippling loss the family feel. "I felt I lost a part of my body. Not my prick, no, can't say a leg, an arm, but a feeling that was physiological and yet an interior loss. A hollowing out, as though I'd been worked on with a chisel" (*ST* 298).

Sabbath's storyline orbits around his effort to fill the hole his brother's death causes. As I noted above, Sabbath's mother, childhood, and dawning of America are all linked to the sea, so it makes sense that Mickey, at the age of seventeen, flees to the Merchant Navy, pursuing the same kind of endlessness he possessed before Morty's death.[4] "He hung around the union hall and—since he had tasted paradise—waited for the 'Romance Run': Santos, Monte, Rio, and B.A. ... Whores, brothels, every kind of sex known to man" (*ST* 99). The last sentence is especially illustrative of my point: Sabbath seeks out an infiniteness in sex that would symbolically return to him an innocent beginning, one without the pain of grief. The word "paradise" is likewise telling, highlighting how he craves the taste and touch of heaven, the same celestial warmth he felt as a child. Yet this return, as it were, is always contorted

---

[4] Sabbath tells Norman, an old associate of his, how their home was marked with a gold star in the window, which symbolized that they had suffered a loss during the war. Mickey suggests this was the reason he fled to the sea, "to get the fuck away from the gold star" (*ST* 144).

Jews in the Garden 93

by the grief loss has induced in him; death alters Mickey into something ugly, and so his will toward the prelapsarian is determined by his intent to control and dominate those around him.

Hence Sabbath's attraction to Nikki—his first wife, whom he manipulates and controls—and his affinity for puppets, objects which he can govern absolutely. Regarding the latter, Sabbath claims there "was nothing false or artificial about puppets, nor were they 'metaphors' for human beings. They were what they were, and no one had to worry that a puppet would disappear, as Nikki had, right off the face of the earth" (*ST* 21). The matter-of-factness of the puppet, the object that signifies nothing else other than itself, symbolizes—for Sabbath— the absoluteness he craves. There is, dare I say it, a purity to the art form for Mickey, as he tells Nikki: "puppets were not for children; puppets did not say, 'I am innocent and good.' They said the opposite" (*ST* 96). The puppet is a symbol of authenticity, an art form that enables him to communicate a message that troubles the childish numbing anesthesia he sees in the Muppets (sorry, Kermit): "all the decent Muppets, making people happy with their untainted view of life: everything is innocent, childlike, and pure, everything is going to be okay— the secret is to tame your prick, draw attention away from the prick" (*ST* 208). The mind-numbing decency of the Muppets represents the sanitizing force of capitalism, a disabling commodifying culture that Sabbath seems to suspect of de-centering and disempowering "the prick." The prick here represents both male power (the phallus) and libido, two facets fundamental to the Sabbath's Indecent Theater.

For Mickey, puppetry is a unique craft precisely because it is a sexually explicit art form: "shoving your hand up a puppet and hiding your face behind a screen! Nothing like it in the animal kingdom!" (*ST* 244). The verb "shove," of course, has a penetrative overtone, a mustardy residue of phallic dominance underscores the sentence, and yet despite, or maybe precisely because of this, Mickey is enamored with puppeteering.

Nikki, for a while, serves as Mickey's puppet ("Nikki his instrument, his implement" [*ST* 201]), a figure he can metaphorically (and literally) insert himself into, control, and manipulate, as her director and husband. Both "instrument" and "implement" render Nikki as an object, reflecting the crude way Sabbath sees his wife as a nonhuman entity for him to use. If this sounds insidious, imbalanced, and sexist, it's because it is, despite Sabbath's protestation he "did not care to make people suffer beyond the point that he wanted them to suffer; he certainly didn't want to make them suffer any more than made him happy"

(*ST* 171).[5] There's a bizarre logic underpinning Sabbath's thought process here, as though he can control the thoughts and feelings others have. Sabbath sees himself as a kind of Prospero, a figure with an otherworldly ability to control and manipulate people, yet this is part of his theatricality. Mickey routinely spirals into rages, crying fits, and outbursts of grief; he conflates Norman for Morty (his brother), rubs his foot up against Norm, believing it to be his wife, Michelle, and chases a woman on the subway who he believes to be Nikki. At times, Mickey demurs from the seriousness of the episodes: "He was fairly sure that he was half faking the whole collapse. Sabbath's Indecent Theater" (*ST* 185), but this descent—despite Mickey's quasi protestations—feels very real. "Something horrible is happening to Sabbath" (*ST* 78).

The horror of grief desolates Mickey. As Ranen Omer-Sherman points out, "Sabbath's lifelong embrace of the transgressively erotic is an attempt to compensate for the losses he has never come to terms with, including Morty's, his mother's, Nikki's, and finally Drenka's" (2005: 175). Sabbath's erotic engorgements, read as compensatory acts, entwine the novel with William Shakespeare's final play, *The Tempest* (2006), as both orient around loss and power. "Every third thought shall be my grave" (*ST* n.p.) is the epigraph of *Sabbath's Theater*, signaling its primary concern: death, death, and more death. But the reference also alludes to questions of phallic power and control, as Sabbath targets women who—at least on the surface—appear vulnerable. Essentially, Mickey—like Prospero does with his daughter Miranda—manipulates and controls his wives for his own amusement and to regain that which he has lost. Unlike Prospero, of course, Sabbath is not interested in recapturing any status in society; instead, he seeks to control (and immerse himself in) the flesh of others as a means of returning to the endlessness of his childhood.

Sabbath's relationship with Drenka is the closest Mickey comes to re-creating the sense of infiniteness he grew up with. While his marriages with Nikki and Roseanna are imbalanced, predatorial, and cruel, Sabbath and Drenka share a

---

[5] I disagree with Alan Cooper's claim "Sabbath is not a misogynist. If he constantly hurts weak women, it is in a continual search for strong ones. In only one is he not disappointed, and her death is the hardest blow of his adult life" (1996: 287). If Sabbath does, as Cooper claims, judge women according to their strength, then such undertaking is misogynistic in and of itself, as he values and scores women against whatever criteria he has constructed. Shostak offers a more considered view that Sabbath serves to "critique … the mythology of masculine power" (2004: 47), a point I find more palatable than an absolute denial of Sabbath's obvious sexism. Kaplan, likewise, presents a counterargument to Cooper (regarding Sabbath's [and Roth's] misogyny). "Tracing the 'crisis of masculinity' does not mean one is free of misogyny; in fact, one could say that some crises of masculinity include a denigration of women in order to construct a counterpart that is figured as more powerful" (2015: 84–5).

genuine connection built on each's seemingly never-ending libidos. "She was his last link with another world, she and her great taste for the impermissible. ... they were interconnected by the instinctual and together could eroticize anything (except their spouses)" (*ST* 27).

Drenka and Sabbath, as I see it, are pitted as equals, both as depraved and as foul as each other. However, Mickey is repeatedly referred to as Drenka's teacher and instructor, and she as his pupil and student. Likewise, Drenka is defined only in relation to Mickey: "Inside this woman was someone who thought like a man. And the man she thought like was Sabbath. She was, as she put it, his sidekicker" (*ST* 9). In both Drenka and Mickey, Roth probes and explores the elastic performativity of gender. Brauner argues that Roth's fiction highlights "a fluid, plastic male sexuality" (2016: 88), but I would argue that in Drenka he explores a volatile sexuality that does not hinge on a gendered binary; instead, they flow and flit between such monikers. Kaplan takes issue with the masculinization of Drenka and asks why Roth's strongest and most memorable female character "need[s] to be configured as male-ish" (2015: 80). This is a fair criticism, yet I find in the last phrase ("sidekicker" [*ST* 9]) a comical nod to the biblical Eve, one that perhaps acknowledges the masculinization of Drenka's character. Drenka, much like Genesis's Eve, is constructed as a metaphorical side kick of Sabbath's, just as Eve is made from the rib of Adam.

Drenka is not merely a sidekick; rather, she is a side-kicker, a physical force that offers Mickey new erotic knowledge and knocks him from his position of power. Her malapropisms, for example, are adopted by Mickey, who delights in her solecisms, subtly alluding to the even dynamic between the two. As Frank Kelleter points out, "Drenka is able to shape Sabbath's language and imagination in much the same way as he contrives to chisel hers" (2003: 176).

Mickey and Drenka's relationship is yet another example of a counterlife, "a pornutopian 'beyond' in a beyondless world" (Kelleter 2003: 177). Crucially, the two rendezvous at a "love nest" in a wooded hillside where they "retreated to renovate their lives. ... [Where] no human presence had ever threatened their secret encampment" (*ST* 5). The grotto, as they call it, represents—or parallels—"the pastoral ideal used to define the meaning of America ... the dream of a retreat to an oasis of harmony" (Marx 1964: 3). The paradisical image of Mickey and Drenka hidden away in a clandestine, unspoiled garden links them to Adam and Eve, yet their idyll is rooted in one another's *impurity*, rather than innocence. The intimiacy of the two represents an evolution for Roth, a relationship that anticipates the Edenic pairing in *American Pastoral*.

For Sabbath, Drenka's body abounds in the same porousness his mother possessed; indeed, in the most perverse of fashions, Roth entwines the two. "Lately, when Sabbath suckled at Drenka's uberous breasts, the root word of *exuberant,* which is itself *ex* plus *uberare,* to be fruitful, to overflow like Juno lying prone in Tintoretto's painting ... he was pierced by the sharpest of longings for his late little mother" (*ST* 13, italics in original). The litany of springlike verbs and adjectives ("fruitful" "overflow" and "uberous") reflects how Mickey conceives of Drenka as a woman overflowing with life. Sabbath's "suckling" positions him as an infant, a childlike deviant drawing life from his lover; if Mickey, as I alluded to earlier, is Drenka's superior, their sexual encounters show a different power dynamic, where Drenka, not Sabbath, assumes the dominant role. Indeed, as the simile indicates, Drenka (like Juno) offers Mickey the promise of a fantastical immortality; not literally, of course, but within her he finds the same sort of infinite libido that drives him. It is no surprise, therefore, that Mickey remembers the piercing memory of his "late little mother" (*ST* 13), a woman whom he also associates with endlessness. Yet the word "piercing" tellingly reflects the sharp pain his mother's memory induces, and likewise serves as an ironic twist, as Sabbath, too, is penetrated in his sexual encounter with Drenka.

Mickey's "fantasy of endlessness" (*ST* 31)—paralleling Tintoretto's painting— is eviscerated by the "fact of finitude" (*ST* 31), as Drenka tells Mickey she is suffering from terminal cancer. During her reveal, "the oddest thing happened ... a helicopter flew over the woods and then circled back and hovered directly above them. This time it had to be his mother" (*ST* 32). It is befitting Mickey believes his mother is sat in the helicopter as this strange scene unfolds. Once again, Sabbath faces the agony of losing someone he loves: "Mother, he thought, this can't be so. First Morty, then you, then Nikki, now Drenka. There's nothing on earth that keeps its promise" (*ST* 32).

The cruel irony, of course, is that death does in fact keep its promise. The question, though, is why does Roth feature a helicopter in this scene? What is it doing here? As Drenka speaks to Mickey, "the helicopter's energy roared above them, a dynamic force to magnify the monstrous loneliness, a wall of noise tumbling down on them, their whole carnal edifice caving in" (*ST* 32). The helicopter is a literal machine in the garden, an invasive force that amplifies Mickey's feeling of isolation and desolation, as the structures of their affair crumble. The penetrative destructiveness of the helicopter reflects not only the devastation Drenka's cancer has and will inflict on the pair but represents the corruptive socio-technological changes American society has undergone since Mickey's self-enforced exile. Death brings Sabbath into the spotlight, forcibly removing him from the Edenic sex-den he and Drenka have forged together, drawing him back to the places of his past.

Springtime Mud

The novel's climax takes place at Drenka's grave, a site where her former lovers come (literally) to masturbate. At one point, Mickey spies Drenka's paramour, Lewis, masturbating onto the grave, and proceeds to lick "from his fingers Lewis's sperm and, beneath the full moon, chanting aloud, 'I am Drenka! I am Drenka!'" (*ST* 78). The declarative sentences at the end are, for Joel Diggory, "an outrageous example of Sabbath's attempt to incorporate Drenka's identity into his own" (2016: 59). Indeed, this "strange" (*ST* 78) act signifies Sabbath's effort to undo *him*self, to collapse the border between himself, Lewis, and Drenka.

The novel's ending is a resumption of Mickey's effort, as he—draped in the American flag and wearing his brother's "red, white, and blue satin ... patriot's yarmulke" (*ST* 404)—pisses over his lover's grave. Initially, Mickey cannot go ("Perfect metaphor: empty vessel" [*ST* 444]), but then, almost miraculously ...

> a trickle at first, just some feeble dribbling, as when your knife slices open an onion and the weeping consists of a tear or two sliding down either cheek. But then a spurt followed that, and a second spurt, and then a flow, and then a gush, and then a surge, and then Sabbath was peeing with a power that surprised even him, the way strangers to grief can be astounded by the unstoppable copiousness of their river of tears. He could not remember when he had peed like this last. Maybe fifty years ago. To drill a hole in her grave! To drive through the coffin's lid to Drenka's mouth! But he might as well try, by peeing, to activate a turbine— he could never again reach her in any way.
>
> (*ST* 444)

There is a bizarre poignancy in this scene, a tenderness dripping in grief and mourning, as evidenced by the referral to the knife cutting through the onion. The scene also borders on the supernatural, such is the inexplicability of Sabbath's "flow." Mickey's piss makes him feel as though he has regenerated ("He could not remember when he had peed like this last"), and he fantasizes (albeit briefly) about reviving Drenka. As Garth Greenwell notes of this iconic moment, "the very restlessness of the book calls all finality into question, even the finality of finality itself" (2023). Such questioning is dampened at the end (the dead remain dead here), but Greenwell highlights the fluidity of *Sabbath's Theater*, and such volatility orbits around the penis of its titular protagonist.

Sabbath's liquid mourning is brought to a shuddering halt by Drenka's son, Matthew, who shines a light on his naked body (his penis is referred to as a "spout without menace or significance of any kind" [*ST* 445], negating the earlier phallic thrum Roth imbues his dick with), and asks Mickey, "What *are* you?" (*ST* 445). Light, here, offers no consolation to Matthew, nor any explication of what or who stands before him. The question frames Sabbath as borderless, subjectless, an abjection that cannot be situated or demarcated. After arresting him, Matthew reveals that Drenka had been writing a diary during their affair: "She left a diary! ... He read the things you made her do! Even my *cousin*—my little kid *cousin*! 'Drink it, Drenka! Drink it!'" (*ST* 446). Drenka's diary—in a similar fashion to Faunia Farley in *The Human Stain*—remains concealed from the protagonist (and reader); instead, we are given only this small snippet, a reference to the two's most intimate sexual act where each urinated on one another. There's an irony here as Matthew is "so swept away ... by his own tears" (*ST* 446) given the porous fluidity of Mickey. Roth subtly here links the two men, both of whom are yoked together by their mutual grief, the porosity of their bodies, and the inevitability of death.

Mickey relentlessly teases Matthew, declaring his urination as "a religious act" (*ST* 446). Disgusted, Matthew hurls Mickey from the car ("You sick fuck ... You filthy sick son of a bitch!" [*ST* 451]), literally and metaphorically expelling him. Sabbath is left "ankle-deep in the puddling of the springtime mud, blindly engulfed by the alien, inland woods, by the rainmaking trees and the rainwashed boulders—and with no one to kill him except himself" (*ST* 451). The novel ends almost as it began: in the wilderness, Mickey finds himself surrounded by the moisture of the land; such sogginess summons memories of Drenka and Mickey's mother, returning us to his childhood of American endlessness. Befittingly, Sabbath decides "He could not fucking die. How could he leave? How could he go? Everything he hated was here" (*ST* 451), an apt ending for such an acerbic character. However, the wetness surrounding him offers an oddly hopeful climax, as the backdrop teems with virility. Ejected from society (yet again), Mickey renounces death, here, reaffirming his commitment to the abject ("everything he hated was here"). This paradoxical proclamation aptly reflects the multitudinous and contradictory porosity of Mickey Sabbath, the dirtiest Jew to have ever sullied the pages of American literature.

Jews in the Garden   99

Entering the Green

If Mickey Sabbath is Roth's filthiest creation, Seymour "Swede" Levov may be his purest and most innocent. In *American Pastoral*, Nathan Zuckerman's fantasy of self-renewal is oriented around an actual male body rather a pastoral landscape or non-Jewish woman's body; the Swede is the brave, strong, "whole" Portnoy fatalistically pursues, and the tangibility of the Swede echoes the pastoral fantasy of America itself. The Swede's body is for Zuckerman what America was for its first explorers: a perceptible, real site that makes possible the fantasy of self-renewal.

This section focuses on the role of myth in Roth's novel and the gendered imagery that imbues the Swede as a figure of the American pastoral. David Houston and Joseph Darda have, among others, been attentive to Roth's dismissive attitude toward the pastoral itself, but my interest here centers on the gendered body politic of *American Pastoral* and its relation to the pastoral-impulse Kolodny outlines.[6] My effort follows and departs from Marshall Bruce Gentry, who argues the novel's beauty rests in its "feminist subversion of male authority" (2000: 76), highlighting the ways in which women "seem to win a battle over the dominant male voice of its main character Swede Levov, the narrator Nathan Zuckerman, and even, to some extent, Philip Roth himself" (2000: 76). I seek to expand on Gentry's work by exploring the role of the abject in Roth's novel, and how Merry and Rita's inassimilable bodies eviscerate the Swede's fantasy of American innocence.[7]

This chapter asks how Zuckerman wields his power as a mythmaker to deconstruct the Swede's pastoralism. I contend that in Zuckerman's re-telling of Seymour's life, the Swede reduces his wife and daughter to figures of alterity.[8]

---

[6] See Houston (2014: 125–39) and Darda (2015: 77–94). Ross Posnock's *Rude Truth: The Art of Immaturity* (2006b) features a chapter on *American Pastoral*, which is particularly noteworthy in its analysis. Posnock highlights how the novel "examines the seduction, delusion, and power of antitragic 'utopian thinking'—in this case, its function as the motor of American faith in war triumphalism" (2006b: 103). Elsewhere, David Brauner defines Roth's use of the term "pastoral" as "an ahistorical, Utopian dream world in which man lives in harmony with nature, his fellow man (and woman), and himself" (2007: 149). This is an especially useful definition that I carry forward in my consideration of how women, like the land itself, are transformed into mythological objects that help maintain the illusion of the utopian fantasy.

[7] Hobbs (2010: 69–83) is particularly excellent in its discussion of the body and the gender politics underpinning the elevation of Seymour into the mythic "Swede." See also Staudte (2015: 55–66).

[8] This chapter works with and departs from Aliki Varvogli (2007: 101–13). Varvogli contends that there is a "certain degree of identification between the narrator and the terrorist character" (2007: 103). By stressing the moral ambiguities of the novel, Varvogli complicates earlier readings of the text that positioned the Swede as the sympathetic hero. Likewise, I seek to stress the Miltonic complexities of Merry as a Satanic figure whose terrorism reads as a reaction to the patriarchal oppressiveness of the Swede's American Eden.

By stressing Seymour's othering of Dawn, Merry, and Rita, I make connections between *American Pastoral* and John Milton's epic, *Paradise Lost*. Developing from Lee Morrissey's "Eve's Otherness and the New Ethical Criticism," this chapter contends that the Swede, like Milton's God and Adam, fetishizes Dawn into an Eve-like figure of his paradise.[9] In doing so, I highlight how the Swede denies Dawn a voice and autonomy by ossifying her into an Eve-like figure of perfection. By focusing on how Zuckerman's recreates the Swede's relationship with his wife, daughter, and Rita Cohen, I consider how the Swede's pastoral is representative of the American dream and to what extent America's pastoralism is predicated on the oppression and control of women's bodies. Before considering how Roth's novel fits within Kolodny's theory, I want to explore the definitions and traits of America's pastoral. Doing so helps contextualize Roth's engagement with the literary form, and better understand the ways in which *American Pastoral* illuminates the racial and gendered body politics underpinning American mythologies surrounding its lands.

Zuckerman's Jewishness is an important factor in Roth's reconstitution of the pastoral-impulse narrative originally outlined by Kolodny. Roth's narrator seeks to "enter" into the body of another man rather than the "maternal womb" of the land itself. The disparity points to an underlying foreignness felt by Zuckerman, one that stems from his Judaic heritage. As I discussed in Chapter 1, a metaphorical return to his mother's womb would maintain Nathan's connection to Judaism, which he sees as disconnected from America. The conceptualized Jew has been a signifier of displacement and exile; a perennial wanderer, the Jew has repeatedly been defined as nationless. If the Jew has no nation to impose their dominance or power over, then they are excluded from partaking in the pastoral impulse. Therefore, the stereotype denies Jews mastery over any land, as they are a landless people. The image of the dispossessed Jew influences Zuckerman's perception of his own connection to America as he feels alienated from the gentiles. The Swede, however, can transcend the schism that haunts Zuckerman through his physique and non-Jewish appearance.

To be self-assertive and virile, Zuckerman (and the other Jews of Newark) fetishizes the body of the Swede as a way of experiencing life as Americans

---

[9] Morrissey stresses how Adam turns "Eve into an other with repeated insistence that she is like him, but perfect" (2001: 336). By doing so, Adam "leaves Eve with few alternatives for showing him that she is not what he thinks she is. In order to break through this otherness, Eve would need to show Adam that she is neither like him nor perfect" (2001: 336). My reading of *American Pastoral* borrows from Morrissey's. Dawn is very much like Eve in Roth's novel, fetishized into a figure of perfection whose voice and complexity is repeatedly denied and repressed.

rather than as Jews: "through the Swede, the neighborhood entered into a fantasy about itself and about the world, the fantasy of sports fans everywhere: almost like Gentiles (as they imagined Gentiles), our families could forget the way things actually work and make an athletic performance the repository of all their hopes. Primarily, they could forget the war" (*AP* 3). The twice-repeated "fantasy" ameliorates the Swede with a mysticism that centers on his separateness from the Jewish community, enabling Newark's Jews to temporarily "forget the way things actually work" through his sporting prowess. The metaphorical retreat into the life and body of the Swede signals a collective desire to escape from the tumult and terror of American reality during the Second World War. The desire to imagine themselves as "gentiles" is animated by a collective uneasiness surrounding their identity as Jews, and it is this apprehensiveness that fuels their yearning to "forget the war" (*AP* 3) and begin again.

Essential to this renewal is the reinvention of the Jewish body to be more like the gentiles. The Swede is ardently fetishized because he is so stereotypically non-Jewish looking. As Nathan observes, "The Jewishness that he wore so lightly as one of the tall, blond athletic winners must have spoken to us too—in our idolizing the Swede and his unconscious oneness with America, I suppose there was a tinge of shame and self-rejection" (*AP* 20). The Swede's athleticism as well as physical strength correlates with the masculine ideal that was particularly prevalent during the Second World War in America but separates him from certain pernicious anti-Jewish stereotypes that represented the Jew as weak and effeminate. "The topos of the Jewish man as a sort of woman is a venerable one going back at least to the thirteenth century in Europe, where it was widely maintained that Jewish men menstruate" (Boyarin 1997: 210). The myth was born from the Jewish man's circumcised penis, which was, Boyarin writes, "interpreted as feminizing" (1997: 211). Zuckerman recognizes his Jewishness as shameful because his circumcised penis represents a masculine "lack" that denigratingly delineates him as a symbolic "woman."

The Swede, however, is a strong, athletic "winner" (*AP* 20), whose non-Jewish appearance and "marvelous body" (*AP* 20) render his Jewishness (and thus, femininity), unidentifiable, leaving Nathan to wonder, "[w]here was the Jew in him? You couldn't find it and yet you knew it was there" (*AP* 20). The Swede's appearance "hides" his Jewishness, which enables him to metaphorically penetrate the American landscape and "escape" the shameful stigma of being Jewish.

For Zuckerman, the Swede is a metonym for the American pastoral itself, as his hyper-masculine body enables Nathan to imagine mastering "the beautiful and bountiful femininity of the new continent" (Kolodny 1975: 139). Thus, when Nathan hears Seymour has married Dawn Levov, a former Miss New Jersey model, he considers the Swede's meteoric ascent complete: "A shiksa. Dawn Dwyer. He'd done it" (*AP* 15). The punchy, ironical brevity in these three sentences underpins the finality and significance of Seymour's momentous marriage. The meaning of the word "it" is not hard to discern: the Swede's marriage, in Zuckerman's skewed vision, cements Seymour's erasure of his attachment to his Judaism. The Swede, Zuckerman envisages, can only complete this assimilative fantasy by marrying a "shiksa" (a derogatory Yiddish word for non-Jewish woman), which Zuckerman believes reconstructs the Swede not only culturally but also racially. Thus, for Zuckerman (and presumably the Swede, and most certainly for Alex Portnoy) America can be symbolically entered through the white woman's body.

The non-Jewish, white American woman as an elusive symbol of gentility has been a staple of Roth's fiction. Yet the transcendental reverence and loathing Alex Portnoy insidiously imbues the "shiksa" with is absent here. Dawn is a real woman, and the Swede's marriage signifies a sacred moment that ceremoniously secures Seymour's ascension into the mythical plains of "Americanness." The name "Dawn" symbolizes the beginning of a new time, one that explicates the Swede's regeneration as an "American" and signifies a primordial entry into the American land. Thus, when Zuckerman wryly observes that "*Swede Levov's life, for all I knew, had been most simple and most ordinary and therefore just great, right in the American grain*" (*AP* 31, italics in original), Roth is tacitly returning to a pastoral ideal that orients the land-as-female. The word "grain" (*AP* 31) connects the Swede's unification with Dawn to the land itself; without her, the Swede's life could not be the pastoral ideal Zuckerman envisages it to be. Through Dawn, the Swede can "grow" within the American land, obliterating his connection to Judaic history and culture, much to young Zuckerman's admiration and envy.

Dream, Dream, Dream

The Swede's supposed freedom from his Jewish identity makes him, in the eyes of Zuckerman, what R.W.B. Lewis defines as the American Adam, "an individual emancipated from history, happily bereft of ancestry, untouched and undefiled by

Jews in the Garden

103

the usual inheritances of family and race" (1955: 5).[10] Yet the Swede's purification from history and the identity politics associated with family, ancestry, and race creates a subjective vacuity, as Zuckerman discovers upon re-acquainting with his hero. Roth ties Seymour's (supposed) lack of character with the pastoral itself, and by doing so, uses the fairy tale of the Swede as a way of commenting on the shallowness of America's pastoral mythos.

Roth highlights the Swede's alleged lack of subjecthood in the novel's opening chapter, as Nathan describes Seymour as an "*instrument* of history" (*AP* 5, italics in original) who "walked about the neighborhood in possession of all that love, looking as though he didn't feel a thing ... the love thrust upon the Swede seemed actually to *deprive* him of feeling" (*AP* 5, italics in original). Seymour's dense, thick body seems to lack any emotive depth, operating as a passive tool rather than as a person. Seymour's apparent lack of complexity is made evident when Zuckerman and the Swede have dinner together after running into one another at a baseball game. As the two eat, Roth's narrator wonders, "what did he do for subjectivity? What *was* the Swede's subjectivity? There had to be a stratum, but its composition was unimaginable" (*AP* 20, italics in original). The Swede's grandiose superfluity, once tantalizingly unimaginable, now seems vacuous and hollow to Roth's beguiled narrator, who seeks to locate in his former idol a shred of humanity.

The Swede's superhuman imperviousness that was once so mesmeric to Nathan is now tedious and shallow. Zuckerman observes that the Swede "is not faking all this virginity. You're craving depths that don't exist. This guy is the embodiment of nothing" (*AP* 39). Seymour's apparent subjective absence is connected to Zuckerman's mythologizing of him. Roland Barthes contends that "[t]he function of myth is to empty reality: it is, literally, a ceaseless flowing out, a hemorrhage, or perhaps an evaporation, in short a perceptible absence" (2009: 143). Zuckerman empties the reality of Seymour by creating "the Swede," and in doing so, the subjective reality of Nathan's hero is made absent, as he is mythologized into a fetishized object of Zuckerman's desire.

The myth of the Swede perniciously centers on an unconscious collective yearning to efface Newark Jewry's identity as Jews. The transformation of Seymour into the Swede enables Zuckerman to realize "the strongest fantasy I had of being someone else" (*AP* 88). Barthes highlights how myth functions

---

[10] See Mcdonald (2004: 27–40) for an extensive overview of the ways in which *American Pastoral* critiques the American Adamic tradition.

as "a type of speech defined by its intention ... much more than by its literal sense ... and that in spite of this, its intention is somehow frozen, eternalized, *made absent* by this literal sense" (2009: 124, italics in original). Subsequently, the Swede becomes a frozen, eternalized emblem of a fantasy, but is deprived of any knowable or identifiable subjectivity; he exists beyond the realms of possibility for Zuckerman, which is precisely why Seymour is so ardently fetishized.

However, the myth of the Swede as superhuman proves false. During a school reunion, Nathan learns from Jerry Levov, the Swede's brother, that Seymour's life was not as idyllic as Zuckerman had assumed: "He had a big, generous nature and with that they really raked him over the coals, all the impossible ones. Unsatisfiable father, unsatisfiable wives, and the little murderer herself, the monster daughter. The monster *Merry*" (AP 67, italics in original). Jerry obliterates the fantasy Zuckerman had of the Swede's perfect existence, divulging Seymour's recent demise from prostate cancer, and that his daughter Merry blew up a post office and killed a man to protest the war in Vietnam. During their dinner together, the Swede reveals to Nathan he had suffered from cancer but seems to lie when he tells Zuckerman the operation went "just fine" (AP 28). Seymour's deceptiveness regarding his health combined with Jerry's revelations regarding Merry and Dawn re-humanize the Swede, destroying the mythological invincibility Seymour seemed to possess.

The fallibility of the Swede inspires Zuckerman to rewrite Seymour as a tragic hero who tries and fails to understand the motivations of his terrorist daughter and adulterous wife. Merry and Dawn transgress the Swede's Eden to formulate their own subjectivities that are free from Seymour's influence. Zuckerman dreams a "realistic chronicle" (AP 89) that centers on the Swede's inability to comprehend his wife and daughter's subjectivities, parodying Nathan's own failure to conceptualize Seymour. The parodic function of the chronicle is what Barthes calls an "*artificial myth*," which undermines and satirizes his childhood idolization of the Swede which was predicated on Jewish self-hatred. "The best weapon against myth is perhaps to mystify in its turn, and to produce an *artificial myth*: and this reconstituted myth will in fact be a mythology. Since myth robs language of something, why not rob myth?" (Barthes 2009: 135, italics in original). To undo the myth of the Swede, Zuckerman ironically wields his power as mythmaker, creating a Miltonic mock-epic centered on the Swede's fall from the idyllic hamlet of Old Rimrock.

"Subtlest beast of all the field"

"The Fall" of *American Pastoral*, the second section of the novel, begins by introducing the enigmatic figure of Rita Cohen, whose inexplicability stems from her indeterminate bodily appearance. Roth describes Rita as a "tiny, bone-white girl who looked half Merry's age but claimed to be six years older" (*AP* 117), who was so "ineffectual-looking that he [the Swede] could barely believe she was at the University of Pennsylvania's Wharton School of Business and Finance ... let alone the provocateur who was Merry's mentor in world revolution" (*AP* 117). Seymour struggles to specify Rita's age and underestimates her intellectual prowess based on how small and pale she is. Rita's indeterminate appearance enables her to deceive Seymour into believing that she is a research student wanting to write a paper on his glove factory. At the end of the tour, she reveals who she really is by telling Seymour, "very softly, '[s]he [Merry] wants her Audrey Hepburn scrapbook'" (*AP* 132). The deceptive mystery of Rita's character is a recurrent motif that repeatedly leaves the reader wondering who Rita is and whether she knows Merry.

Rita is a semantically overloaded character whose ambiguity and lack of symbolic cohesiveness threatens the Swede's indomitability. She summons him to a hotel room, demanding he bring ten thousand dollars in cash, and it is here that Rita sets the Swede his challenge. She will only take him to see his daughter if he has sex with her. Rita mimics Merry's speech impeded voice as she attempts to lure him into bed. "Let's f-f-f-fuck, D-d-d-dad" (*AP* 143), Rita says, as she exposes herself to the Swede, "rolling the labia lips outward with her fingers, expos[ing] to him the membranous tissue veined and mottled and waxy with the moist tulip sheen of flayed flesh" (*AP* 145). Merry's voice becomes inescapably entangled with Rita's genitalia here, as the latter metaphorically assumes the role of the Swede's daughter and looks to have Seymour enact a fake form of incest. Just as Milton's Satan enters the mouth of the sleeping serpent "[l]ike a black mist" (2003: 190), Rita transgresses her embodied subjectivity by demonically parodying Merry's stutter. In doing so, she returns him to a particular memory (that Zuckerman has created) in which father and daughter share a passionate kiss after Merry begs Seymour to "kiss me the way you k-k-kiss umumumother" (*AP* 89).

Rita (and Merry) serves as Zuckerman's Miltonic serpent, as they attempt to entice Roth's Adam and Eve into sin. Rita is compared to an "imp of upheaval" (*AP* 146), which connects her to Milton's Satan, who transforms into "[t]he subtlest beast of all the field. ... [A] Fit vessel, fittest imp of fraud, in whom/ To enter, and his dark suggestions hide/ From sharpest sight" (2003: 188). The chaotic instabilities of Satan's bodily transformation center on his becoming invisible, as his entering into the serpent enables him to hide from God's vision. The Swede struggles to clearly see Rita, as her age, appearance, and actions repeatedly deceive and confound him. The excessive visibility of Rita's flesh is contrasted by her hidden and unknowable subjectivity that remains invisible to the hapless Swede. Like Satan, Rita disrupts subjective borders through her demonic slipperiness (both symbolically and literally) as she attempts to remove Seymour from what she describes as his "dead center" (*AP* 146).

Rita's body and sexuality threaten the Swede's "good" life in its perverse female excessiveness: "Her dark child's eyes. Full of excitement and fun. Full of audacity. Full of unreasonableness. Full of oddness. Full of *Rita*. And only half of it was performance" (*AP* 146, italics in original). Rita is a hypersexual woman entrapped in a child's body; she overflows with contradictory meanings that are so extreme she seems paradoxically vacuous in her excess. I contend that Rita's sexual exorbitance inverts the metaphor of "the land-as-woman" that Kolodny recognizes in America's pastoral-impulse. Instead of an idyllic garden or Eden, Rita's body is presented as a site of uncultivated chaos. "Step right up and take a whiff," she commands the Swede, "[t]he swamp. It *sucks* you in. Smell it, Swede" (*AP* 146, italics in original). Her directives to "smell" and "whiff" center on Seymour's mouth, an orifice she seeks to penetrate through the primordial scent of her genitalia. By comparing Rita's vagina to a bog, Roth presents Seymour with a bountiful body that is uncontainable and impossible to master; Rita represents a "wild" femininity that seeks to penetrate man, rather than be penetrated.

Rita's excess represents what Marx calls America's "counter force." In *The Machine in the Garden* (1964), Marx examines two contradictory chronicles that shaped Elizabethan perceptions of America: one defined America as an unspoiled garden capable of realizing and hosting "a pastoral retreat" (1964: 36), while the other depicted America as a savage site without order or civilization; a "hideous wilderness" (Marx 1964: 43). The Swede's "pastoral retreat" (Marx 1964: 36) collides with the hideous wilderness Merry and Rita represent, "bring[ing] a world which is more 'real' into juxtaposition with an idyllic vision" (Marx 1964: 25, italics in original). Ironically, the "realness" of Rita's counterforce is steeped in an unreality that Nathan fashions through his dreamlike "realist chronicle"; to deconstruct the myth of the Swede, Zuckerman constructs a new fable centered on the monstrous bodies of Rita and Merry.

In *American Pastoral*, the female body becomes the counterforce, which opposes the pastoral impulse Seymour harbors. The "hideous wilderness" (Marx 1964: 47) overruns the Edenic wonderland the Swede fetishizes; Rita's infinite, sexual abundance becomes a grotesque nightmare for the Swede. Roth reverses a pastoral trope of American literature that Marx outlines in *The Machine in the Garden*: "the machine [is] a sudden, shocking intruder upon a fantasy of idyllic satisfaction ... It invariably is associated with crude, masculine aggressiveness in contrast with the tender, feminine, and submissive attitudes traditionally attached to the landscape" (1964: 29). In Roth's novel, the interconnection between the land-as-female and the sexual tenderness of the landscape Marx posits as being traditional of American literature is skewed. Rita's body, intertwined with the wilderness of the American land, is symbolically positioned as an aggressive counterforce to the Swede's pastoral, which is defined as an ideological fantasy of idyllic satisfaction, upholding pernicious narratives of the American land-as-female.

Zuckerman's Rita disrupts the wholeness that the Swede represented for Nathan as a child. The immaculate unity of the Swede's masculine body is penetrated by the overwhelming smell of Rita's vagina. As Seymour hovers over her, Rita begins to "reach inside herself with her hand" (*AP* 146), and then extends the very same hand upward, as "[t]he tips of her fingers bore the smell of her right up to him. That he could not shut out, the fecund smell released from within" (*AP* 146). Rita collapses the divisions between the bodies' interior and exterior that simultaneously disrupts the fantasy of the Swede as an absolute figure of masculinity. Rita, whom Seymour identified initially as weak and insignificant, manages to violate Seymour through her genitalia; it is she who seizes power by penetrating the Swede's passive and powerless body.

The sexual disempowerment Seymour feels destabilizes him from his "dead center" (*AP* 146) and creates a conflict that perversely centers on paradoxical emotions of disgust and desire. Seymour, Roth writes, "was bursting so with impulse and counter impulse that he could no longer tell which of them had drawn the line that he would not pass over" (*AP* 147). The explosive language suggests a sexual desire here, one that is affirmed by the word "impulse," as the Swede has an ashamed urge to submit to his tormenter. Yet in the final moments of this climactic scene (pun intended), Rita "slipped each finger between her lips to cleanse it. 'You know what it tastes like? Want me to tell you? It tastes like your d-d-d-daughter.' ... Here he bolted the room. With all his strength. ... Faced with something he could not name, he had done everything wrong" (*AP* 147).

The word "slipped" appropriately reflects the transgressive fluidity of bodies here, as Rita and Merry's orifices spill out from Rita's mouth in a borderless heap. Seymour flees the moment his daughter's insides are prolapsed by Rita. The Swede, one suspects, is still erect when Rita reveals that she has had sex with his daughter and is overwhelmed by the shame and terror of being aroused the moment his daughter's vagina is verbally externalized. The contradictory feeling of disgust and desire, combined with Rita's performance as his daughter, confounds the Swede, whom Roth, through Zuckerman's earlier hypothesis, positions as a figure of singularity. That is, Seymour is a "good man" faced with a grotesque figure who attempts to eviscerate the Swede's pastoral fantasy life. The Swede's world is defined as a whole: a completed American model of living that is singular, solid, and unified, reified by Roth's emphasis on the Swede's muscular frame. Rita's grotesqueness destroys Nathan's childhood fantasy of Seymour's godlike solidity, as Zuckerman imagines Seymour becoming undone when faced with the abject and unruly female body that symbolizes the counterforce of the American pastoral.

The Monster *Merry*

Like Rita, Merry acts as a counterforce to the Swede's pastoral. Nathan Zuckerman's reconstruction of Merry Levov heavily borrows from Jerry's description of her as a "monster daughter" (*AP* 67). I am interested in how Merry's monstrousness connects her with Milton's Satan and the ways in which she influences Dawn's decision to abandon the Swede. Jerry informs Nathan that "Seymour was into quaint Americana. But the kid wasn't. He took the kid out of real time and she put him right back in. My brother thought he could take his family out of human confusion and into Old Rimrock, and she put them right back in" (*AP* 68). Jerry's summary of the struggle between Merry and her family animates Nathan's retelling of the story, as Merry, like Rita, assumes a Serpent-like role in destroying Seymour's Edenic life in Old Rimrock. I read Dawn and Merry differently from Catherine Morley, whose salient analysis posits the latter as a Miltonic Eve, who "sends the Adamic Seymour spiraling towards the Fall, unleashing a complicated anger at the nation and its unfulfilled promises" (2009: 103). I suggest, however, that Merry's bomb is the cataclysm that instigates Dawn's desire to transgress from the Swede, which is the turning point in Seymour's fall from "quaint Americana" (*AP* 68).

The comparison between Merry and Milton's Satan may seem incongruous at first, particularly given the latter's infamy for his eloquent soliloquies. In Book Nine of *Paradise Lost*, Satan is compared to "some old orator renowned/ In Athens or free Rome, where eloquence/Flourished" (2003: 203), and "his words replete with guile/Into her [Eve's] heart too easy entrance won" (2003: 204). The guileful, considered eloquence of Satan's rhetoric is essential to the Fall of Adam and Eve, as Katherine Cox concisely points out: "[f]or the Fall to occur, the serpent must speak" (2016: 234). Merry, in contrast, suffers from a speech impediment and repeatedly struggles to articulate her political dissonance to her rather bewildered family. I contend that both Merry and Satan's speeches are connected by their transgressive desires. As Christopher Eagle has observed, Merry's speech impediment serves as a symbolic form of protest against the formalistic structures of American English the Swede uses to create his Eden-like fantasy. Eagle reads this impediment as a "refusal to conform to her family's perfectionist demands ... [which allows her to resist] gender and generational expectations" (2012: 21). Thus, when Merry tells the Swede, "I want to be f-f-f-free!" (*AP* 106), the dragging repetition of the consonant "f" underscores her unwillingness to conform to the normative standards of American language and culture, but simultaneously affirms her inability to break free from the social and linguistic structures she is bound by.[11]

Merry's resistance to America's political and social hierarchies is illuminated when Merry and her grandfather debate the ensuing war in Vietnam. The latter, to appease his granddaughter, sends Merry copies of letters he wrote to President Johnson in protest against the war in Vietnam. Unimpressed by her grandfather's actions, Merry tells Lou, "He's not going to s-s-s-stop the w-w-war, Grandpa, because you tell him to" (*AP* 288). He retorts with an impassioned defense of American democracy: "Honey, we live in a democracy. Thank God for that. You don't have to go around getting angry with your family. You can write letters. You can vote. You can get up on a soapbox and make a speech" (*AP* 289). Both of their ideological disparities are illuminated within this telling scene. Lou, a democrat and stout proponent of American liberalism, fails to see beyond the social edifices he has successfully advanced through, ignoring the racial inequalities of American society.

---

[11] See also Bylund (2010: 13–30). Bylund highlights how Merry's excessive consumption of food serves to "dismantle the complacent pastoralism of the bourgeoisie American dream" (2010: 14).

110   *Philip Roth and the Body*

Merry, on the other hand, seeks to destroy those institutions Lou celebrates. By bombing the post office in Hamlin's store, Merry ideologically retorts against her grandfather's letters. By destroying a place where letters (and, thus, language) are sorted, cataloged, and disseminated, Merry is rejecting the racist American democracy her grandfather advocates. In other words, Merry destroys the unified, coherent, racially exclusionary American language her grandfather supports; her bombing of the post office is an extension of her stuttering voice, marking out her unwillingness to conform to the regular political and social processes she is expected to exist within.

Merry's body, like Rita's, threatens the Swede's idyllic existence through its abject excess. After receiving a tip-off from the mysterious Rita Cohen, Seymour rediscovers his daughter in a desolate hovel. Merry has become a Jain, devoting herself to a life of purity. She refuses to speak in anger or lie, renounces any form of sexual pleasure, repudiates any kind of material or emotional attachment, and rejects any form of killing (*AP* 239). Rita's extremes, her unaccountability, unknowability, and excessive sexuality, are superseded by Merry's excessive material negation; Seymour's daughter becomes a unified, singular non-being by abandoning herself to an extreme ideology centered on a grotesque ideal of selflessness.

Merry's uncleanliness initially makes her unrecognizable to the Swede. Confronted by his daughter, whom Roth describes as "not a daughter, a woman or a girl; what he [the Swede] saw, in a scarecrow's clothes, stick-skinny as a scarecrow, was the scantiest farmyard emblem of life, a travestied mock-up of a human being" (*AP* 239). Twice compared with a scarecrow, Merry is defined as a nightmarish reversal of the pastoral, a nonliving stick figure that barely resembles a human. She is neither a daughter, nor a woman, nor a girl in Seymour's eyes, but is instead defined as a scant emblem of life, a half-formed, half-alive mutilated mock-up of the Swede's daughter. Merry's physical collapse marks the breach of the border between Self/Other, a dark and violent revolt, beyond the scope of the Swede's understanding: Merry is defiling the logic of existence by willing herself toward self-destruction.

In a telling act, the Swede attempts to take control of his daughter's body by grabbing open her mouth, symbolizing his facile effort to reassert his authority over his unruly daughter and her body. Nevertheless, when he opens her mouth, he is overwhelmed by the stench of her breath:

> what he smelled now, while pulling open her mouth, was a human being and not a building, a mad human being who grubs about for pleasure in its own shit. Her foulness had reached him. She is disgusting. ... Her smell is the smell of

everything organic breaking down. It is the smell of no coherence. ... A spasm
of gastric secretions and undigested food started up the intestinal piping and,
in a bitter, acidic stream, surged sickeningly onto his tongue, and when he cried
out, "*Who are you!*" it was spewed with his words onto her face.

(AP 265–6, italics in original)

The embodied humanness of Merry's foulness is what Seymour finds most
horrifying. The return to a primordial mode of being, the negation of
order in favor of incoherent mess and madness—this is what Seymour is
faced with when he opens his daughter's mouth. The intoxicating stink is a
grotesque opening into the abject where every facet of postwar American
wholesomeness is eviscerated by the disturbing stench emanating from
his daughter. Ann Basu rightly highlights how "[t]he Swede's revulsion at
Merry's embodiment of this uncontrollability, this breaching of boundaries,
leaves him unable any longer to contain his own bodily reactions" (2015: 69–
70), but his vomit, in Kristevan terms, also marks his desire to reaffirm his
own subjectivity. As Julia Kristeva explains, "I expel *myself*, I spit *myself* out,
I abject *myself* within the same motion through which 'I' claim to establish
myself" (1982: 3, italics in original). The Swede's act of vomiting is doubled:
it exhibits his disgust but affirms his subjectivity. The Swede's outcry of "*Who
are you!*" synthesizes with his vomiting. By interlinking the question of
Merry's identity with the Swede's expulsion of himself, Roth highlights how
Seymour, faced with the abject, attempts to recreate and redefine the borders
between him and his daughter.

Seymour abandons Merry to preserve his fantasy life in Old Rimrock. He
leaves his daughter in the hovel, rather inexplicably, at Merry's request. The
Swede realizes. "This was his daughter, and she was unknowable. This murderer
is mine. His vomit was on her face, a face that, but for the eyes, was now most
unlike her mother's or her father's. The veil was off, but behind the veil there was
another veil. Isn't there always?" (*AP* 266). Seymour's use of the word "this," an
indeterminate pronoun, marks the ambiguous space Merry occupies, existing
between subject and object, human/nonhuman, daughter/stranger. There
is a Zuckerman-inflected reflexivity in this passage that stretches beyond the
intellectual capacity Roth grants Seymour, which is particularly prevalent in
the final two lines regarding Merry's veil. The last question is too epistemologically
laden to belong to the ideologically naïve Seymour; Zuckerman's presence is
explicit in this passage to forcibly underscore the parallels between hero and
monster.

112   *Philip Roth and the Body*

Both the Swede and Merry are defined through their obscured faces. Zuckerman compares the Swede's face to a "Viking mask" (*AP* 3), and Merry's veil symbolically echoes her father's cloaked appearance. The pair are ideological opposites, yet they are intertwined. As Ross Posnock observes, "Merry … is at once her rational, orderly father's nightmare opposite but also a grotesque version of his own project of purity" (2006b: 112).[12] The Swede recognizes his daughter; he understands that she belongs to him, and thus he chooses to abandon her, because she is both his daughter and his monstrous foe. In forsaking Merry, he attempts to re-enclose his Eden, but as I have highlighted, it is Dawn, not Merry, who finally instigates the Fall from Old Rimrock.

Through Eden Took Their Solitary Way

The Swede's fantasy of "entering into the green" (Bellow [1959] 2007: 283) is centered in America, which focuses on the pastoralist house in Old Rimrock. Despite his father's remonstrations regarding the historic proximity of the Klu Klux Klan, Seymour naively equates his purchase of the house with the expeditions of the first settlers in America:

> Next to marrying Dawn Dwyer, buying that house and the hundred acres and moving out to Old Rimrock was the most daring thing he had ever done. What was Mars to his father was *America* to him—he was settling Revolutionary New Jersey as if for the first time. Out in Old Rimrock, all of America lay at their door.
>
> (*AP* 310, italics in original)

The correlation Seymour makes between his marriage to Dawn and the American landscape startlingly resembles Alexander Portnoy's puerile proclamation, "through fucking I will discover America" (*PC* 235). The latter explicitly connects the non-Jewish woman's body to his own subjective identity as a man and as an American. Portnoy jests, but the desire to belong as an American rather than as a Jewish American is a real and serious point of concern for Roth's beguiled narrator. As such, Portnoy identifies the non-Jewish woman's body as a means of making himself into the mythologized version of the American he fetishizes.

---

[12] Likewise, Chris Gair highlights how Merry's "vow of purity, while apparently offering a 'renunciation' of her earlier actions, are in fact an extension of them, representing a symbolically murderous twist to Whitman's language of democratic freedom that, as we have seen, seeks to preclude the forms of human empathy upon which Whitman's America depends" (2008: 247).

The Swede, albeit more meekly and less obscenely, makes the same correlation. The marriage to Dawn and the purchase of their home in Old Rimrock enact the same American endlessness Portnoy envisages in the "shiksa."

The Swede's fantasy of being an American is not as aggressively or directly predicated on conquering the female body; rather, his American fantasy is rooted in the myth of Johnny Appleseed, whom Seymour envisages himself as being: "Wasn't a Jew, wasn't an Irish Catholic, wasn't a Protestant Christian—nope, Johnny Appleseed was just a happy American. Big. Ruddy ... a great walker was all Johnny Appleseed needed to be. All physical joy. Had a big stride and a bag of seeds and a huge, spontaneous affection for the landscape, and everywhere he went he scattered the seeds" (*AP* 316). The Swede creates a false binary: separating history and myth, failing to understand the ways in which the two are inseparably bound together. Thus, the Swede seeks to remove himself from the complex histories he associates religious identities with, aspiring instead to live in an alternate, mythologized version of America he envisions through the figure of Johnny Appleseed. The oversexed explicitness of Alexander Portnoy's rhetoric is absent, but the same carnal, malignant desire underpins the Swede's fantasy. His fetish for Appleseed's "physical joy" stems from the latter's freedom to spread his seeds across the land of America; the language is manifestly bodily: "big stride," "bag of seeds," "huge," and "scattered" (*AP* 316) are all pervasively sexualized and suggestive, exhibiting the over-masculinized rhetoric inherent in the myth Seymour defines America through.

Dawn is central to the Swede's Appleseed identification. Her name, as I discussed earlier, signifies a new beginning and closely correlates with the Hebrew word for Eve (Chavah), which means "Mother of all life." Both women are constructed in relation to their male counterparts: Eve is constructed from the rib of Adam, while Dawn is imagined and reconstructed as the wife of Swede; her origins and life are told in relation to Zuckerman's fallen hero. Following Merry's bombing of the post office, Dawn has a mental breakdown, and accuses the Swede of objectifying her and holding him responsible for her hospitalization: "How have I wound up *here*? You, that's how! ... You were like some *kid!* You had to make me into a *princess*. Well, look where I wound up! In a madhouse! Your princess in a *madhouse!*" (*AP* 178, italics in original). Dawn unravels not only because of her daughter's actions but because of the pain induced through her newfound critique of the Swede's ideology. She recognizes the ways in which her husband has objectified her into a sublimated figure of his pastoral drama, a princess for his American fantasy.

114   *Philip Roth and the Body*

Dawn's outburst against the Swede and her repudiation of her work as a beauty pageant model are vehemently blotted out by the doting husband: "It was a great help to him, driving home after one of those visits, to remember her as the girl she had really been back then" (*AP* 180). The Swede refuses to confront his wife's feelings by remembering Dawn as he wishes her to be: a perfect, happy, and young girl whom he was enraptured with. The Swede effectively others Dawn. Just as Milton's Adam loftily heralds Eve as his a "woman whom thou mad'st to be my help, / And gav'st me as thy perfect gift, so good,/So fit, acceptable, so divine" (2003: 221), the Swede denies Dawn her own subjectivity by returning to his version of Dawn's experience during the pageantry, obscuring and outright denying her a voice.

Like Eve, Dawn refuses to conform to the patriarchal authority. Merry's bomb serves the same function as Satan's acoustical charm: to enable man's Fall. Both Milton and Roth's Eve seek knowledge to no longer be "low and ignorant" (2003: 203), and both women's transgressions are framed through their bodily desires. After the Serpent tempts Eve with the promise that she will be "[o]pened and cleared, and ye shall be as gods" (2003: 204), Milton heavily sexualizes Eve's gaze upon the Tree of Knowledge: "Fixed on the fruit she gazed/ … An eager appetite, raised by the smell/ So savoury of that fruit, which with desire,/ Inclinable now grown to touch or taste,/ Solicited her longing eye" (2003: 204).

The word "fixed" returns us to the first moment in Milton's epic in which Eve sees herself. In Book IV, Eve finds a lake and sees her reflection in the water which has "answering looks/Of sympathy and love; there I had fixed/Mine eyes till now, and pined with vain desire" (2003: 85). The word "fixed" suggests a stiffness, as though she were "erect" at the sight of herself, while "desire" elucidates Eve's fancy for her own likeness. The yearning for her own reflection symbolizes her longing to assume her own subjectivity, which would free her from the patriarchal authority of Adam and God. Milton employs the same carnal language when Eve gazes upon the fruit. She is inflamed with sensory desires. Her mouth, eyes, and nose are all enticed, as Eve's appetite "raises her." On the one hand, Eve feels uplifted by the possibilities of the fruit and the knowledge it possesses, but I suspect there is a playful secondary meaning here: the fruit empowers Eve with the possibility of possessing the phallus which would symbolically enable her to be "raised" and thus erect.

Dawn's act of transgression is imbued with the same bodily desires that underpin Eve's consumption of the fruit. After Merry's bomb, Dawn begins to reinvent herself: "[t]he heroic renewal," Roth writes, "began with the face-lift

Jews in the Garden

at the Geneva clinic she'd read about in *Vogue*" (*AP* 187). Conjunctively, Dawn begins to "build a small contemporary house on a ten-acre lot the other side of Rimrock and to sell the big old house" (*AP* 188), as she reveals to their neighbor and architect Bill Orcutt that she had always hated their house (*AP* 189). Dawn seeks to re-create her body and home, both of which symbolically serve as a refutation of the Swede's pastoral. Like Milton's Eve, Dawn's "longing eye" (2003: 204) is set on erecting a space for herself away from her Adam.

Ironically, Seymour cannot "see" his wife's emotional complexity. When Dawn chooses to have a facelift, the Swede naively believes his wife has fully recovered from the ordeal of Merry's bomb: "He [the plastic surgeon] did a great job ... Erased all that suffering. He gave her back her face. No longer does she have to look in the mirror at the record of her misery. It had been a brilliant stroke: she had got the thing out from directly in front of her" (*AP* 298). The Swede fails to grasp the complexities of the trauma he and Dawn still suffer and struggle with; his oversimplification of Dawn's emotional depth mirrors Zuckerman's misidentification of the Swede, and accurately reaffirms his superficial understanding of Dawn's subjectivity. Moreover, it is the almost invisible mother, Mrs. Levov, who observes that Dawn's pain is still viscerally present: "Maybe you erase the suffering from the face, but you can't remove the memory inside" (*AP* 298). Of course, the Swede only conceptualizes his wife through her exterior, and therefore believes "[s]he's fine" (*AP* 299).

The turning point arrives when Seymour sees his wife with Bill Orcutt, standing tightly together shucking corn, leaving the unwitting husband to ponder, "if he was only helping her learn to shuck corn, why, beneath the florid expanse of Hawaiian shirt, were his hips and his buttocks moving like that?" (*AP* 335). The shucking of the corn is emblematic of Dawn's intentions to strip herself away from the Swede, which has a dual meaning, as Seymour sees the bare desires and intentions of his wife for the first time.

At last, the pastoral fantasy has been upturned, as the Swede reflectively declares to himself: "The outlaws are everywhere. They're inside the gates" (*AP* 366). His Eden has been corrupted by the transgressive desirousness of his wife, whose disobedience was born from the Satanic actions of his daughter, Merry. Rita, Merry, and Dawn's sexually porous bodies disrupt and perturb the gender roles Seymour conceptualizes his Johnny Appleseed mythology through, which ties into the novel's final setting.

The climatic moments of the text are set during a dinner in which Roth explores the evolving political, moral, and cultural landscape of America. The conversation focuses on Watergate and the pornographic film *Deep Throat* and are predominantly driven by the overemphatic Lou, the alleged moralist, Bill, and the provocateur, Marcia Umanoff, who provocatively proclaims, "[w]ithout transgression there is no knowledge" (*AP* 360). Umanoff is referring to the story of Adam and Eve, mockingly satirizing Lou's understanding of the tale that "when God above tells you not to do something, you damn well don't do it" (*AP* 360). Lou accepts the commandments and their authenticity in terms of authority, but Umanoff, as her name suggests (you-man-off!), seeks to resist and rebel against the absolutism of patriarchy; she, like Rita, Merry, and Dawn, refuses to submit.

Roth correlates the unruly female body with the American landscape in the novel's concluding moments. As the Swede dreams of his daughter walking through "the lovely Morris County countryside that had been tamed over the centuries by ten American generations" (*AP* 419), Lou Levov is stabbed in the face by the drunk Mrs. Orcutt. The Swede's reverie of the "tamed" landscape is violently overthrown by the untamable Mrs. Orcutt. She strikes out after Lou attempts to spoon-feed her, telling him, "*I feed Jessie*" (*AP* 422, italics in original). Mrs. Orcutt seeks to reclaim her authority and autonomy over her body by violently stabbing the face of the Levov patriarch, which symbolically serves as a refutation of the Swede's reverie of the tamed countryside. The novel ends with Roth's female characters lashing out against American patriarchy that has posited the land-as-female. Dawn is set to leave Seymour; Marcia loudly (and proudly) protests against Lou's patriarchy; Jessie, perhaps aware of her husband's infidelities, drinks herself into a stupor and violently attacks Lou; and Merry, the symbol of resistance, seems to have finally broken down her father's pastoralist dream: "the breach had been pounded in their fortification, even out here in secure Old Rimrock, and now that it was opened it would not be closed again. They'll never recover" (*AP* 423).

The women in *American Pastoral* break down what Kolodny calls "America's oldest and most cherished fantasy: a daily reality of harmony between man and nature based on an experience of the land as essentially feminine" (1975: 4). In the final two lines of the novel, Zuckerman's voice returns, satirizing the innocence of his own Swedian fantasy that the book began with: "what is wrong with their life? What on earth is less reprehensible than the life of the Levovs?" (*AP* 423). The seraphic purity of the Swede's harmonious existence is obliterated by Nathan's chronicle, as the ironic inflections of his questions signify a rupturing from the Swedian innocent that echoes the end of *Paradise Lost*. Nathan, in rewriting the Swede, goes hand in hand with his hero, wandering steps and slow, but "Through Eden took their solitary way" (Milton 2003: 288).

4

Black Skin, Jewish Masks

The Blackness of the Jewish Body

Shortly after being violently thrown out of "the famous white whorehouse Oris's" (*HS* 180) for being an African American, Coleman Silk—the protagonist and tragic hero of *The Human Stain*—retreats to a "colored bar" (*HS* 181) to patch himself up in the toilet and hide from the Shore Patrol (who would prosecute him for passing as a white man). Written as a flashback, Coleman remembers "how he'd struggled to stanch his cut face and how he'd swabbed vainly at his white jumper but how the blood dripped steadily down to spatter everything. The seatless bowel was coated with shit, the soggy plank floor awash with piss … he threw up onto the wall he was facing rather than lower his face into all that filth" (*HS* 181). This scene throngs with abjection: piss, shit, blood, and vomit come together in this grotesque dive, as Coleman—violently ejected from the white identity he has ensconced himself in for so long—is forcefully hurled back into a racial appellation he had previously absconded from. Coleman desperately tries to clean the blood from his white jumper, but fails, signifying his inability to wash away the racial violence inflicted on him; forced into a space abounding with bodily waste, Coleman's battered, bloodied body exemplifies the racial abjection Brandon R. Davis describes as the "abolition of the subject" (2023: 158).

This chapter begins by contextualizing the interrelations between Blackness and Jewishness, and how Roth explores the indeterminacy of race in America through his symbolically abject bodies.[1] Thereafter, I offer an extensive close reading of *The Human Stain* (2000) that connects Coleman's Emersonian quest to become the "raw I" (*HS* 108) through the psychoanalytical works of Franz Fanon. Coleman dismissively identifies women as sexual objects, literally and metaphorically penetrating their bodies to make his Blackness invisible. I

---

[1]   For more on the symbolic function of dirt in *The Human Stain*, see Newman (2019: 84–100).

118   *Philip Roth and the Body*

question the sexist objectification of women in *The Human Stain* and how the novel's problematic phallocentric focus on women's bodies illuminates and potentially reinforces America's patriarchal social structures. I conclude the chapter by examining how whiteness represents death in *The Human Stain*, and questioning how Roth fictionalizes a Jewish difference that resists what Herman Melville's Ishmael calls the "dumb blankness" of whiteness (2012 [1851]: 228).

Before discussing *The Human Stain*, I first must unpack how Blackness has been racially constructed in opposition to whiteness, and how the body operates in this racialized binary. In the seventh chapter of *The Jew's Body* (1991), Gilman asks an important and telling question: Are Jews white? (1991: 169). The significance of the question will become evident as I examine the racial ambiguities of Ashkenazi Jewry, but what is telling is how Jewishness is approximated in relation to whiteness rather than Blackness.[2] My focus is on how white American racism constructs Blackness in opposition to whiteness, and the ways in which Jewishness has likewise been positioned as a threat to white identities. Gilman's research is hugely important because it examines "how the category of race present within Western, scientific, and popular culture, has shaped Jewish self-perception" (1991: 170), and the ways in which the Jew's body has been constructed both symbolically and literally as Black. Gilman illuminates a pattern within nineteenth-century scientific literature that connects the Black, Jewish, and diseased body: "By the mid-century, being black, being Jewish, being diseased, and being 'ugly' come to be inexorably linked. All races, according to the ethnology of the day, were described in terms of aesthetics, as either 'ugly' or 'beautiful'" (1991: 173). The body determined and imbued individuals with a socioeconomic value as physiognomies of ethno-racial groups were hierarchized based on stereotypes that were constructed somatically.

Essentially, Gilman stakes that Jewishness was racially defined as Black: "The general consensus of the ethnological literature of the late nineteenth century was that the Jews were 'black' or, at least, 'swarthy'" (1991: 171). Recently, Ran HaCohen has challenged this claim, contending Gilman's readings of certain sources are from mistranslations. Essentially, HaCohen argues that the "notion of a pervasive 'Jewish blackness' from early times to the twentieth century thus

---

[2] Jewish studies scholarship has often overlooked Black Jewish lives. The Blackness of the Jew is analyzed as a metaphor or is considered in terms of antisemitic conceptualizations of Jewishness. My research likewise examines antisemitism's depiction of Jews as "black," but I feel it necessary here to address the dangerous potential of erasing Jews of color. See Parfitt (2013) as an example of scholarship that works to highlight Black Jewish lives.

seems to rely on an undifferentiated conceptual framework and inattentive reading of the source" (2018: 7).[3] HaCohen's re-evaluation of Gilman's research raises important questions concerning the overarching argument regarding Jewish Blackness, particularly the distinction between racial conceptualizations of the Jewish and Black body.

My interest here is to parse how the Jewish body in America was marked out and how this racialization compares with conceptualizations of Blackness.[4] In *Black Bodies, White Gazes* (2016), George Yancy highlights that the "Black body has been historically marked, disciplined, and scripted materially, psychologically, and morally invested in to ensure both white supremacy and the illusory construction of the white subject as a self-contained substance" (2016: 17). As Gilman's work shows, modern antisemitism used the Jew's body in an almost identical manner, conceptualizing Jewish difference somatically to construct the white European subject as a separate and "beautiful" entity. Yet within an American context, the Jew's body is racially abstracted in a way that is distinct from the corporeal racialization of the Black body.

Daniel Itzkovitz highlights how Jews in modern America were both "[w]hite and racially other, American and foreign, deviant and normative, vulgar and highly cultivated ... all of which made them seem at once inside and inescapably outside of normative White American culture" (1999: 38). The Jew signifies instability; their bodies are uncannily like conceptualizations of whiteness, but as Itzkovitz points out, "Jewish difference is a difference with no content, or, more exactly, with a fluid and ever-shifting content that cannot mark Jewishness as distinct" (1997: 179–80). The Jew is positioned as a threat because Jewish difference cannot be defined within the parameters of race or religion.

The insider/outsider status Jews inhabited in American society imbued Jewish people with a particularly distinct socio-economic position in that they were legally recognized as white. The concept that Jews (or indeed any other group of peoples that migrated from Europe) "became" white has recently been challenged by sociologists Philip Yang and Koshy Kavitha. They examine the

---

[3] See Parfit's "The Color of Jews," 1–13 in *Black Jews in Africa and the Americas*, for a fuller exploration of how Jews were conceptualized as "black" and the correlations made between Black and Jewish bodies. Parfit builds and develops from Gilman and gives a more expansive account of how Jews were corporeally conceived of as "black."

[4] My capitalization of "Black" follows from George Yancy, whose work has hugely influenced this chapter; it is a small gesture to bring to focus how Black Lives Matter and the racial inequalities are inherently present within American and European social structures.

120 *Philip Roth and the Body*

US censuses and highlight how these European minorities were always able to identify and bracket themselves within the category of white.[5]

While I am wary of promulgating the notion that Jews have always been white given the socio-economic barriers Jews have faced in American society, I raise Yang and Kavitha's research to underscore an important distinction between Jewish and Black bodies.[6] Within the context of America, the Jewish body has not been posited in opposition to whiteness; instead, whites feared Jews precisely because their bodies were uncannily approximate to conceptions of whiteness.

However, as Frantz Fanon and George Yancy have shown, the Black body has been positioned into an antithesis of whiteness. "The structure of whiteness is binary," Yancy writes, "[w]hiteness requires the so-called degraded and dangerous Black body. It is this structural requirement that reveals both the social constructed nature of whiteness and its deep fragility" (2016: xiv). Yancy's *Black Bodies, White Gazes* (2016) explores how the "white gaze" (de)constructs Black bodies into monstrous figures of otherness, highlighting the ways in which America's legal system sought to separate white and Black bodies. The "one drop of blood" rule exemplifies the ways in which racial differences are legally codified. If an individual has any trace or mark of African American lineage, they are marked and defined as Black.[7] As Neil Gotanda contends, "[t]he metaphor is one of purity and contamination: White is unblemished and pure, so one drop of ancestral Black blood renders one Black. Black is a contaminant that overwhelms ancestry" (qtd. in López 2006: 20). Jews were likewise positioned as contaminants and threats, but the racial ambivalence of the Jewish body meant that Jews were able to "hide" their differences from the view of whites. Yancy contends that the fundamental difference between the Black and European immigrant was the way in which the law was used to separate white and Black bodies: "Anti-miscegenation laws and the so-called one-drop rule kept ... [racial divisions] firmly in place for Blacks, while for Irish or Italian immigrants their alleged 'essence' might be said to dissipate eventually through assimilation" (2016: 19).

---

[5] See Yang and Koshy (2016: 1–27). The argument seems to overlook the symbolism of whiteness referred to by scholars such as Roediger and Brodkin. The very idea of "becoming" white is inherently impossible because whiteness itself is a social construct that is not fixed or stable.

[6] Antisemitism flourished in universities across America, particularly within the Ivy League institutes. See Karabel (2006) and Pollack (2010).

[7] *The Plessy v. Ferguson* case (1896) is the most cited example of the "one drop of blood" rule. Plessy was 7/8 white and 1/8 Black, and contended that he should be allowed to sit on the whites-only railroad car. Plessy ultimately lost the case and was demarcated as Black. Yancy contends that ultimately the "white gaze as a racist socio-epistemic aperture will 'see' a threatening Black body in white" (2016: 31). That is, the Black body is transfixed by the dangerous stereotypes associated with Blackness, even if the body identified as Black seems to be white.

While the Jewish body in America threatens whiteness because of its somatic instability, the Black body has been trapped by the "white gaze" that transfixes Blackness into whiteness's opposite: "the Black body has been confiscated to serve the needs of whiteness. The white gaze has fixed the Black body within its own procrustean frame of reference" (Yancy 2016: 4). In other words, the white gaze immobilizes Black bodies within a particular category of presumed racist stereotypes, while the Jewish body threatens precisely because it seems to resist categorical immobilization. As Yancy observes, "[t]he Black body ... *is* by nature criminal, because the white body ... *is* by nature innocent, pure, and good" (2016: 37, italics in original). Yancy's work follows Frantz Fanon's groundbreaking text, *Black Skin, White Masks* ([1952] 2021), a psychoanalytic exploration of race that unpacks the ways in which colonized peoples' identities are constructed through white gazes. Fanon, following Jean-Paul Sartre's essay, *Anti-Semite and Jew* (1995), argues, *"it is the racist who creates his inferior"* ([1946] 1995: 93, italics in original). The displacement of the colonized subject imprisons them within an objectified space that robs them of their autonomy.

Fanon is particularly interested in examining how the individual becomes representative of their racial category. In the fifth chapter of *Black Skin, White Masks*, Fanon recounts a moment in which he is racially abused: "'Dirty nigger!' Or simply, 'Look, a Negro!' I came into this world anxious to uncover the meaning of things, my soul desirous to be at the origin of the world and here I am an object among other objects" ([1952] 2021: 89). The command "Look" underpins the ways in which race is conceptualized through a visual ontology; the Blackness of the body is constituted as both abject and inhuman through the utterance of the racial slur etched onto the skin. Racism destroys Fanon, annihilating his aspirations to uncover meaning in the world that centered on an understanding of himself as a human being. The racist appellation assailed upon his body blows him up, reducing him to an object that represents a collective racial group. Fanon writes later that the "body schema, attacked in several places, collapsed, giving way to an epidermal racial schema" ([1952] 2021: 92). The subject is replaced by a racial body that begins with the flesh being marked as Black. As Fanon contends, "the *biological* cycle begins with the black man" ([1952] 2021: 139 italics in original).

Fanon's work is concerned with the individual's struggle to assert themselves against a system of identification that categorizes individuals within racial castes that dehumanizes and destroys subjects. Fanon ends *Black Skin, White Masks* with a powerful proclamation and prayer that seeks to move beyond

122   *Philip Roth and the Body*

racial classifications: "At the end of this book we would like the reader to feel us with the open dimension of every consciousness. My final prayer: O my body, always make me a man who questions!" ([1952] 2021: 206). Fanon desires mutuality: his Whitman-inflected call to see the open door of humanity's collective consciousness seeks out a world that does not castigate bodies into static categories. The construction of race, or rather the process of racialization, imbues bodies with social and economic values. In American society, Pellegrini contends, "[w]hiteness dissimulates its own race relations ... Whiteness produces itself as the unmarked, the universal term by projecting the burden of difference onto other bodies" (1997: 92). In other words, the white, unmarked body is symbolically clean and untouched. The Black (or indeed, Jewish) body is literally marked out and thus made into a racialized stain.

In *The Human Stain*, Roth explores how the racialized body is made abject and follows Fanon's examination of how the marked body can resist, deconstruct, and surpass colonialism's racial schema. Roth's bodies are deceptive, unstable, and porous, signifying a symbolic resistance to the crystallization of subjects within the specific category of race. Roth transforms the porosity and volatility of the body into a symbolic site of meaning that disturbs social divisions that rely on bodies to be cohesive and orderly. Leaking orifices assume a significant symbolic function in *The Human Stain*, representing "sites of cultural marginality, places of social entry and exit, regions of confrontation or compromise" (Grosz 1994: 193). I look at how Roth's bodies rupture the rigidity of categorical markings by stressing the intersecting links Roth creates between sex and race in America's social structures.

The Human Stain explores the intersectional ways race and sex are used to create distinctions between pure and impure bodies. The novel asks whose lives matter in America. How are American lives measured and valued, and how do race and sex influence the ways in which American lives are defined as American and as human?[8] In *The Counterlife*, Nathan Zuckerman proclaims "we are all the invention of each other, everybody a conjuration conjuring up everyone else. We are all each other's authors" (*CL* 149). *The Human Stain* continues *The Counterlife*'s exploration of how subjects are constructed through a constellation of narratives but expands its subject to the matter of race in America that includes

---

[8] In "Violence, Mourning, Politics," Judith Butler asks, "[W]ho counts as human? Whose lives count as lives? And, finally, what makes for a grievable life?" (2003: 10, italics in original). These questions underpin the chapter's focus on Roth's novel, and the ways in which bodies are positioned as "grievable."

Black Skin, Jewish Masks   123

and develops beyond the multiplicities of Jewishness. Through the characters of Coleman Silk, Nathan Zuckerman, and Faunia Farley, Roth explores how individuals are invented and reinvented through the imaginations of others, and what is a stake in this collective (re)constructing when bodies are defined in terms of race and sexuality.

Narrated by the isolate and impotent Nathan Zuckerman, the novel begins shortly after Clinton's failed impeachment, which Roth's narrator defines as "the summer when a president's penis was on everyone's mind, and life, in all its shameless impurity, once again confounded America" (*HS* 3). For Roth, the obsession with Clinton's penis represents a continuation of what Nathaniel Hawthorne called "the persecuting spirit" (*HS* 2) of America. The affair between Clinton and Monica Lewinsky represents an act of immorality that is categorized as dirty. Elizabeth Grosz contends this symbolic dirt "signals a site of possible danger to social and individual systems, a site of vulnerability insofar as the status of dirt as marginal and unincorporeable always locates a site of potential threat to the system" (1994: 192). The affair creates a moralistic frenzy in which "some kind of demon had been unleashed in the nation and, on both sides, people wondered 'Why are we so crazy?'" (*HS* 3).

The semen stain on Lewinsky's dress represents her and Clinton's vulnerability as human beings. "I myself," Zuckerman observes, "dreamed of a mammoth banner, draped dadaistically like a Christo wrapping from one end of the White House to the other and bearing legend *A HUMAN BEING LIVES HERE*" (*HS* 3). The reflexivity of the first-person pronoun highlights the separateness Nathan feels in relation to the rest of the American public, many of whom he describes as "confounded" (*HS* 3) by Clinton's libidinous recklessness and potential abusiveness. The Dadaist banner reflects the absurd excessiveness of American outrage, but the underlying message is potentially problematic in its apologetically sympathetic treatment of Clinton given the numerous sexual assault allegations against the former president.[9] Anthony Hutchison has argued that "*The Human Stain* is a novel not so much concerned with Bill Clinton but with the values of an age in which he could emerge as such a divisive figure" (2007: 136). Hutchison is correct, but I think it fair to highlight the simple fact that Roth's choice of Clinton as a metaphor has aged poorly. Clinton does not represent a debased

---

[9] Bill Clinton was accused of sexual assault and sexual harassment on numerous occasions. Paula Jones, a former Arkansas state employee, sued Clinton during his presidency for allegedly exposing himself to her when he was a governor. Kathleen Willey claimed Clinton fondled her in the Oval office in 1993, and Juanita Broaddrick has accused Clinton of rape during his 1978 campaign for Arkansas governor (Matthews 2016).

124 *Philip Roth and the Body*

and democratic humanity; rather, he symbolizes the corruptibility of white male power and privilege. Nevertheless, the hysteria surrounding Clinton reflects America's obsession with purity, a fixation structured on the body politic.

The Persecuting Spirit

The Human Stain is a continuation of Hawthorne's *The Scarlet Letter* in terms of its exploration of how bodies are marked as impure. Mark Shechner calls *The Human Stain* a "moral romance, a *Scarlet Letter* about race" (2003: 188), neatly encapsulating how Roth's novel interlinks Hawthorne's exploration of sexual politics and Fanon's examination of race.[10]

At the center of *The Human Stain* is Nathan Zuckerman, Roth's hermit-like writer who remains committed to a life of isolation and separation in a two-room Berkshire cabin. Zuckerman returns to the "goyish wilderness" (*GW* 68) he fled to in *The Ghost Writer*, but instead of seeking the validation of E.I. Lonoff, Nathan abandons himself to nature and writing. The monasticism of Zuckerman's isolation is apoplectically extirpated by the inconsolably rancorous Coleman Silk, who bursts into Nathan's home following the death of his wife, Iris, demanding Zuckerman write Coleman's story to clear his name and repudiate the charges of racism.

The initial discussion between the two instigates one of the text's central concerns: the interdependencies of individuals to be seen, heard, and thus recognized as human beings. *The Human Stain* asks how individuals are defined as Americans, and what happens to those that are excluded from this national identity.[11] Roth's grandiose exploration begins with the microcosmic "spooks" episode, where Coleman is publicly disgraced and labelled as a racist after asking if the two absentee students "exist or are ... spooks?" (*HS* 6). The two students transpire to be African American and register a complaint against Coleman for using a racial slur. The incident tarnishes Coleman's reputation as a respected academic who had been instrumental in the radical restructuring of Athena College that brought in its first African American professor.

---

[10] For more on Hawthorne's influence on *The Human Stain*, see Seeley and Rubin-Dorsky (2011: 93–111).
[11] Mark Maslan observes that "*The Human Stain* is only nominally about an individualists' struggle against the group; it is essentially about an American's struggle to realize his nationality" (2005: 379).

Black Skin, Jewish Masks

Ironically, Coleman was the target of antisemitism when he first arrived at Athena. Coleman, Nathan explains, "was one of a handful of Jews on the Athena faculty and perhaps the first of the Jews permitted to teach in a classics department in America" (*HS* 5). Furthermore, Coleman was the only Jew to ever serve as dean of faculty, and during his tenure he became a target of antisemitism because "he brought in competition, he made the place competitive, which, as an early enemy noted, 'is what Jews do'" (*HS* 9). The antisemitism Coleman experienced shows how he has faced racial prejudice, and perhaps make doubtful his alleged racism. Of course, this is not to suggest that Coleman is immune to intolerance because he has experienced antisemitism, but the inclusion of this scene serves to complicate the accusation.

Nevertheless, Coleman is branded a racist, and is effectively denounced and isolated by his colleagues and peers, many of whom he hired. Friendless and widowed, Coleman seeks out Nathan to write his story because if he did so, "nobody would believe it, nobody would take it seriously" (*HS* 11). Coleman's reliance on Nathan seems in part to stem from his position as a "professional writer" (*HS* 11), as the accused academic seeks to undo the charges of racism. In effect, Coleman wants to write a new narrative of himself that corrects the "false image of him" which "had not merely misrepresented a professional career conducted with the utmost seriousness and dedication—they had killed his wife of overt forty years" (*HS* 11). Coleman's story underpins the dangerous underside of *The Counterlife*'s thesis that "[w]e are all each other's authors".

The collapse of the imperious dean is a spectacle for Nathan, who admits that "[t]here is something fascinating about what moral suffering can do to someone who is in no obvious way a weak or feeble person" (*HS* 12). Coleman's extravagant unravelling is likened to a decapitated chicken: "His head had been lopped off ... and what I was witnessing was the amputated rest of him spinning out of control" (*HS* 11). Coleman is effectively castrated. The power he once possessed as an academic and former dean is ruthlessly cut from him, and what Nathan is confronted by is a flailing, headless carcass. Though tragic, Nathan finds Coleman's collapse captivating and almost comedic in its calamity.

Unlike the tragic Ira Ringgold of the preceding novel, or the hapless Swede of *American Pastoral*, Coleman can reinvent and remove himself from the controversy he is mired in. Two years after the "spooks" episode, he reveals to Nathan that he is having an affair with Faunia Farley, a thirty-four-year-old janitor who is illiterate. After Coleman tries and fails to write his own account of the spooks saga, which he laments as a "parody of the self-justifying memoir" (*HS* 19), he appears to be liberated. "Now that he was no longer grounded in his hate, we were going to talk about women. This *was* a new Coleman. Or perhaps an old Coleman ... the Coleman contaminated by desire alone" (*HS* 20, italics in original). Unfettered by rage and grief, Coleman is unbound, and singularly defined by his desire which is inherently connected to Faunia's body. Yet the unitary insulation of Coleman's desire seems suspiciously approximate to the "spooks" encounter in terms of how Zuckerman relays the events. As Peter Brooks highlights, desire is rooted in "a desire to possess, and also a desire to know" (1993: 11), and it seems Coleman's yearning for Faunia remains rooted in his wish to be seen and recognized as he demands.

Faunia is encoded politically; her body represents a kind of canvas for Coleman to express himself through. As such, Coleman's fetishization of Faunia threatens to overlook her subjectivity by sexualizing her into a fantastical object. Coleman reveals to Nathan that he has nicknamed her as "Voluptas" (*HS* 34), the name of the daughter born from Cupid and Psyche whose name means pleasure. She assumes a problematically mythic quality, verging (in a similar manner to Merry Levov) into the unrealistic, the unbelievable. Indeed, Nathan compares Coleman to "Aschenbach feverishly watching Tadzio" (*HS* 51), affirming the crazed excess in which Faunia's body is metamorphosed into a site of sexual desire. Faunia is presented purely in terms of how both Zuckerman and Coleman see her: she is defined and described by the gazing Zuckerman, whose interpretation of her is greatly influenced by Coleman.

In a particularly telling scene, Coleman and Nathan visit Faunia at her place of work, the Organic Livestock, whose produce is heralded in the local paper as though it were a "redemptive religious rite" (*HS* 46). The farm itself becomes a tantalizing space for Roth to examine the entwining images of pure and impure, and the ways in which Faunia's body is enmeshed as an almost biblically central figure monastically herding and milking the cows within the field:

> There was, at first glance, little to raise unduly one's carnal expectations about the gaunt, lanky woman spattered with dirt, wearing shorts and a T-shirt and rubber boots, whom I saw in with the herd that afternoon and whom Coleman identified as his Voluptas. The carnally authoritative-looking creatures were those with the bodies that took up all the space, the creamy-colored cows with the free-swinging, girderlike hips and the barrel-wide paunches and the disproportionately cartoonish milk-swollen udders, the unagitated, slow-moving, strife-free cows,

Black Skin, Jewish Masks

each a fifteen-hundred-pound industry of its own gratification, big-eyed beasts for whom chomping at one extremity from a fodder-filled trough while being sucked dry at the other by not one or two or three but by four pulsating, untiring mechanical mouths—for whom sensual stimulus simultaneously at both ends was their voluptuous due. Each of them deep into a bestial existence blissfully lacking in spiritual depth: to squirt and to chew, to crap and to piss, to graze and to sleep—that was their whole raison d'être.

(*HS* 47–8)

There is nothing flattering or sexual in Nathan's description of Faunia here; instead, she is described as haggard and spindly in height. Yet it is precisely this imperfectness that both men find so captivating. Faunia exists here as an exulted figure of the impure—the pastoral-shepherd of "crap and piss" (*HS* 48) that is the absolute antithesis of the Swede's Johnny Appleseed. She immerses herself in the dirtiness of life, surrounded by cows, whose lives revolve around bodily excretions and secretions, digestions, and expulsions. The peculiar romanticism of this scene places Faunia as a symbolic matriarch of sexual and spiritual virility. As Derek Parker Royal rightfully contends, "[t]he associations of feminine or maternal wholesomeness give emphasis to Coleman's newfound vivacity and what it might represent to the aging novelist" (2005: 130). Yet Faunia's femininity is far removed from the biblical innocence of Maria in *The Counterlife* or the Eve-like immaculacy of Dawn in *American Pastoral*. Faunia's vivaciousness seems to stem from her willingness to embrace the shitty, impurities of life.

Coleman and Faunia's relationship instigate Nathan's return to the material world. As Coleman and Nathan discuss the former's libidinous past affairs, Coleman directs Nathan to "[c]ome on" and "[g]et up" (*HS* 25), an ironic set of commands given the author's incontinence and impotence. Nevertheless, Zuckerman acquiesces, and the two dance the fox trot together, with Coleman assuming the lead position:

There was nothing overtly carnal in it, but because Coleman was wearing only his denim shorts and my hand rested easily on his warm back as if it were the back of a dog or a horse, it wasn't entirely a mocking act. There was a semi-serious sincerity in his guiding me about on the stone floor, not to mention a thoughtless delight in just being alive, accidentally and clownishly and for no reason alive—the kind of delight you take as a child when you first learn to play a tune with a comb and toilet paper.

(*HS* 26)

128 *Philip Roth and the Body*

Coleman's warm, naked back creates for Zuckerman a "delight in just being alive," enabling Nathan to embrace the adventitious, comedic absurdity of life that almost returns to him an infant-like state of "delight" (*HS* 26). I agree with Debra Shostak's contention that "the dance is the sign of Nathan's renewed receptivity to human contact ... [that signals] his willingness to *engage* with others" (2004: 263, italics in original). Coleman leads Nathan back to the world of infantile delight that sex and play initiates.

Coleman's virile "rebirth" (*HS* 27) enthralls Roth's narrator so much so that he wets himself: "I'd been so engaged by Coleman and his story that I'd failed to monitor myself" (*HS* 36). Nathan's urinary "accident" symbolically registers a letting-go of his solitary life, as Coleman's revelations unravel the author's reclusive existence. Nathan's leakage does not simply represent finality; rather, it represents the return of the material, the acceptance of life as a porous, unpredictable, and chaotic which is fundamentally tied to the body.

Nathan's asexual existence is obliterated by the intrusive and abrupt entrance of Coleman Silk, who, despite first appearing as severed and impotent, comes to possess a penetrative sexual power that pierces Nathan's solitary and sexless life. In other words, Coleman destroys Nathan's equilibrium (*HS* 37) and returns him to the matter of bodily desires: "How can one say, 'No, this isn't a part of life,' since it always is? The contaminant of sex, the redeeming corruption that de-idealizes the species that keeps us everlastingly mindful of the matter we are" (*HS* 37). Sex is positioned as a pollution, a sullying act that symbolizes an impurity that refutes the possibility of purification. For Nathan (and Roth), the corruptive de-idealization sex signifies grounds human beings within their bodies and thus redeems us from the pollutive corruptibility that purification represents.

Prior to meeting Coleman, Nathan had attempted to foster a purified existence that is removed from desire. Coleman's sexual awakening with Faunia contaminates Nathan's self-imposed exile on the account of his incontinence, but Coleman disregards propriety in favor of carnal pleasure. Without Viagra, Coleman explains, "I could continue, in my declining years, to develop the broad impersonal perspective of an experienced and educated honorably discharged man who has long ago given up the sensual enjoyment of life" (*HS* 32). There is a prescribed social role here for Coleman to follow that involves a disavowal of the libido. Nevertheless, as Zuckerman observes, Coleman

> wish[es] to let the brute out, let that force out—for half an hour, for two hours, for whatever, to be freed into the natural thing ... At seventy-one you're not the high spirited, horny brute you were at twenty-six, of course. But the remnants

of the brute, the remnants of the natural thing—he is in touch now with the remnants. ... It's not family, it's not responsibility, it's not duty, it's not money, it's not a shared philosophy or the love of literature, it's not big discussions. No, what binds him to her is the thrill. Tomorrow he develops cancer, and boom. But today he has this thrill.

(HS 32–3)

The twice-repeated "brute" evokes a primordial animalism that signifies a separation from the Coleman Silk of the past, the academic family man whose life centered on shared philosophies, love of literature, and "big discussions." Nathan sees Coleman's libidinousness as an absolute return to the body itself, an apolitical, nonracial, nonideological affair based on nothing but the "thrill" itself. One must wonder, though, given the excessive use of the word "brute" (which itself denotes a violent primitivism), to what extent Coleman's rather aggressive sexual language is predicated on a masculinist reclamation of phallic empowerment? Should we as the reader be wary of taking Coleman (and Nathan) at face value given the biases imprinted within the narrative? Considering the novelist in question, we as readers must tread carefully: *The Human Stain*—much like *The Counterlife*—exposes the precarity of language and narrative in the construction and maintenance of racialized and gendered bodies.

Coleman and Faunia are—like Mickey and Drenka—Zuckerman's prelapsarian Adam and Eve, but with a significant twist. Their naked commitment to one another centers on an exclusion and/or rejection of epistemology and language itself. Faunia, Coleman tells Nathan, is illiterate. She demands Coleman promise he never try to teach her how to read, effectively dismissing the power of language and knowledge. Unlike the biblical or Miltonic Eve, Faunia has no desire to taste the Tree of Knowledge and has no desire to assume any kind of authority the enlightenment of learning might provide: "Do anything you want with me, anything ... Bad enough having to hear people speak. Start teaching me to read, force me into that, push reading on me, and it'll be you who push me over the edge" (*HS* 34). Coleman replies by telling her, "I'm going to fuck you ... for just what you are" (*HS* 35). The two seek to create a relationship that dispenses with language and form a connection solely based on bodily pleasure. As Zuckerman observes of the two in a later scene, "[t]hey are, together, a *pair* of blanks" (*HS* 213, italics in original). Both Coleman and Faunia attempt to exist outside of language, away from the politics of being marked and labeled within categories that create and maintain social order. Ironically, however, the "blankness" the

130   *Philip Roth and the Body*

two seek is identified and detailed by Zuckerman, affirming the inescapability of the mark or stain language inevitably imprints on the body.

The two's attempt to exist away from the politics of being categorized or marked is confounded by Delphine Roux, the current dean of faculty, who sends Coleman an anonymous letter denouncing him for sexually exploiting Faunia: "Everyone knows you're/ sexually exploiting an/ abused, illiterate/woman half your/ age" (*HS* 38). Faunia is stripped of her subjectivity and becomes an "abused, illiterate woman half [Coleman's] age" (*HS* 38). The enjambment of the first and fourth line ends on "you're" and "your," stressing the direct accusatives of the letter that firmly focuses on Coleman's role as abuser. Conversely, the accuser (Delphine Roux) places "abused" and "illiterate" alone, which singularly defines Faunia as a victim, as the last line again places emphasis not on Faunia's subjectivity but her age in relation to Coleman's.

The words "Everyone knows" creates the impression of a universalistic understanding, a complete and shared knowledge that Coleman is a perpetrator and Faunia is a victim; the accusation is dependent on the absolute certainty that Coleman's age and social status makes him an exploiter of Faunia. Delphine's letter reduces Faunia to a victim of abuse whom Coleman has manipulated in his assumed position of power. The accusation effectively dismisses and/or denies Faunia's agency. All that matters here are the identity markers: Coleman and Faunia's disparity in age and class signifies an unequal and unacceptable social relation that must be "fixed" through public condemnation. I want to return to the question Butler poses of whose lives matter here as an ending point, because at this moment Faunia, positioned as victim, seems to be the figure of priority here. Delphine's letter claims to privilege and serve to protect Faunia from the exploitative Coleman, yet the letter seems to suggest that their lives only matter in that they exist outside of societal norms. What matters, then, is that social order be restored through a collective and public shaming.

The Raw Singular I

Thus far, my focus has been limited to the novel's opening and the sexual politics of Coleman's relationship with Faunia. To expand on the intersectional links between sex and race in *The Human Stain*, I will briefly clarify the novel's rather striking narrative structure. Adam Kelly contends, "*The Human Stain* has the structure of an observer-hero narrative ... [which] may be defined in brief as a story told by a dramatized first-person narrator about a significant relationship or encounter he has had with another person" (2013: 93). Kelly's description risks oversimplification, as the novel's first three chapters flit between Zuckerman's first-person observations of Coleman and the third-person perspectives of Coleman, Faunia, Les, and Delphine that extend beyond the hero-observer framework.

At the beginning of the novel, Zuckerman identifies Coleman as a Jew, describing him as "the small-nosed Jewish type with the facial heft in the jaw, one of those crimped-haired Jews of a light yellowish skin pigmentation who possess something of the ambiguous aura of the pale blacks who are sometimes taken for white" (*HS* 15–16). Furthermore, Coleman tells Nathan his father was "one of those Jewish Saloon keepers" who died in his final year of high school, and that he was the only child—"[t]he adored one"—who wasn't even allowed to work in the saloon (*HS* 22). Right from the novel's beginning then, readers are to understand that Coleman and his family are Jewish.

Yet ten pages into the second chapter, the novel diverges from Coleman's account of his upbringing. The narrative flashes back to Coleman's childhood where Dr. Fensterman, a Jewish physician, attempts to bribe the Silk family to allow their son Bert to finish above Coleman in school because universities had placed quotas on how many Jewish applicants they would take. "Dr. Fensterman knew that prejudice in academic institutions against colored students was far worse than it was against Jews ... He knew the kind of obstacles that the Silks themselves had had to overcome to achieve all that distinguished them as a model Negro family" (*HS* 86). Intuitively, the reader understands that the Silk family are not African American Jews; rather, Fensterman, a Jew, is bribing the non-Jewish African American family to allow Bert to become the class valedictorian and finish above Coleman. Fensterman's remark that he knows how the Silk family has struggled not only is hollow sounding but highlights a separation between the two families as demonstrated by the father's rather shameless appraisal of the Silks as a "model Negro family" (*HS* 86). In other words, Fensterman is attempting to appease the Silks with an empty and manufactured empathy centered on their mutual experiences of racial exclusions as Jews *and* as African Americans.

The incongruity between the two stories is not explained until the fourth chapter, after Coleman and Faunia have been murdered. At the former's funeral, Zuckerman meets Coleman's estranged sister, Ernestine. As Jerry Levov does with the Swede, Ernestine reveals the "truth" to Nathan. Coleman had been

132 *Philip Roth and the Body*

born an African American and after his father died, Coleman decided to pass as Jewish, eventually marrying Iris Gittelman and abandoning his family altogether. Nathan is "seized by his story, by its end and by its beginning, and, then and there, I began this book" (*HS* 337). The preceding chapters and the events that transpired turn out to have been reinvented works of fiction by the transfixed Zuckerman. The story has been repeated, retold, and reconstructed through the figure of Nathan-the-novelist, bringing into focus the ways individuals' lives are constructed as narratives.[12]

If we are in fact each other's authors (*CL* 149), then the authorial (re)writing each of us enacts is always recognized in Roth's American Trilogy as being subjective. As Zuckerman observes in *American Pastoral*, "[w]riting turns you into somebody who's always wrong" (*AP* 63). The letter Delphine sends to Coleman that claims, "Everyone knows" (*HS* 38) is challenged by the narrative form of the text itself; that which the reader assumes and understands as an objective portrayal of events is a re-interpretation. For Nathan, "[w]hat we know is that, in an unclichèd way, nobody knows anything. You *can't* know anything … Intention? Motive? Consequence? Meaning? All that we don't know is astonishing. Even more astonishing is what passes for knowing" (*HS* 209). Unlike Delphine, whose letter proclaims and propounds an epistemological certainty, Nathan embraces the unknown enigma of Coleman's character, and transforms this lack through writing.[13]

Nathan reconstructs Coleman into a tragic hero that attempts to realize the entrenched American ideal of self-reinvention: "To become a new being. To bifurcate. The drama that underlies America's story, the high drama that is upping and leaving—and the energy and cruelty that rapturous drive demands" (*HS* 342).[14] The dramatic impulse Nathan sees as distinctly American once again centers on the symbolic penetration of the land-as-female, metaphorically

---

[12] As Calvin Hoovestol points out, "Zuckerman's twice-told tale about Coleman supposedly repeats information or gossip he heard from Coleman's sister Ernestine and from his own fictional characters" (2016: 45).

[13] Connolly saliently observes how "the work of imagination occupies the void that opens from the knowledge that 'nobody knows anything' by breathing new energy into life's desiccated 'facts'" (2017: 176).

[14] Mark Maslan challenges the way Roth grounds the concept of self-reinvention as a distinctly American phenomenon. Maslan argues that calling imaginative identification "an American activity requires us to identify those doing it as an American beforehand, which means that the basis for such identification must lie elsewhere" (2005: 389). Compellingly, Maslan calls into question the inherency of American self-reinvention and its supposed particularity to American culture. Likewise, I am troubled by Roth's portrayal of Coleman, but particularize my focus to the sexist objectification of women's bodies in Coleman's attempt to create a new identity for himself.

embodied by the white (non-Jewish) woman's body. For Coleman, however, a man born as an African American, it is the Jewish woman's body that symbolically finalizes the possibility of being "free" from the racial borders of Black and white. *The Human Stain* follows and disrupts *Portnoy's Complaint*, *The Counterlife*, and *American Pastoral*, as Coleman's fantasy of Americanness centers on a heteronormative penetration of the (Jewish) woman's body. Roth uses Coleman to examine the intersections between sex and race in American society by considering how Jewishness is couched between Blackness and whiteness, and what this racial indeterminacy reveals about American race and class.

For Nathan, Coleman's pursuit of self-reinvention is a heroic form of individual artistry: "every day you woke up to be what you had made yourself" (*HS* 345). Coleman can achieve what Nathan could only dream of: escaping his family and reinventing himself; it is hardly surprising Roth's narrator is so enamored by Coleman's triumphant story given the events that transpired in "Zuckerman Bound." Yet Coleman's performance of Jewishness is not self-affirmed. He requires others to accept his identity as a Jewish man, and selfishly exploits women's bodies to ensure his passing is unquestioned. Coleman's pursuit of individuality is selfish and destructive, but his actions are not condemned. Coleman remains tragic and at times, deeply sympathetic: he is, as so many of Roth's protagonists are, a morally ambiguous figure with a profoundly unhealthy attitude toward women.

Coleman's passing is rather unique in that he chooses to assume an identity as Jewish rather than white. Jewishness represents a separation from the black-white binary of American racism, which signifies a unique form of freedom. In an almost Swede-like proclamation, Zuckerman's Coleman denounces both Blackness and whiteness: "All he'd ever wanted, from earliest childhood on, was to be free: not black, not even white—just on his own and free" (*HS* 120). For Coleman, freedom means to exist beyond the racial appellations of Black and white, finding in Jewishness an identity that does not easily fit within either rubric.[15]

Coleman's decision to pass as Jewish is explained by his sister, who tells Nathan about the Silk family's life in East Orange. Her version of events shapes much of

---

[15] Timothy Parrish and Eric Sundquist both connect *The Human Stain* to Ralph Ellison's *Invisible Man*. Parrish contends Roth's text "can be read as a sequel to Ellison's novel" (2004: 422), while Sundquist connects the theme of self-masking and self-making with the two novelists.

what we read, but it is Nathan's imagination that brings Coleman's story to life. Fensterman's influence on Coleman is substantial, and it seems rather befitting (and problematic) that Coleman's story and life is rewritten by a Jewish author. Dr. Fensterman teaches Coleman the value of his own intellect. Fensterman's three-thousand-dollar bribe signifies for Coleman his intellectual uniqueness: "Yet another record-breaking triumph for the great, the incomparable, the one and only Silky Silk!" (*HS* 88). The offer signifies Coleman's ability to rupture and dislocate America's social structures; as Roth (via Zuckerman) writes, "Dr. Fensterman's proposal meant no more to him than that he was of the greatest importance to just about everyone. The larger picture he didn't get yet" (*HS* 88). Coleman is too young to understand the racial inflections of Fensterman's proposal; all he can see is his own intellectual value being affirmed here by the Jewish doctor's bribe.

While Dr. Fensterman shows Coleman the value of his intellect, it is Doc Chizner, Coleman's boxing teacher, who educates him how to move both as a boxer and more broadly within racial categories. Chizner teaches Coleman "how to stand and how to move and how to throw the punches ... How to move his head. How to slip punches. How to block punches. How to counter" (*HS* 90). The bodily movement essential to boxing initiates Coleman's journey into slipping away from his identity as an African American.[16]

Chizner starkly contrasts Coleman's father, whose affinity for English and the works of Chaucer, Shakespeare, and Dickens teach Coleman the importance and meaning of language: "They learned things had classifications. They learned the power of naming precisely" (*HS* 93). For Clarence Silk mastering the English language (and its white, canonical male authors) is vital. In learning the importance and nuances of language, Clarence's father hopes his children (and their friends) can become metaphorically assume an approximate position of whiteness.

Clarence's efforts to control the language of the colonizer bring us back to *Black Skin, White Masks*, as Fanon underlines how important it is for the colonized to learn the colonizer's language: "To speak a language is to appropriate its world and culture. ... It should be understood that historically the black man wants to speak French, since it is the key to open doors which only fifty years ago still remained closed to him" ([1952] 2021: 21). Clarence Silk wants his children to be adroitly

---

[16] As John G. Rodwan Jr. observes, "[b]oxing teaches Silk the pleasures and uses of concealment" (2011: 87).

proficient in their usage of English to become resplendent representatives of the African American community. Roth (or rather, Zuckerman) extensively details Clarence's commitment to teaching his children American literature, art, and theatre: "In the Silk family they had read all the old classics. In the Silk family the children were not taken to prizefights, they were taken to the Metropolitan Museum of Art to see the armor" (*HS* 93–4). Clarence seeks, as Fanon would say, to have his son become "a complete replica of the white man" ([1952] 2021: 19) by mimicking and perfecting a culture that has colonized, oppressed, and dehumanized Black bodies.

Chizner, on the other hand, appreciates the power of moving precisely. When Chizner takes Coleman to a boxing match at West Point, he tells Coleman not to mention to an interested coach that he is Black. Importantly, Chizner does not tell Coleman to lie about his race, but just to avoid the subject altogether. By not stating his race, Chizner explains, the coach will automatically assume he is Jewish: "You look like you look, you're with me, and so he's going to think you're one of Doc's boys. He's going to think that you're Jewish" (*HS* 99). Chizner has no interest in language and the particularities of speaking precisely. Yet he, like Clarence, seeks for Coleman to mimic or replicate the Jewish body here; by saying nothing, Chizner intends for Coleman to assume a new identity as a Jew. In doing so, Coleman makes his Blackness invisible, and discovers an autonomy and power in his body that is markedly distinct from the English (i.e., colonizer's) language that seeks to delineate individuals within a particular identity.[17] Coleman believes he has found a way to slip the punch of white America's violent racism by silently "becoming" a Jew, without realizing that his replication of Jewishness remains within the racial schema that wordlessly denounces Blackness as a negative.

Coleman's father forces him to stop boxing with Chizner and sends him to Howard, the African American university, "to become a doctor, to meet a light-skinned girl there from a good Negro family, to marry and settle down and have children who would in turn go to Howard" (*HS* 102). The social ascension Coleman's father fantasizes is centered on a Blackness that is "light," highlighting Clarence's internalization of American racism that positions Blackness as undesirable.

---

[17] Joe Holroyd makes a similar observation, noting how boxing "enables Silky to discover the possibility of emotional release through physical action ... [which allows him] to see through a more objective, dispassionate lens the challenges posed to his will to self-determine, such as his father's antagonism" (2016: 64).

136 *Philip Roth and the Body*

The implications of remaining Black in America are very quickly made apparent. Coleman and his roommate, "a lawyer's son from New Brunswick" (*HS* 102), are on their way to see the Washington Monument when they stop in Woolworth's to get a hot dog and are racially abused in the store:

> he was called a nigger. His first time. And they wouldn't give him the hot dog. Refused a hot dog at Woolworth's in downtown Washington, on the way out called a nigger, and, as a result, unable to divorce himself from his feelings as easily as he did in the ring. At East Orange High the class valedictorian, in the segregated South just another nigger.

> (*HS* 102)

Coleman and his roommate's educational achievements and family's professional position grant them a particular degree of social privilege within the African American community. Yet their identities as intellects and academic achievers are obliterated by the violent singularity of the word "nigger," which freezes the slippery Coleman, suspending the fluid, transgressive boxer into a solid object. "In the segregated South ... there were no separate identities, not even for him and his roommate. No such subtleties allowed, and the impact was devastating. Nigger—and it meant *him*" (*HS* 103, italics in original). Coleman's sliding, slippery subtleness is violently denied in the segregated South. Like Fanon, Coleman is obliterated and reconstructed by racism, rooted in a word that denies and creates meaning onto his body that is entirely beyond his control.

Coleman is frozen into a racial appellation that denies him autonomy. Boxing enables a movement that grants Coleman power through his body, but when he is called the *n* word, his body is turned against him. Like Fanon, Coleman's subjectivity is brutalized by the realization that he is defined in the South as an object. Despite how successfully Coleman has replicated whiteness through his institutional achievements, he is racially disregarded as an abjection. Clarence's attempts to mimic whiteness through education are violently undermined here, further enhancing Coleman's disillusionment with his father. In a particularly revealing scene, Coleman recalls a moment in which his father was confronted by a racist: "'What happened, Dad?' Coleman would ask. But, as much out of pride as disgust, rarely would his father elucidate. To make the pedagogical point was enough. 'What happened,' Coleman's mother would explain, 'is beneath your father even to repeat'" (*HS* 103). Clarence's passivity, signified by his silent inactivity, represents the same masculine failure that Alex Portnoy sees in his father's inability to play baseball. Clarence cannot even speak of the event; it is his mother who informs Coleman of his father's passivity. Racism violently

Black Skin, Jewish Masks

strips Clarence of agency; he becomes, in Coleman's eyes, a castrated, powerless, inanimate object.

Coleman laments his father's culpability in enabling American racism to impose itself against the Silk family. Coleman, Roth writes, "finally recognized the enormous barrier against the great American menace that his father had been for him" (*HS* 102). The very language Clarence celebrates for its articulacy and nuance serves as a violent weapon used to deprive African Americans of their humanity. Clarence, in the disenfranchised son's view, enables American racism to maintain the socio-racial barriers that denigratingly ossify African Americans into racial objects. Clarence's failure to act signifies a masculine lapse; he is, unlike Doc Chizner or Dr. Fensterman, incapable of action when faced against American racism. Fensterman's social mobility, and Chizner's physical slipperiness, symbolizes American Jewry's ability to slip past America's institutional racism, a feat Clarence Silk cannot achieve. Coleman seems attracted to the metaphorical Jew's slipperiness that I discussed in the Introduction. The conceptual "Jew," as Bauman outlined, puts categories into crisis.

When Clarence dies, Coleman sees his father's passing as his opportunity to reinvent himself beyond the prescribed social role his father had constructed for him. Clarence's death represents an "exhilarating" (*HS* 107) opportunity for the disobedient son, as the patriarchal authority that dictated his life has finally been removed:

> He saw the fate that was awaiting him, and he wasn't having it. Grasped it intuitively and recoiled spontaneously. You can't let the big they impose its bigotry on you any more than you can let the little they become a we and impose its ethics on you. ... Instead the raw I with all its singularity. *Self*-discovery—*that* was the punch the to the labonz. Singularity. The passionate struggle for singularity. The singular animal.
>
> (*HS* 108, italics in original)

Racial categorization appalls Coleman because it means being subjected to institutional racism. Coleman refuses to succumb to any kind of "we" group-think politic and chooses instead to create himself as an individual. He does this by becoming what he (or rather, Nathan) calls the "raw I with all its singularity" (*HS* 108). Raw represents an unblemished and unprocessed life: a life free from the determinations of others seeking to impose their bigoted ideologies upon Coleman and his body. To live as a "singular animal" (*HS* 108) is to exist alone, free from the social structures governed by group-think ideologies.

Coleman's quest for singularity and isolation indelibly links to the American Renaissance writer, Ralph Waldo Emerson. I contend the "raw I" (*HS* 108) reads as a homophonic allusion to Emerson's transparent eyeball in his essay "Nature." As Emerson wanders through the woods, he envisages a subliminal moment in which he becomes detached from his very body: "Standing on the bare ground,—my head bathed by the blithe air and uplifted into infinite space,—all mean egotism vanishes. I become a transparent eyeball; I am nothing; I see all; the currents of the Universal Being circulate through me; I am part or parcel of God" ([1836] 2003: 39). Roth strips the Emersonian spiritualism away here; the transparent eyeball is torn from its naturalist context and placed within the discourse of race in America. The naked transparency of Emerson's eye is sought after by Coleman, whose Black body has been brutalized by the language of racism; Coleman seeks to make himself into an Emersonian nothing by refuting racial markings. Yet while Emerson's transparent eyeball is stripped of its materiality (in part, because of Emerson's whiteness), Coleman's "raw singular I" (*HS* 108) is pure flesh. Indeed, I read Coleman's capitalized, singular, "I" as a literal erection. To become transparent and immaterial, Coleman immerses himself into the flesh of others. His body becomes the primary force and function in which he attempts to return to an unmarked nothing.

The Big White Thing

Coleman's quest for singularity repeatedly positions women as objects of desire, in a manner that strikingly parallels Fanon's sexist objectifications. Gwen Bergner contends Fanon's *Black Skin, White Masks* positions women "almost exclusively in terms of their sexual relationships with men; feminine desire is thus defined as an overly literal and limited (hetero)sexuality" (1995: 77). As I discussed in the previous chapter, women in Roth's fiction are usually positioned as objects of male desires, meaning that their characterizations tend to be limited. Having said that, Roth critically interrogates his characters' provocative sexualization of women through his satire, parody, and narrative strategies that ensure a critical distance between the narrator and author and continues to do so in *The Human Stain*.

For Coleman, women represent what Luce Irigaray defines as "fetish-objects." Women are made into symbols of male-worth through "the circulation of a power of the Phallus, establishing relationships of men with each other"

Black Skin, Jewish Masks   139

(Iragaray 1985: 183). For Coleman (and Portnoy, and Zuckerman, and Levov), women's bodies become sites in which their masculinities and heterosexuality are recognized and affirmed, serving to accredit them within what Bergner calls the "homosocial matric" (1995: 81). While Roth certainly does not endorse his protagonist's attitudes, and Zuckerman is used as a narrative device to interrogate both the Swede and Coleman's characters, there is a recurring trope within his fiction of men attempting to claim a position of power vis-à-vis the penetration of women's bodies.

For Fanon, the phallus is white, and if the Black man wishes "to be acknowledged not as *black* but as *white*" ([1952] 2021: 45 italics in original), they can only achieve this through the acceptance of the white woman. "Between these white breasts that my wandering hands fondle, white civilization and worthiness become mine" (Fanon [1952] 2021: 45). Fanon's hands are grasping, restless, insecure; there is a knowing diffidence here as he recognizes the impossible divide that separates his Black hands from the white woman's breasts. Fanon seeks to become an autonomous subject through the white woman's body, but in doing so, Bergner explains, he silences women, "rendering their sexuality spectacular—in sum, excluding them from occupying a place as subjects within the scopic systems of signification" (1995: 79).

Coleman, like Fanon, denies women subjectivity by fetishizing their bodies into symbolic spaces that represent social and economic mobility. While reminiscing with Nathan about his sexual endeavors in New York, Coleman declares, "[i]t was like fishing down there. Go down into the subway and come up with a girl" (*HS* 21). Women are consumable objects for him to swoop down and hunt, and my choice word of "swoop" is quite intentional, as it is used to describe him by his former lover, Steena: "You were incredibly good at swooping, almost like birds do when they fly over land or sea and spy something moving, something bursting with life, and dive down—or zero in—and seize upon it" (*HS* 24). Coleman gushes with a sexual vitality that positions him as forceful, tactical, and almost dangerous.

The first relationship Coleman has is with Steena Palsson, "an eighteen-year-old exile from Minnesota" (*HS* 23). Coleman first mentions her in the novel's opening chapter, describing her as an "[i]ndependent girl from Minnesota. Sure-of-herself girl, or seemed so. Danish on one side, Icelandic on the other. Quick. Tall. Marvelously tall" (*HS* 23). Intriguingly, Coleman uses the same nickname for Faunia as he did for Steena: "Used to call her Voluptas. Psyche's daughter. The personification to the Romans of sensual pleasure" (*HS* 23). For Coleman, both women's white bodies represent a racial site of difference inherently tied to Coleman's own phallic empowerment. What separates the two women, however, is the way Coleman uses Steena's white body to propagate himself within American patriarchal society.

Coleman, like Fanon, tries fondling "white civilization" ([1952] 2021: 45) and reforms himself as white. While I am aware Coleman explicitly rejects the racial binary of Black and white, his attempt to exist as a pure, unmarked body represents whiteness, and his relationship with Steena only further accentuates Coleman's unspoken and perhaps unintentional desire to become "white." Steena unknowingly writes Coleman's body into whiteness through her poetic portrait of him: "He has a body./ He has a beautiful body—/ the muscles on the backs of his legs and the back of his neck./ ... I am almost dangerous for this man./ How much can I tell/ of what I see in him?/ I wonder what he does/ after he swallows me whole" (*HS* 112). Steena's letter operates as a mirror for Coleman, enabling him to see himself through her gaze. Steena's lack of description or detail here in her recreation of Coleman is instructive: the body is unmarked; it is pure and beautiful precisely because it lacks any kind of categorical imprint. The absence of racial signifiers gestures toward a whiteness that erases or makes invisible Coleman's Blackness. In the second last verse, Steena declares herself a danger to Coleman. The line is alone: separated and singularized, it represents a rupturing of the poem's stream. Its suddenness suggests a momentariness, a fleeting realization that is vague and uninformed. Does Steena sense Coleman's secret? Does she realize that he is hiding his racial past from her? If so, the danger she conceives of is rooted in the unspoken, unseen, and unheard racial dichotomy silently orchestrating the two's relationship. Fanon is instructive in explaining the danger Steena stumbles upon: "We know historically that the Negro guilty of lying with a white woman is castrated" ([1952] 2021: 53). As Yancy has highlighted, the Black body represents a violent threat to whiteness. Coleman and Steena's relationship signifies a rupture to racially drawn divisions; their coupling threatens the absoluteness of whiteness, as it is no longer separated from the Black body.

The last stanza reflects Steena's uncertainty regarding her position in relation to Coleman. She muses over what she can communicate to him, and envisages him swallowing her whole, as though he were a predator, and she prey. The irony of course is that Steena's poem is greatly revealing for Coleman. By failing to identify or mark Coleman out as Black, Steena authenticates Coleman's identity. The additional irony is that Steena feels as though Coleman is swallowing her, without realizing how much agency and power she has over him. Coleman relies on Steena to see and define him, creating a power dynamic within the relationship that Steena is entirely unaware exists. Coleman misreads the third line of the poem, believing Steena writes "negro" instead of "neck" (*HS* 112). The connection Coleman makes between the words reveals his vulnerability; it is as if Steena's poem strips him bare and threatens to strangle or submit him back into the racial schema he is fleeing.

Steena's whiteness gives her a power and authority over Coleman that is indeterminately marked through her body. As the two listen to the radio, Steena, as Faunia does later, dances for Coleman: "Prompted by a colored trumpet player playing it like a black torch song, there to see, plain as day, was all the power of her whiteness. That big white thing" (*HS* 115).[18] What does the noun refer to here? What is Steena's thing? Is it her vagina, or her breasts, or her body writ large? The word "thing" refers to an object that has no specific name, and by naming Steena's body (if it is in-fact her body that is being referred to) as an undetermined "thing," Coleman effectively dismisses Steena into an object. Does Steena's life matter here to Coleman? It seems unlikely. There is a very clear correlation between Coleman's sexism here and the racism he has endured: Black bodies and white women are positioned as nonhuman objects. For Coleman, the white woman's body is commodified into a metonym for whiteness, while the Black body symbolizes an abject monstrousness.

Coleman's sexism is part of his attempt to make himself into the singular raw I he strives to be. He attempts to follow Doc Chizner's advice, "if nothing comes up, you don't bring it up" (*HS* 118), but Coleman's plan is foiled when Steena meets his family. Moments after they leave the Silk household, Steena flees from Coleman, crying, "'I can't do it'" (*HS* 125). Here we have yet another indeterminate marker: "it"—the third person singular pronoun that is supposed to refer to something easily identifiable. Steena cannot be with Coleman because he is Black, and she is white. This scene affirms Fanon's proclamation that he is "a slave not of the 'idea' others have of me, but to my appearance" ([1952] 2021: 95); or in this case, Coleman is a slave to the idea others have of his family's appearance. The severing of the relationship represents the limits of Coleman's autonomy as the author of his own subjectivity. Steena's rejection

---

[18] Sinéad Moynihan highlights how "Steena's dance evokes the endlessly interrelated forms of cultural exchange and appropriation that have taken place between black, white and Jewish American's" (2010: 120); this is an important observation that underpins the myriad of racial tensions underscoring The Human Stain, tensions that remain unresolved and vividly ever-present.

142   *Philip Roth and the Body*

of the ambiguous "it" (*HS* 125) returns Coleman to a racial category that he does not identify with.

If Steena is "too white" for Coleman, then Ellie Magee, his next partner, is "too Black." Coleman does not hide his family's racial past from Ellie, as he believes they have a mutual understanding based on their shared identity as African Americans. He tells her about his family, his trouble at Howard, and his willingness to allow others to identify him whichever way they see fit. Initially, Coleman revels in the easiness of the relationship: "In the beginning, he luxuriates in the solution to his problem. Losing the secret, he feels like a boy again. The boy he'd been before he had the secret" (*HS* 135). The return symbolizes his rejuvenation in releasing himself from the secrecy and deception that he undertook in his relationship with Steena. Yet the easiness with Ellie becomes problematic for Coleman precisely because it is too comfortable and disrupts the illusion Coleman harbors of himself as an American pioneer.[19]

Shortly after meeting Ellie, she points out other African Americans who are passing as white. Ellie's revelations throw into question Coleman's self-assuredness that centered on his uniqueness. "'You're wrong,' Coleman tells her, 'he can't be.' 'Don't tell me that I'm wrong'—she laughs—'*you're* blind'" (*HS* 134, italics in original). If, as I have argued earlier, Coleman's I is a metonym for the Emersonian transparent eyeball, then Coleman's blindness represents a phallic lack that suggests his singularized raw identity is not as absolute as he thought. Coleman's failure to see or recognize other African Americans who pass represents his flaw: in pursuing the raw singular I he so desperately craves, Coleman fails to recognize other African American experiences.

Coleman ends his relationship with Ellie because "some dimension is missing. The whole thing lacks the ambition—it fails to feed that conception of himself that's been driving him all his life" (*HS* 135). The language, especially in Roth's use of the words "ambition" and "drive," highlights how Coleman sees women as instruments rather than as people, tools for him to mobilize socially and economically. For Coleman, their relationship accords with America's social and racial order, as Ellie threatens to make visible Coleman's Blackness. Effectively, his autonomy and individualism are vulnerable in the presence of a self-identifying African American.

---

[19] Coleman's affinity for reinvention seems to correlate with Alex Portnoy and Seymour "Swede" Levov, particularly about how he positions himself as a pioneering figure.

Black Skin, Jewish Masks

If Steena is too white, and Ellie is too Black, then Iris, a Jewish woman, is just right. Iris's character arc has all the markings of a typical Rothian protagonist: "Iris Gittelman [Gittel is a Yiddish word, which translates to 'good'] had grown up willful, clever, furtively rebellious—secretly plotting ... how to escape her oppressive surroundings" (*HS* 127). Iris's family is aggressively atheistic ("[they] spat on the ground when a rabbi walked by" [*HS* 127]) and, significantly, "called themselves what they called themselves freely, without asking permission or seeking approval from what her father contemptuously described as the hypocritical enemies of everything that was natural and good—namely, officialdom, those illegitimately holding the power" (*HS* 127). Clarence cannot speak out against the racism he suffers from, but passively seeks for his children to live within the parameters of their racialized identities, but Iris's father represents a new modality for Coleman. He understands the racism of America and enables his children to resist by allowing them freedom to self-identify as they wish. The self-authorship Iris's father encourages starkly contrasts the rigidity Coleman grew up with, and Iris's Jewishness, indeterminate and loosely defined, is enticing to the self-inventing Coleman, who sees in the Gittelmans' religious identity a category that is open, fluid, and free.

There has been a tendency to highlight the ways in which Zuckerman valorizes Coleman as a heroic figure for his self-reinvention. Parrish, for example, contends that for Roth, "Coleman's choice ... gives him a life, viewed from an individualist perspective, as complicated and as courageous as choosing to be known as black would have given him" (2004: 439). Nevertheless, Coleman remains a complex Rothian protagonist. Coleman fetishizes women into social capital, enabling him to mobilize himself beyond the racial appellation of Blackness. In other words, Coleman transfers the racism he suffers onto women's bodies to escape the racial oppression he faces.

The categorical separation Coleman creates between himself and Iris is predicated on his sexist desire to maintain his singularity. Coleman lies to Iris by telling her that he too is Jewish, even though he intuitively knows she would be entirely accepting of his decision to pass: "To be two men instead of one? To be two colors instead of one? ... To her there was nothing frightening about such deformities" (*HS* 130). Yet in refusing to reveal himself to Iris, Coleman attempts to singularize himself into a solid, staid entity. As Godfrey observes, Coleman seeks "not to transgress social conventions but to benefit from them" (247). Crucially, Coleman's commitment to social convention maintains patriarchal structures that transfix women's bodies into objectified socioeconomic commodities.

144 *Philip Roth and the Body*

Coleman fetishizes Iris's body, or more specifically her hair, for its sinewy curliness that represents the racial ambiguity of Jewishness:

> Her head of hair was something, a labyrinthine, billowing wreath of spirals and ringlets, fuzzy as twine and large enough for use as Christmas ornamentation ... Iris's hair, that sinuous thicket of hair that was more Negroid than Coleman's ... all that he had ever wanted from Iris Gittelman was the explanation her appearance could provide for the texture of their children's hair.

(*HS* 129, 136)

Coleman sees in Iris's hair his opportunity to create a maze that will enable him to metaphorically hide his racial identity. In other words, Coleman intends to make himself invisible through Iris's Jewish body. Dean Franco argues that "[b]eing Jewish for Coleman is finally a way of trading in one set of assumptions, rigid, and dichotomous, for another, fluid and malleable. Jewishness is finally an *ethnicity* subsumed within the larger black-white racial sphere" (2004: 94, italics in original). However, the socioeconomic fluidity Jews enjoyed in America meant that they became closer in proximity both culturally and racially to whites than African Americans. In other words, I read Coleman's decision to pass as Jewish both as a subversion to racial structures and as a commitment to America's racially inflected social order.

Coleman's decision to assume a Jewish identity culminates in the symbolic murder of his mother, and this matricidal impulse—as discussed in Chapter 1—is a prominent theme in Roth. The relationship with Steena teaches him that he cannot adopt an identity if his family remain visibly present; to pass as Jewish, Coleman must fully remove himself from his family in a purifying act of sacrificial "murder" that exceeds Doc Chizner's logic of passive silence. Coleman "murder[s] her on behalf of his exhilarating notion of freedom!" (*HS* 138), but this matricide is hardly definitive or as final as Coleman would like. Coleman's mother accuses him of "think[ing] like a slave ... You're as white as snow and you think like a slave" (*HS* 139). The twice-repeated "slave" operates as a reaffirmation of Coleman's doubled identity; it reminds him of his Blackness that he has chosen to hide and the instability of his Jewishness that he has chosen to assume. Ultimately, Coleman's secret transfixes him within the singular phallic "I" that represents a negation of his own complex humanness.[20]

---

[20] Pierpont counters by contending "Silk has escaped his race not because he longs to be white but because he longs to be unrestrictedly human" (2014: 245), yet this is perhaps the very problem of the racial schema Coleman attempts to resist. Racism denies Black bodies the fundamental identity as human, meaning that Coleman can only be unrestricted by assuming an identity that closely approximates with whiteness.

Black Skin, Jewish Masks

As other critics have noted, the "spooks" episode represents the return of his racially repressed past.[21] In defining the two absentee students as specters, he conjures his secret other racial identity into being. It seems befitting and intentional that Coleman is referring to two African American students as ghost-like. After all, Coleman's pursuit of the singular I is predicated on a desire to eradicate the DuBosian doubleness thrust upon him by America's racial schema. The inherent contradictory logic of the novel is perhaps what makes the text so tragic, as Coleman's efforts are so obviously futile. He is haunted by his own doubled identity that he has attempted to repress, hide, and violently singularize.

Writing in the Dark

The "spooks" episode is the moment in which Coleman is supposed to reveal his racial identity; it affords him the chance to expose himself to his friends, family, and community and render the charges of racism ridiculous. However, Coleman refuses to reveal his secret and resigns from the institute in a commitment to his singular I. Upon exiting the university and initiating an affair with Faunia, Coleman removes himself from the social order he has blissfully existed within. While Coleman's passing is a fraught deconstruction of racial hierarchies, he remains committed to linearly ascending through the social ranks. The affair with Faunia signals a rejection of society altogether; it extends beyond Coleman's singular Emersonian I, toward a hybridized multiplicity that very visibly and publicly violates social structures.

As I discussed in the previous section, Coleman calls both Steena and Faunia "Voluptas."[22] Yet while the former's identity is marked almost exclusively by her racial genealogy and the social value her whiteness represents for Coleman, Faunia represents an abjection.[23] "Faunia has nothing," Coleman tells Nathan,

---

[21] Shechner is most adroit in surmising it "would not have been lost on Roth, that old Freudian, that in uttering the word 'spooks' when he did, Silk meant just what everyone thought he meant. If ever there was a classic return of the repressed, there it is" (2003: 191).

[22] Parrish likewise highlights the correlation between Faunia and Steena: "Faunia can be seen as the return of Steena to Coleman—a chance to resolve before death the specific conflict that ultimately clinched his choice to pass for white" (2004: 454).

[23] Luminita Dragulescu highlights how "Faunia deconstructs the class element of her identity by renouncing her upbringing and passing for an illiterate janitress" (2014: 100). Faunia attempts to remove herself from the social structures entirely, mirrors Coleman's effort to "pass" as Faunia, and creates a new guise for herself. Unlike Coleman, however, Faunia's re-invention of herself is centered on a desire to evade rather than exploit social hierarchies.

146   *Philip Roth and the Body*

> she began life a rich, privileged kid. Brought up in a big sprawling house south of Boston. ... But she's dropped so far down the social ladder from so far up that by now she's a pretty mixed bag of verbal beans. Faunia's been exiled from the entitlement that should have been hers. Declassed. There's a real democratization to her suffering.
>
>   (*HS* 28)

Faunia's life has been stripped and emptied of the privilege and wealth she once had. In a sense, Faunia is Coleman's direct opposite: she begins her life within the confines of white privilege, but is flung into abject poverty, violence, and abuse. Coleman narrates her suffering to Nathan: Faunia was sexually abused by her stepfather and eventually flees home, meets, and marries Les Farley, a Vietnam veteran who physically and mentally abuses Faunia. The two's marriage disintegrates as their dairy farm financially crumbles, and their two children die in a house fire.

For Coleman, Faunia is a nymph-like figure of sexual pleasure and is positioned solely in terms of her body: "In bed nothing escapes Faunia's attention ... [h]er flesh has eyes. Her flesh sees everything. In bed she is a powerful, coherent, unified being whose pleasure is in overstepping the boundaries. In bed she is a deep phenomenon. Maybe that's a gift of the molestation" (*HS* 31). In bed, Faunia's flesh becomes Emerson's transparent eyeball: her body becomes a site of sublime pleasure that has an otherworldly autonomy and power. The last line is the most striking and unsettlingly revealing as it underpins the troubling sexual politics of their relationship that Coleman is publicly denounced for, and almost authenticates the acerbic claims laid against him. Faunia, Coleman implies, is only recognizably human when she is having sex.[24] Faunia's symbolic lack is what defines her in the eyes of her lover Coleman and the narrator, Zuckerman. For the former, her rejection of societal statuses excitingly represents a libidinous return to the enthralling empowerment being "Silky Silk" induced for Coleman.

For Zuckerman, Faunia becomes a far more symbolically weighted figure, particularly after the two dies, because she re-enters a symbolic order; in death, she re-enters the world of language and letters. Faunia and Coleman—ejected and expelled for their relationship—exit into the abject, the abyssal point of

---

[24] Hoovestol argues, "Faunia's body might be her only power or weapon in the cruel, patriarchal world of her lived experiences, but she appears, at least according to Nathan, to use it with adroit dexterity" (2016: 49). The point stands, of course, but risks overlooking the problematic ways in which Faunia's character is positioned solely as a body.

Black Skin, Jewish Masks   147

non-being, retreating into their own Edenic den much like Drenka and Sabbath. Farley's murderousness, of course, annihilates such escapism, violently returning to them to the gory politic of racial, class, and gendered labelling.

In the fifth and final chapter of the novel, entitled "The Purifying Ritual," Zuckerman attends Faunia and Coleman's funerals and is perturbed by the myriad of counter-narratives being constructed about the two. Faunia, for example, is eulogized by Sally, the manager of the dairy farm, whose encomium Zuckerman smarmily defers to as an "environmentalist Rousseauism" (*HS* 286), a banal speech imbued with reverences harking back to Faunia's fondness for the farmyard. Smoky Hollenbeck (Faunia's manager and former lover) also delivers an uninspiring eulogy that recalls her proficiency as a cleaner. On the "Athena fac.discuss [*sic*] news group" (*HS* 288) an anonymous poster accuses Coleman of physically and mentally abusing Faunia. They suggest Coleman intentionally drove into the river to commit suicide and kill her "[s]o as to annihilate not only the two of them, but, with them, all trace of his history as her ultimate tormentor" (*HS* 293). Nathan meets Faunia's father and stepmother, and learns she kept a diary, and that her illiteracy was in fact an act. He attempts to convince the stepmother to give him the journal, but she dismisses Faunia's words as "[f]ilth! There is a record of filth there!" (*HS* 301). Nathan is unable to retrieve the diary, meaning that Faunia's memories, emotions, and version of events are lost: her life can only be retold and reimagined through the fictional reinvention of Zuckerman. Faunia is dismissed as waste, an abjection that should be disregarded.

Faunia is rejected by her stepmother and father because she represents an aberration, a sullying force that has stained the lives of those around her. At Coleman's funeral, his family attempt to purify their father's reputation by re-constructing a new narrative of him as a tragic fallen hero. The act of rewriting the deceased is the purifying ritual the chapter alludes to: Coleman and Faunia's lives are purified of the symbolic "dirt" that they lived as, and both lives are rewritten by their friends, family, and associates. Coleman's colleague, Herb Keble delivers the eulogy at his funeral. He was the first African American whom Athena hired under Coleman's jurisdiction and refused to defend Coleman during the "spooks" episode. Keble repents and compares Coleman to America's Renaissance writers such as Hawthorne, Melville, and Thoreau, declaring him "an American individualist who did not think that the weightiest things in life

148   *Philip Roth and the Body*

were the rules" (*HS* 310–11).[25] Disgusted, Zuckerman decries him for this public act of self-righteousness: "Herb Keble was just another one out trying to kosher the record ... and so I thought, on Coleman's behalf, Fuck him" (*HS* 312). This koshering represents a cleansing to Zuckerman, a purifying eulogy for a man vilified and demonized by the very people now commemorating and celebrating him.

Essential to the cleansing of Coleman's reputation is the erasure of Faunia's very being from his life. Shortly after the funeral, Jeffrey and Michael (Coleman's sons) tell Zuckerman, "Faunia Farley's was a name they never wanted to hear again." Jeffrey tells Nathan, "[s]he is not the ideal woman to have linked with our father's legacy" (*HS* 308), while Michael viciously decries her as a "cheap little cunt [that] has nothing to do with anything" (*HS* 308). The use of the word "cunt" (*HS* 308) disparagingly dismisses Faunia as a commodified body; the son dismisses Faunia as a mere sexual orifice that "cheapens" their father's esteemed reputation as the fallen hero of Athena.[26] Claudia Roth Pierpont laments the portrayal of Faunia, contending Roth "tries too hard to make Faunia an interesting woman" (2014: 249). I agree but argue Faunia's character is being aggressively reclaimed by Zuckerman, who seeks to dramatically mythologize her as a figure of the impure, a fictional tool resisting America's persecuting and purifying spirit.

Faunia is arguably the hero of the narrative: she is the central figure who almost sermonically proclaims the novel's title. Furthermore, her name is porous with meaning; it signifies a multiplicity that offers several interpretations. Rankine suggests Faunia's name connects with "Faun" (2005: 108), a Greek and Latin demigod that has a male torso and head, but also possesses a goat's legs and cloven hooves. Typically, the Faun was associated with a powerful sex drive that were usually found in the woodlands, which does to a certain degree link with the way Roth depicts Faunia.[27] Gustavo Sánchez Canales, however, contends the name links to the roman goddess of fertility, Fauna. "This goddess ... was worshipped throughout Italy as a bestower of fruitfulness on people and fields, serves as an embodiment of life; Faunia, however, ... serves as an embodiment of disgrace

---

[25] Ironically it seems Zuckerman seems to adopt Keble's eulogy for his own narrative, constructing Coleman as an Emersonian figure in the quest to become the singular I.

[26] Godfrey highlights how the erasure of Faunia and Les's antisemitism serves to "rest[ore] both Coleman's unsullied character and his whiteness" (2017: 251), an astute observation that underlines how American racism and antisemitism are repressed to maintain the illusion of American innocence.

[27] See Weinstock (2014: 233–6).

Black Skin, Jewish Masks

149

and death" (2009: 115). Both Canales and Rankine provide two meaningful interpretations that reflect Faunia's symbolic indeterminacy. Her very name represents a destabilization of symbolic order.

Hence Faunia's affinity for Prince, the crow at the Audubon society that has been raised by humans and has subsequently been rejected by the other birds. "He doesn't have the right voice. He doesn't know the crow language. They don't like him out there" (*HS* 242). The crow's inability to mimic and adapt to "proper" culture has been read by some as a doubling of Coleman.[28] Prince, like Coleman, seeks to make invisible his past by ripping apart newspaper clippings that detail the crow's history: "He didn't want anybody to know his background! Ashamed of his own background! Prince! ... You're ashamed of your notorious past?" (*HS* 240). Additionally, Roth creates a triptych between Faunia, Coleman, and Prince, as all three are unable to exist within the parameters of their given identities.

For Faunia, Zuckerman, and Roth, humanness begins not with purity, but impurity; the human condition is fundamentally chaotic, unstable, and disorderly. Faunia reflects that what happened to Prince is "what comes of being hand-raised ... That's what comes of hanging around all of his life with people like us" (*HS* 242). The touch of the human hand on Prince leaves a mark that corrupts, deforms, and destabilizes Prince's identity as a crow. Humans, the third-person narrator (presumably Zuckerman) asserts, "leave a stain, we leave a trail, we leave our imprint. Impurity, cruelty, abuse, error, excrement, semen—there's no other way to be here" (*HS* 242). The impure, unclean, dirty, violent, filthiness of human bodies is what for Faunia and Zuckerman defines us as human: this is Roth's ode to the abject.[29] The inherency of mess, Zuckerman contends, makes the concept of purity an absurdity: "The stain ... *precedes* disobedience, that *encompasses* disobedience and perplexes all explanation and understanding. It's why all the cleansing is a joke. A barbaric joke at that. The fantasy of purity is appalling. It's insane. What is the quest to purify, if not *more* impurity?" (*HS* 242, italics in original). The body begins as a messy viscous entity entrenched in impurity; thus, humanness begins with stains. In other

---

[28] Ross Posnock, for example, contends "[i]f Prince is a strutting, black category mistake—described as a 'crow that doesn't know how to be a crow'—Coleman Silk is a human version, a black man who won't be a black man" (2006b: 220).

[29] Pozorski calls Faunia's "reflection on the fate of the crow ... a religion of the stain, of impurity" (2011: 51). I agree but see Zuckerman's voice as quite distinct within this particular passage; Faunia's speech is highlighted by the quotation marks, but the mythic-like soliloquy that follows seems to belong to the voice of Nathan rather than Faunia, though, of course, Faunia's speech is itself Zuckerman's creation.

150 *Philip Roth and the Body*

words, humans begin life as porous, leaky entities; to live as human is to exist impurely. For Roth the very concept of racial or sexual purity is inherently impossible because the subject always begins as a porous instability that renders categorization of the human body farcical.

Roth connects the act of categorization and the desire for purity through the isolated figure of Les Farley, the alleged murderer of Coleman and Faunia.[30] Les is a self-described "loyal American who'd served his country with not one tour but two, who'd gone back [to Vietnam] to finish the goddamn job" (*HS* 64). Les serves America, committed to the singular nation-state ideal of his country, which is inherently connected to the same racist schema Coleman resists. Farley's racist logic creates a separation between us and them which is weaponized in the army: "you see the enemy you kill the enemy" (*HS* 69), and his enemies are always demarcated racially. Les laments the multiculturalist diversity he perceives has changed America's cultural solidity:

> He serves his country and he can't even get a doctor who fucking speaks English. All round Northampton they've got Chinese restaurants, they've got Vietnamese restaurants, Korean markets—but him? If you're some Vietnamese, you're some Chink, you make out, you get a restaurant, you get a market, you get a grocery store, you get a family, you get a good education. But they got fuck-all for him. Because they want him dead.
>
> (*HS* 69)

The expansion of ethnic minorities into America threatens Les: the polyphony of voices and cultural nuance of these various constellations is reductively obliterated into racial appellations such as "Chink" (*HS* 69). Les seems transfixed by the logic of war: the enemy remains a threat to him, and he is still trying to wage his war against them. Unsurprisingly, Les decries his wife's relationship with Coleman because he is "a two bit-kike professor ... Jew bastard" (*HS* 70). Every other group whom Les identifies as non-white is racially marked out with a vicious appellation that dehumanizes them into threats, enemies that must be killed.

Les Farley is an isolated figure: like Coleman, he exists as a singular I, but his singularized subjectivity is a violent one, motivated by a desire to exclude minorities and maintain American culture as unified and "pure." Pozorski

---

[30] The name Les Farley seems to link with the word "Farleigh," which refers to a woodland clearing. Therefore, Les Farley may well be a synonym for "the woodlands," symbolically linking Les (and his whiteness) with the land.

Black Skin, Jewish Masks 151

convincingly argues that Farley's separateness from the rest of the characters stems from the narrative structures that detail his character: "starting from the moment Les' voice is heard on page 64," Pozorski argues, "the monologue reads very much like stream of consciousness" (2011: 92). The stream-of-consciousness style breaks semantic forms, and Pozorski argues Zuckerman would not "betray the rules of paragraphing in this way" (2011: 92). Pozorski's reading is particularly compelling when read alongside Hoovestol's analysis of Farley. Hoovestol compares Farley to Shelley's monster, highlighting the ways in which both authors position their monsters as alone, surrounded by the wintry snow and ice (2016: 41). Farley stands alone in *The Human Stain* because he must, because he represents the deathly destructiveness of whiteness.

At the end of *The Human Stain*, Nathan and Les confront one another in a "pristine" setting that Zuckerman imagines being "what the world was like before the advent of man" (*HS* 345). Roth seems to return us to what Toni Morrison has identified as a recurrent motif within the American tradition: "the snow," Morrison explains, "is the wasteland of unmeaning, unfathomable whiteness" (1992: 58). Zuckerman describes himself as having "trespassed" (*HS* 345) upon this space, again affirming his commitment to sullying the very ideal of purity itself. The two make idle chitchat, as Zuckerman anxiously attempts to wheedle out a confession from Farley, all the while facing his auger, "a metal shaft about four feet long ending in a wide, cylindrical length of corkscrew blade, a strong, serious boring tool" (*HS* 346). The impotent and incontinent Nathan stands against Les and his threateningly penetrative weapon used fertilely to break the ice and fish.

The Human Stain ends with Zuckerman leaving Les alone on the ice, promising to send him a copy of his forthcoming novel upon its release. Les is left on his bucket, surrounded by

> the icy white of the lake encircling a tiny spot that was a man, the only human marker in all of nature, like the X of an illiterate's signature on a sheet of paper. There it was, if not the whole story, the whole picture. Only rarely, at the end of the century, does life offer up a vision as pure and peaceful as this one: a solitary man on a bucket, fishing through eighteen inches of ice in a lake that's constantly turning over its water atop an arcadian mountain in America.
>
> (*HS* 361)

The X becomes the metaphor for the human stain that Roth links with the "illiterate" figure of Faunia, signifying a blotch that spoils the purity of the Arcadian ending. The simile brings us back to the impure figures of Coleman and Faunia, whose presence haunts and upsets the pristineness of the peaceful serenity Farley seeks. *The Human Stains* ends by reflecting on the immutable deathliness of purity that Roth connects with whiteness. "Whiteness, alone, is mute," writes Morrison, "meaningless, unfathomable, pointless, frozen, curtained, dreaded, senseless, implacable" (1992: 59). For both Morrison and Roth, whiteness represents a purification of the body that is not only senseless but violent, deathly, and violating.

Conclusion: Goodbye, Philip

Roth's legacy is a complicated and messy one, which is befitting for a novelist whose oeuvre abounds in bodily expulsions, secretions, and ejaculations. His fictive enterprises exhibit a disgust against what he terms purity. As Zuckerman notes in *The Human Stain*, "the fantasy of purity is appalling. It's insane. What is the quest to purify, if not *more* impurity?" (*HS* 242, italics in original). His fiction upturns and resists white fantasies of racial superiority by exposing us to the volatility of the body, reminding us that the starting points we define ourselves through are leaky and porous.

In his early fiction, Roth explored the absurdity of purification through his protagonist's fantasies of renewal that hinged around white women's bodies. As his literary career ballooned, however, so too did the scope and scale of his fictive imagination. Roth became more attentive toward the racial body politic of America and Europe, the racialization of Jewishness in the latter, and the systemic racism of the former (though, of course, the latter, too, is plagued by racism). What remained, however, was his investment in the complex multiplicities of Jewry and the brittleness of the body.

Roth wrote vociferously about Jews, sex, and race; he did so crudely, thunderously, and haphazardly. Recall the lines from *Deception*: "*Caprice* is at the heart of a writer's nature. Exploration, fixation, isolation, venom, fetishism, austerity, levity, perplexity, childishness, *et cetera*. The nose in the seam of the undergarment—*that's* the writer's nature. *Impurity*" (*D* 99, italics in original). The doubling of Roth as the speaker means we the reader must be cautious in taking this quotation too seriously; its stately rhetoric is called into question by the narrative structures that imbue the impure as the natural starting point of literature itself. Ironically, of course, this proclamation encapsulates the spirit of Roth's novels that centers on the impurity of human desires; for Roth, writing serves as an act of resistance against those seeking to establish social orders based on purified racial hierarchies. Roth's fiction attempts to encapsulate the impure

154 *Philip Roth and the Body*

messiness of life as a human being. Nevertheless, the passage above returns us to the issue of Roth's playfulness: the gendered imagery here reminds us that within Roth's writing, women's bodies are fetishized sites of impure desires, and the human subject Roth envisages is almost always a Jewish male.

This book has attempted to highlight the gendered body politics within Roth's fiction, and the ways Roth explores how the Jewish body has been used to define Jewish differences within America and Europe. The book has questioned the ways in which Roth's literature destabilizes racist conceptualizations of Jewish bodies and has done so by incorporating a considered analysis of Roth's gendered imagery. I have argued that Roth's fiction undermines racial concepts of Jews-as-different and attempted to explicate how the bodies in his work symbolically undermine white supremacy ideations of racial divisions.

Equally, Roth highlights how antisemitism has perniciously influenced Jewish men's conceptualizations of Jewish women. Jewish mothers are marginalized within Roth's fiction, problematically reflecting the ways in which Jewish women were disregarded as Jewish men assimilated into American society. Within the texts discussed here, non-Jewish white women are fetishized because they represent a racial and social form of Americanness that is regarded as superior to Jewishness. Even though Roth fails to imagine a Jewish woman as a literary subject, his novels serve as powerful critiques of how Jewish men have become embroiled in a culture of racial and sexual classifications, as they sought to establish themselves as white in post–Second World War America. Similarly, Roth's fiction highlights (whether intentionally or otherwise) the complicity of American (and European) Jewry in upholding the racist schemas that prop up white men. As Berlinerblau notes, Roth's protagonists are beneficiaries of racism, and do not attack or undermine the system from which they reap their rewards. Roth remains hyper-alert to the threat of antisemitism and its effects on Jewish identities but is perhaps less surefooted when describing America's racial schema.

Looking forward, I believe more work can and needs to be done on the topic of Roth and embodiment. Lee Trepanier's article "The Paradoxes of the Body in Philip Roth's Last Novels" reads Roth's novels through Merleau-Ponty, exploring how "the body is a source of both hope and betrayal for the protagonists' aspirations and ambitions" (2023: 131). Trepanier's approach—novel in Roth Studies—could and should be expanded in application to the rest of Roth's fiction. Regarding my own approach, I recognize the narrowed concentration on a single author foreclosed the possibility of creating intersectional discussions with other Jewish novelists and artists. The ghost of Philip Roth is a haunting one, and I admit to feeling relief at the thought of foreclosing this long and ghoulish chapter of my life. Interestingly, the topic of looking Jewish has reared its head of late, with writers such as Joshua Cohen, Melissa Broder, and Charlie Kauffman producing novels that—in a very Rothian manner—probe the subject of Jewish embodiment. There is much left to be said on the topic of Jewish literary responses to antisemitism, Jewish difference, and racism.

Over the course of writing both this book and doctoral thesis, I have witnessed the rise, fall, and potential return of Donald Trump in America. I was finishing my thesis as white supremacists took to the streets of Charlottesville, chanting, "Jews will not replace us." I watched in horror and sadness as my country—Great Britain—voted to leave the European Union. Now, Israel and Palestine are at war. Islamophobia, antisemitism, and violence against both Jews and Muslims continue to escalate, and my Twitter (X) feed is full of division and anger.

Roth remains relevant precisely because he was invested in how the body has been used to divide and define us. Reading Roth's novels offers an intricate excavation of how Jews have mobilized in terms of race, gender, and class, and the ways Jews have overcome and been made to confront antisemitism. Roth is an important (and problematic) writer; he is a significant figure of American letters because his works repeatedly confronts, confounds, and undermines antisemitism. Roth was a "satirist of the clamoring body … a writer who broke taboos, fucked around, indiscrete, stepped outside that stuff deliberately" (*CL* 223). He was a filth merchant, an uproarious, cantankerous novelist whose books abound in abjection that always hark back to Jews, Jewry, and America, to a people who are endless and inassimilable: "inside every Jew there is a *mob* of Jews. The good Jew, the bad Jew. The new Jew, the old Jew. The lover of Jews, the hater of Jews. The friend of the goy, the enemy of the goy. The coarse Jew, the gentle Jew. The defiant Jew, the appeasing Jew. The Jewish Jew, the de-Jewed Jew" (*OS* 334, italics in original). Such multiplicities always orbit around the body. Roth wrote about the gooey, gnarly, knotted corporeality the self cleaves and clings to; his novels abound in the slippery, slimy, impossibility of selfhood that was always entwined with Jewishness, gender, and race. As Henry Zuckerman observes of his brother Nathan, so too the same can be said for his creator: Roth, the poor bastard, always had Jew on the brain.

References

Primary Texts

Roth, P. ([1959] 2016) *Goodbye, Columbus: And Five Short Stories*. London: Vintage.

Roth, P. ([1969] 1999) *Portnoy's Complaint*. London: Vintage.

Roth, P. ([1985] 1989) *Zuckerman Bound: A Trilogy and Epilogue*. London: Penguin Books.

Roth, P. ([1986] 2005) *The Counterlife*. London: Vintage.

Roth, P. (1988) *The Facts: A Novelist's Autobiography*. London: Vintage.

Roth, P. (1990) *Deception*. London: Vintage.

Roth, P. ([1991] 1999) *Patrimony: A True Story*. London: Vintage.

Roth, P. (1994) *Operation Shylock: A Confession*. London: Vintage.

Roth, P. (1995) *Sabbath's Theater*. London: Vintage.

Roth, P. ([1997] 2016) *American Pastoral*. London: Vintage.

Roth, P. (2000) *The Human Stain*. London: Vintage.

Roth, P. (2002) *The Dying Animal*. London: Vintage.

Roth, P. (2004a) "The Story Behind 'The Plot against America,'" *The New York Times*, 19 September. Available at: https://www.nytimes.com/2004/09/19/books/review/the-story-behind-the-plot-against-america.html.

Roth, P. (2004b) *The Plot against America*. London: Vintage.

Roth, P. (2011) *Nemesis*. London: Vintage.

Roth, P. (2012) "An Open Letter to Wikipedia," *The New Yorker*, 6 September. Available at: https://www.newyorker.com/books/page-turner/an-open-letter-to-wikipedia.

Roth, P. (2017) *Why Write? Collected Nonfiction, 1960–2013*. New York: The Library of America.

Secondary Sources

Aarons, V. (2000) "Is It 'Good-for-the-Jews or No-Good-for-the-Jews'?: Philip Roth's Registry of Jewish Consciousness," *Shofar: An Interdisciplinary Journal of Jewish Studies*, 19(1), pp. 7–18.

Abrams, N. (2012) *The New Jew in Film: Exploring Jewishness and Judaism in Contemporary Cinema*. New Brunswick, NJ: Rutgers University Press.

Ahmed, S. (2005) *Revolt, Affect, Collectivity: The Unstable Boundaries of Kristeva's Polis*. Edited by T. Chanter and E.P. Ziarek. Albany: State University of New York Press (SUNY series in gender theory).

References

Antler, J. (2007) *You Never Call! You Never Write!: A History of the Jewish Mother*. Cary: Oxford University Press. Available at: http://ebookcentral.proquest.com/lib/gla/detail.action?docID=416062.

Arya, R. *et al.* (eds) (2016) "Introduction: Approaching Abjection," in *Abject Visions: Powers of Horror in Art and Visual Culture*. Manchester: Manchester University Press, pp. 1–13.

Barthes, R. (2009) *Mythologies*. Revised Vintage edition. Translated by A. Lavers. London: Vintage (Vintage classics).

Basu, A. (2015) *States of Trial: Manhood in Philip Roth's Post-War America*. New York: Bloomsbury Academic.

Bataille, G. (1999) "Abjection and Miserable Forms," in *More & less*. Edited by S. Lotringer. Translated by Y. Shafir. Cambridge: MIT Press, 2.

Bataille, G. and Lovitt, C.R. (1979) "The Psychological Structure of Fascism," *New German Critique* (16), pp. 64–87. Available at: https://doi.org/10.2307/487877.

Bauman, Z. (1989) *Modernity and the Holocaust*. Ithaca, NY: Cornell University Press.

Bellow, S. (2007) *Henderson the Rain King*. London: Penguin books.

Bennett, A. and Royle, N. (2004) *An Introduction to Literature Criticism and Theory*. 3rd edition. Harlow: Pearson Longman.

Bergner, G. (1995) "Who Is That Masked Woman? Or, the Role of Gender in Fanon's Black Skin, White Masks," *PMLA*, 110(1), pp. 75–88. Available at: https://doi.org/10.2307/463196.

Berlinerblau, J. (2021) *The Philip Roth We Don't Know: Sex, Race, and Autobiography*. London: University of Virginia Press.

Berlinerblau, J. (2023) "Beware White Male Rothians," *Philip Roth Studies*, 19(2), pp. 82–91.

Bettelheim, B. (2000) "The Ignored Lesson of Anne Frank," in H.A. Enzer and S. Solotaroff-Enzer (eds) *Anne Frank: Reflections on Her Life and Legacy*. Urbana: University of Illinois Press, pp. 185–92.

Bhabha, H.K. (1994) *The Location of Culture*. 2nd edition. New York: Routledge.

Bloom, H. (ed.) (2003) *Philip Roth*. Philadelphia: Chelsea House Publishers.

Boese, S. (2014) "'Those Two Years': Alternate History and Autobiography in Philip Roth's *The Plot against America*," *Studies in American Fiction*, 41(2), pp. 271–92.

Bois, W.E.B.D. (2008) *The Souls of Black Folk*. Oxford: Oxford University Press.

Bousfield, C. (2000) "The Abject Space: Its Gifts and Complaints," *Journal of Gender Studies*, 9(3), pp. 329–46.

Boyagoda, R. (2021) "Why the Other Philip Roth Bio Never Took Off," *The Atlantic*, 5 May. Available at: https://www.theatlantic.com/ideas/archive/2021/05/whyauthorized-biographies-are-best/618797/.

Boyarin, D. (1997) *Unheroic Conduct: The Rise of Heterosexuality and the Invention of the Jewish Man*. Berkeley: University of California Press.

158 References

Boyarin, D. (2022) "The New Jewish Question: To the Memory of Breonna Taylor and George Floyd, ד"יה," *Cambridge Journal of Postcolonial Literary Inquiry*, 9(1), pp. 42–66.

Boyarin, D., Itzkovitz, D. and Pellegrini, A. (eds) (2003a) *Queer Theory and the Jewish Question*. New York: Columbia University Press.

Boyarin, D., Itzkovitz, D., and Pellegrini, A. (2003b) "Strange Bedfellows," in D. Boyarin, D. Itzkovitz, and A. Pellegrini (eds) *Queer Theory and the Jewish Question*. New York: Columbia University Press, pp. 1–18. Available at: http://www.jstor.org.ezproxy2.lib.gla.ac.uk/stable/10.7312/boya11374.4.

Boyarin, J. and Boyarin, D. (eds) (1997) *Jews and Other Differences: The New Jewish Cultural Studies*. Minneapolis: University of Minnesota Press.

Boyd, S.B., Longwood, W.M., and Muesse, M.W. (eds) (1996) *Redeeming Men: Religion and Masculinities*. Louisville: Westminster John Knox Press.

Brauner, D. (2007) *Philip Roth*. Manchester: Manchester University press.

Brauner, D. (2016) "Queering Philip Roth: Homosocial Discourse in 'An Actor's Life for Me', 'Letting Go', 'Sabbath's Theater' and the 'American Trilogy'," *Studies in the Novel*, 48(1), pp. 86–106.

Breines, P. (1990) *Tough Jews: Political Fantasies and the Moral Dilemma of American Jewry*. New York: Basic Books.

Bresnan, M.P. (2016) *America First: Reading "The Plot against America" in the Age of Trump*, *Los Angeles Review of Books*. Available at: https://lareviewofbooks.org/article/america-first-reading-plot-against-america-age-trump/.

Brod, H. (1996) "Of Mice and Supermen: Images of Jewish Masculinity," in S.B. Boyd, W.M. Longwood, and M.W. Muesse (eds) *Redeeming Men: Religion and Masculinities*. Louisville: Westminster John Knox Press, pp. 145–56.

Brodkin, K. (1998) *How Jews Became White Folks and What That Says about Race in America*. New Brunswick: Rutgers University Press.

Brooks, P. (1993) *Body Work: Objects of Desire in Modern Narrative*. Cambridge, MA: Harvard University Press. Available at: http://ebookcentral.proquest.com/lib/gla/detail.action?docID=3300320.

Brühwiler, C.F. and Trepanier, L. (eds) (2017) *A Political Companion to Philip Roth*. Lexington: University Press of Kentucky.

Budick, E.M. (2003) "The Holocaust in the Jewish American Literary Imagination," in H. Wirth-Nesher and M.P. Kramer (eds) *The Cambridge Companion to Jewish American Literature*. Cambridge: Cambridge University Press, pp. 212–30.

Butler, J. (2003) "Violence, Mourning, Politics," *Studies in Gender and Sexuality*, 4(1), pp. 9–37. Available at: https://doi.org/10.1080/15240650409349213.

Bylund, S. (2010) "Merry Levov's BLT Crusade: Food-Fueled Revolt in Roth's American Pastoral," *Philip Roth Studies*, 6(1), pp. 13–30, 117.

Canales, G.S. (2009) "The Classical World and Modern Academia in Philip Roth's The Human Stain," *Philip Roth Studies*, 5(1), pp. 111–28, 149.

Canales, G.S. (2021) "Antisemitism," in M. McKinley (ed.) *Philip Roth in Context*. Cambridge: Cambridge University Press, pp. 241–51.

Castronovo, R. (2023) "The Plot Against Democracy," *American Literary History*, 35(1), pp. 67–80.

Chanter, T. and Ziarek, E.P. (eds) (2005) "The Skin of the Community: Affect and Boundary Formation," in *Revolt, Affect, Collectivity: The Unstable Boundaries of Kristeva's Polis*. Albany: State University of New York Press.

Cheyette, B. and Marcus, L. (eds) (1998) *Modernity, Culture and "The Jew"*. Cambridge: Polity.

Clarkson, S. (2014) "Liver, Lobster and the Law: Gastronomic Identification and Rebellion in Portnoy's Complaint," *Philip Roth Studies*, 10(2), pp. 21–9, 107.

Connolly, A. (2017) *Philip Roth and the American Liberal Tradition*. Maryland: Lexington Books.

Connolly, A. (2021) "Canceling Philip Roth in the Name of Progressive Neoliberalism?," *VoegelinView*, 3 October. Available at: https://voegelinview.com/canceling-philip-roth-in-the-name-of-progressive-neoliberalism/.

Connolly, A. (2022) "An 'Ambiguously Menacing Predicament': Reading The Plot against America in the Age of Donald Trump," *Studies in American Jewish Literature*, 41(1), pp. 60–92. Available at: https://doi.org/10.5325/studamerijewilite.41.1.0060.

Cooper, A. (1996) *Philip Roth and the Jews*. Albany: State University of New York Press.

Coughlan, D. (2016) *Ghost Writing in Contemporary American Fiction*. London: Palgrave Macmillan.

Cox, K. (2016) "'How Cam'st Thou Speakable of Mute': Satanic Acoustics in Paradise Lost," *Milton Studies*, 57(1), pp. 233–60.

Darda, J. (2015) "The Visual Apologetics of Philip Roth's Pastoral America," *Philip Roth Studies*, 11(2), pp. 77–94, 115.

Davis, B.R. (2023) "The Politics of Racial Abjection," *Du Bois Review: Social Science Research on Race*, 20(1), pp. 143–62.

De Boer, K. (2002) "Enter the Ghost/Exit the Ghost/Re-Enter the Ghost: Derrida's Reading of Hamlet in Specters of Marx," *Journal of the British Society for Phenomenology*, 33(1), pp. 22–38. Available at: https://doi.org/10.1080/00071773.2002.11007358.

Deleuze, G. and Guattari, F. (1983) *Anti-Oedipus: Capitalism and Schizophrenia*. Minneapolis: University of Minnesota Press.

Dickstein, M. (2002) *Leopards in the Temple: The Transformation of American Fiction, 1945-1970*. Cambridge, MA: Harvard University Press.

Disch, L. and Hawkesworth, M. (eds) (2015) *The Oxford Handbook of Feminist Theory*. New York: Oxford University Press. Available at: https://doi.org/10.1093/oxfordhb/9780199328581.001.0001.

Dohmen, J. (2016) "Disability as Abject: Kristeva, Disability, and Resistance," *Hypatia*, 31(4), pp. 762–78.

Douglas, C. (2013) "'Something That Has Already Happened': Recapitulation and Religious Indifference in The Plot against America," *MFS Modern Fiction Studies*, 59(4), pp. 784–810. Available at: https://doi.org/10.1353/mfs.2013.0045.

Dragulescu, L.M. (2014) "Race Trauma at the End of the Millennium: (Narrative) Passing in Philip Roth's The Human Stain," *Philip Roth Studies*, 10(1), pp. 91–108.

Duban, J. (2011) "Written, Unwritten, and Vastly Rewritten: Meyer Levin's In Search and Philip Roth's 'Defender of the Faith,' The Plot against America, and Indignation," *Philip Roth Studies*, 7(1), pp. 28–50. Available at: https://doi.org/10.1353/prs.2011.a430869.

Eagle, C. (2012) "'Angry Because She Stutters': Stuttering, Violence, and the Politics of Voice in American Pastoral and Sorry," *Philip Roth Studies*, 8(1), pp. 17–30, 119.

Eilberg-Schwartz, H. (1992a) "Introduction: People of the Body," in *People of the Body: Jews and Judaism from an Embodied Perspective*. New York: State University of New York Press, pp. 1–17.

Eilberg-Schwartz, H. (ed.) (1992b) *People of the Body: Jews and Judaism from an Embodied Perspective*. New York: State University of New York Press.

Emerson, R.W. (2003) *Nature and Selected Essays*. Edited by L. Ziff. New York: Penguin Classics.

Enzer, H.A. and Solotaroff-Enzer, S. (eds) (2000) *Anne Frank: Reflections on Her Life and Legacy*. Urbana: University of Illinois Press.

Ewara, E. (2021) "The Psychic Life of Horror: Abjection and Racialization in Butler's Thought," in A. Halsema, K. Kwastek, and R. van den Oever (eds) *Bodies That Still Matter: Resonances of the Work of Judith Butler*. Amsterdam: Amsterdam University Press, pp. 31–42.

Falla, J.B. (2002) "Disembodying the Body: Allen Ginsberg's Passional Subversion of Identity," *Interdisciplinary Literary Studies*, 3(2), pp. 49–65.

Fanon, F. (2021) *Black Skin, White Masks*. Translated by R. Philcox. London: Penguin.

Feldman, D. (1998) "Was Modernity Good for the Jews?," in B. Cheyette and L. Marcus (eds) *Modernity, Culture and "The Jew"*. 1st edition. Cambridge: Polity, pp. 171–88.

Flood, A. (2011) "Judge Withdraws over Philip Roth's Booker Win," *The Guardian*, 18 May. Available at: https://www.theguardian.com/books/2011/may/18/judge-quits-philip-roth-booker.

Fong, T. (2012) "Matrimony: Re-Conceiving the Mother in Philip Roth's Life Writing," *Philip Roth Studies*, 8(1), pp. 63–80,119.

Foucault, M. (1995) *Discipline & Punish: The Birth of the Prison*. Translated by A. Sheridan. New York: Vintage Books.

Franco, D. (2009) "Portnoy's Complaint: It's about Race, Not Sex (Even the Sex Is about Race)," *Prooftexts*, 29(1), pp. 86–115. Available at: https://doi.org/10.2979/pft.2009.29.1.86.

Franco, D.J. (2004) "'Being Black, Being Jewish, and Knowing the Difference: Philip Roth's 'The Human Stain'; Or, It Depends on What the Meaning of 'Clinton' Is," *Studies in American Jewish Literature*, 23, pp. 88–103.

Frank, A. (1996) *Diary of a Young Girl: The Definitive Edition*. Illustrated edition. Edited by O.H. Frank and M. Pressler. Translated by S. Massotty. New York: San Val.

Freud, S. (1953a) "Medusa's Head," in C.L. Rothgeb (ed.) J. Strachey and A. Freud (trans.) *The Standard Edition of the Complete Psychological Works of Sigmund Freud*. London: Hogarth Press and the Institute of Psycho-Analysis, pp. 273–5.

Freud, S. (1953b) *The Standard Edition of the Complete Psychological Works of Sigmund Freud*. Edited by C.L. Rothgeb. Translated by J. Strachey and A. Freud. London: Hogarth Press and the Institute of Psycho-Analysis.

Freud, S. (1997) *The Interpretation of Dreams*. Hertfordshire: Wordsworth Editions Ltd.

Friedman, M.J. (1973) "Jewish Mothers and Sons: The Expense of Chutzpah," in I. Malin (ed.) *Contemporary American-Jewish Literature: Critical Essays*. Bloomington: Indiana University Press, pp. 156–75.

Gair, C. (2007) *The American Counterculture*. Edinburgh: Edinburgh University Press.

Gair, C. (2008) "The 'Horror of Self-Reflection': Writing, Cancer and Terrorism in Philip Roth's American Pastoral," *Gramma: Journal of Theory and Criticism*, 16, pp. 235–49.

Geller, J. (2007) *On Freud's Jewish Body: Mitigating Circumcisions*. New York: Fordham University Press.

Geller, J. (2011) *The Other Jewish Question: Identifying the Jew and Making Sense of Modernity*. New York: Fordham University Press. Available at: https://doi.org/10.5422/fordham/9780823233618.001.0001.

Gilman, S.L. (1991) *The Jew's Body*. New York: Routledge.

Gilman, S.L. (1995) *Freud, Race, and Gender*. Princeton, NJ: Princeton Univ. Press.

Ginsberg, A. (1974) *Howl: and Other Poems*. San Francisco: City Lights Books.

Godfrey, M. (2017) "Passing as Post-Racial: Philip Roth's The Human Stain, Political Correctness, and the Post-Racial Passing Narrative," *Contemporary Literature*, 58(2), pp. 233–61.

Golash-Boza, T. (2006) "Dropping the Hyphen? Becoming Latino(a)-American through Racialized Assimilation," *Social Forces*, 85(1), pp. 27–55.

Goldscheider, C. and Zuckerman, A.S. (1984) *The Transformation of the Jews*. Chicago: University of Chicago Press.

Gooblar, D. (2014) *The Major Phases of Philip Roth*. London: Bloomsbury Publishing.

Goodman, D.R. (2020) "'The Uncontrollability of Real Things': Operation Shylock, Sabbath's Theater, and Philip Roth's Falstaffian Theology of Judaism," *Philip Roth Studies*, 16(2), pp. 39–59.

Grayson, E. and Scheurer, M. (eds) (2021) *Amputation in Literature and Film: Artificial Limbs, Prosthetic Relations, and the Semiotics of "Loss"*. Cham: Springer International Publishing (Literary Disability Studies). Available at: https://doi.org/10.1007/978-3-030-74377-2.

Greenberg, R.M. (2003) "Transgression in the Fiction of Philip Roth," in H. Bloom (ed.) *Philip Roth*. Philadelphia: Chelsea House Publishers (Bloom's modern critical views), pp. 81–101.

Greene, D. and Rezvani, A. (2020) "In 'Plot Against America,' David Simon Finds Present Day in an Imagined Past," *NPR*, 13 March. Available at: https://www.npr.org/2020/03/13/814602908/in-plot-against-america-david-simon-finds-present-day-in-an-imagined-past.

Greenwell, G. (2023) "A Moral Education", *The Yale Review*. Available at: https://yalereview.org/article/garth-greenwell-philip-roth.

Grosz, E.A. (1994) *Volatile Bodies: Toward a Corporeal Feminism*. Bloomington: Indiana University Press.

HaCohen, R. (2018) "The 'Jewish Blackness' Thesis Revisited," *Religions*, 9(7), p. 222. Available at: https://doi.org/10.3390/rel9070222.

Halio, J.L. and Siegel, B. (eds) (2005) *Turning up the Flame: Philip Roth's Later Novels*. Newark: University of Delaware Press.

Hayes, P. (2014) *Philip Roth: Fiction and Power*. Oxford: Oxford University Press.

Hertzberg, A. (1997) *The Jews in America: Four Centuries of an Uneasy Encounter: A History*. New York: Columbia University Press.

Hillman, D. and Maude, U. (2015a) "Introduction," in D. Hillman and U. Maude (eds) *The Cambridge Companion to the Body in Literature*. Cambridge: Cambridge University Press, pp. 1–9. Available at: https://doi.org/10.1017/CCO9781107256668.001.

Hillman, D. and Maude, U. (eds) (2015b) *The Cambridge Companion to the Body in Literature*. Cambridge: Cambridge University Press. Available at: https://doi.org/10.1017/CCO9781107256668.

Hirsch, M. (1989) *The Mother/Daughter Plot: Narrative, Psychoanalysis, Feminism*. Bloomington: Indiana University Press.

Hirth, B. (2018) "'An Independent Destiny for America': Roth's Vision of American Exceptionalism," *Philip Roth Studies*, 14(1), pp. 70–93. Available at: https://doi.org/10.5703/philrothstud.14.1.0070.

Hobbs, A. (2010) "Reading the Body in Philip Roth's American Pastoral," *Philip Roth Studies*, 6(1), pp. 69–83, 117.

Hobbs, A. (2012) "Family and the Renegotiation of Masculine Identity in Philip Roth's 'The Plot against America'," *Journal of American Studies*, 46(1), pp. 121–37.

Holroyd, J. (2016) "Playful Punches, Words That Hurt, Words That Heal: Dialectically Reading the Human Stain," *Philip Roth Studies*, 12(1), pp. 53–72.

Hoovestol, C. (2016) "Secret Sins, Honest Hypocrites, and Secular Sermons: Hawthorne's Human Stain in Philip Roth's Twice-Told Tale," *Philip Roth Studies*, 12(1), pp. 33–52.

Horn, D. (2018) "Opinion | What Philip Roth Didn't Know about Women Could Fill a Book," *The New York Times*, 25 May. Available at: https://www.nytimes.com/2018/05/25/opinion/sunday/philip-roth-jewish-women-new-jersey.html.

Houston, D. (2014) "Counterpastoral," *Philip Roth Studies*, 10(1), pp. 125–39.

Howe, I. (1972) "Philip Roth Reconsidered," *Commentary*, 1 December, pp. 69–77.

Hutchison, A. (2007) *Writing the Republic: Liberalism and Morality in American Political Fiction*. New York: Columbia University Press.

Hwang, J.-S. (2018) "'Newark's Just a Black Colony': Race in Philip Roth's American Pastoral," *Twentieth Century Literature*, 64(2), pp. 161–91. Available at: https://doi.org/10.1215/0041462X-6941806.

Irigaray, L. (1985) *This Sex Which Is Not One*. Ithaca: Cornell University Press.

Itzkovitz, D. (1997) "Secret Temples," in J. Boyarin and D. Boyarin (eds) *Jews and Other Differences: The New Jewish Cultural Studies*. Minneapolis: University of Minnesota Press, pp. 176–203.

Itzkovitz, D. (1999) "Passing Like Me," *South Atlantic Quarterly*, 98(1–2), pp. 35–57.

James, H. (1987) *The American Scene*. London: Granville.

Jarvis, C. (2010) *The Male Body at War: American Masculinity during World War II*. DeKalb: Northern Illinois University Press.

Kaplan, B.A. (2013) "Do You Just Love Philip Roth?," *Studies in American Jewish Literature*, 32(2), pp. 187–92.

Kaplan, B.A. (2015) *Jewish Anxiety and the Novels of Philip Roth*. New York: Bloomsbury Academic.

Kaplan, B.A. (2020) "'Grotesquery to the Surface': The Leo Frank Case and Philip Roth's The Plot against America Revisited in Trump's Alt-Right America," *Studies in American Jewish Literature*, 39(1), pp. 44–72.

Karabel, J. (2006) *The Chosen: The Hidden History of Admission and Exclusion at Harvard, Yale, and Princeton*. Boston: Houghton Mifflin Company.

Karasik-Updike, O. (2022) "'Momma, Do We Believe in Winter?' Yiddishe Mama and Judaism in Portnoy's Complaint," *Philip Roth Studies*, 18(1), pp. 63–79.

Kartiganer, D.M. (2007) "Zuckerman Bound: The Celebrant of Silence," in T. Parrish (ed.) *The Cambridge Companion to Philip Roth*. Cambridge: Cambridge University Press, pp. 35–51. Available at: https://doi.org/10.1017/CCOL0521864305.004.

Katz, J. (1980) *From Prejudice to Destruction: Anti-semitism, 1700–1933*. Cambridge, MA: Harvard University Press.

Kauvar, E.M. (2011) "My Life as a Boy: The Plot against America," in D. Shostak (ed.) *Philip Roth: American Pastoral, the Human Stain, the Plot against America*. London: Bloomsbury, pp. 130–45.

Kelleter, F. (2003) "Portrait of the Sexist as a Dying Man: Death, Ideology, and the Erotic in Philip Roth's Sabbath's Theater," in H. Bloom (ed.) *Philip Roth*. Philadelphia: Chelsea House Publishers, pp. 163–99.

Kelly, A. (2013) *American Fiction in Transition: Observer-Hero Narrative, the 1990s, and Postmodernism*. London: Bloomsbury Academic. Available at: https://doi.org/10.5040/9781472543394.

Kermode, F. (2001) *Pleasing Myself: From Beowulf to Philip Roth*. London: Allen Lane, The Penguin Press.

Kirsch, A. (2019) *Who Wants to Be a Jewish Writer? And Other Essays*. New Haven: Yale University Press.

Kirshenblatt-Gimblett, B. (2005) "The Corporeal Turn," *The Jewish Quarterly Review*, 95(3), pp. 447–61.

Kolodny, A. (1975) *The Lay of the Land: Metaphor as Experience and History in American Life and Letters*. Chapel Hill: University of North Carolina Press.

Krijnen, J. (2016) *Holocaust Impiety in Jewish American Literature: Memory, Identity, (Post-) Postmodernism*. Leiden: Brill.

Kristeva, J. (1980) "Motherhood according to Giovanni Bellini," in L. Roudiez (ed.), T. Gora and A. Jardine (trans.) *Desire in Language: A Semiotic Approach to Literature and Art*. New York: Columbia University Press, pp. 237–371.

Kristeva, J. (1982) *Powers of Horror: an Essay on Abjection*. New York: Columbia University Press.

Kristeva, J. (1989) *Black Sun: Depression and Melancholia*. Translated by L.S. Roudiez. New York: Columbia University Press.

Lassner, P. and Trubowitz, L. (eds) (2008) *Antisemitism and Philosemitism in the Twentieth and Twenty-First Centuries: Representing Jews, Jewishness, and Modern Culture*. Newark: University of Delaware Press.

Levine, A. (2011) "Embodying Jewishness at the Millennium," *Shofar: An Interdisciplinary Journal of Jewish Studies*, 30(1), pp. 31–52. Available at: https://doi.org/10.1353/sho.2011.0126.

Levitt, L. (2007) "Impossible Assimilations, American Liberalism, and Jewish Difference: Revisiting Jewish Secularism," *American Quarterly*, 59(3), pp. 807–32, 1046.

Levy, P. (2002) "The Text as Homeland: A Reading of Philip Roth's 'The Counterlife' and 'Operation Shylock'," *Studies in American Jewish literature*, 21 (Journal Article), pp. 61–71.

Lewis, R.W. B. (1955) *The American Adam: Innocence, Tragedy and Tradition in the Nineteenth Century*. Chicago University Press.

Lindemann, A.S. (1991) *The Jew Accused: Three Anti-Semitic Affairs (Dreyfus, Beilis, Frank), 1894–1915*. Cambridge: Cambridge University Press.

Lipset, S.M. and Raab, E. (1995) *Jews and the New American Scene*. Cambridge, MA: Harvard University Press.

Lopez, I.H. (2006) *White by Law 10th Anniversary Edition: The Legal Construction of Race*. New York: New York University Press. Available at: http://ebookcentral.proquest.com/lib/gla/detail.action?docID=3025614.

Lotringer, S. (2020) "The Politics of Abjection," in M. Hennefeld and N. Sammond (eds) *Abjection Incorporated: Mediating the Politics of Pleasure and Violence*. Durham: Duke University Press Books, pp. 33–43.

Malin, I. (ed.) (1973) *Contemporary American-Jewish Literature: Critical Essays*. Bloomington: Indiana University Press.

Marcus, L. (2008) "May Jews Go to College? Fictions of Jewishness in the 1920s," in P. Lassner and L. Trubowitz (eds) *Antisemitism and Philosemitism in the Twentieth and Twenty-first Centuries: Representing Jews, Jewishness, and Modern Culture.* Newark: University of Delaware Press, pp. 138–54.

Marx, L. (1964) *The Machine in the Garden: Technology and the Pastoral Ideal in America.* New York: Oxford University Press.

Maslan, M. (2005) "The Faking of the Americans: Passing, Trauma, and National Identity in Philip Roth's Human Stain," *Modern Language Quarterly*, 66(3), pp. 365–90. Available at: https://doi.org/10.1215/00267929-66-3-365.

Matthews, D. (2016) "The Rape Allegation against Bill Clinton, Explained," *Vox*. Available at: https://www.vox.com/2016/1/6/10722580/bill-clinton-juanita-broaddrick.

Maurer, Y. (2011) "'If I Didn't See It with My Own Eyes, I'd Think I Was Having a Hallucination': Re-Imagining Jewish History in Philip Roth's The Plot against America," *Philip Roth Studies*, 7(1), pp. 51–63. Available at: https://doi.org/10.1353/prs.2011.a430870.

Maurer, Y. (2017) "The Body Politic: Philip Roth's American Men," in C.F. Brühwiler and L. Trepanier (eds) *A Political Companion to Philip Roth.* Kentucky: University Press of Kentucky, pp. 172–90. Available at: https://doi.org/10.2307/j.ctt1pc5ftb.13.

Mayo, R. and Moutsou, C. (eds) (2017a) "The Maternal: An Introduction," in *The Mother in Psychoanalysis and Beyond: Matricide and Maternal Subjectivity.* London: Routledge, Taylor & Francis Group, pp. 1–21.

Mayo, R. and Moutsou, C. (eds) (2017b) *The Mother in Psychoanalysis and Beyond: Matricide and Maternal Subjectivity.* London: Routledge, Taylor & Francis Group.

Mcdonald, B. (2004) "'The Real American Crazy Shit': On Adamism and Democratic Individuality in 'American Pastoral'," *Studies in American Jewish Literature*, 23, pp. 27–40.

McKinley, M. (ed.) (2021) *Philip Roth in Context.* Cambridge: Cambridge University Press.

McLennan, R. (2017) *Representations of Anne Frank in American Literature: In Different Rooms.* New York: Routledge.

Mell, J.L. (2017) *The Myth of the Medieval Jewish Moneylender.* New York: Palgrave Macmillan. Available at: https://doi.org/10.1057/978-1-137-39778-2.

Mellard, J.M. (2005) "Death, Mourning, and Besse's Ghost: From Philip Roth's The Facts to Sabbath's Theater," in J.L. Halio and B. Siegel (eds) *Turning up the Flame: Philip Roth's Later Novels.* Newark: University of Delaware Press, pp. 115–25.

Melville, H. (2012) *Moby-Dick.* New York: Penguin.

Merleau-Ponty, M. (2004) *The World of Perception.* London: Routledge. Available at: https://doi.org/10.4324/9780203491829.

Merleau-Ponty, M. (2012) *Phenomenology of Perception.* Milton: Taylor & Francis Group. Available at: http://ebookcentral.proquest.com/lib/gla/detail.action?docID=1433878.

Michaels, W.B. (2006) "Plots against America: Neoliberalism and Antiracism," *American Literary History*, 18(2), pp. 288–302.

Mills, C.W. (1997) *The Racial Contract*. Ithaca: Cornell University Press.

Milowitz, S. (2000) *Philip Roth Considered: The Concentrationary Universe of the American Writer*. New York: Garland.

Milton, J. (2003) *Paradise Lost*. New York: Penguin Books.

Morley, C. (2008) "Memories of the Lindbergh Administration: Plotting, Genre, and the Splitting of the Self in The Plot against America," *Philip Roth Studies*, 4(2), pp. 137–52.

Morley, C. (2009) *The Quest for Epic in Contemporary American fiction: John Updike, Philip Roth and Don DeLillo*. New York: Routledge (Book, Whole). Available at: https://doi.org/10.4324/9780203889534.

Morley, C. (ed.) (2016) *9/11: Topics in Contemporary North American Literature*. London: Bloomsbury Academic.

Morris, K.J. (2012) *Starting with Merleau-Ponty*. London: Bloomsbury. Available at: http://ebookcentral.proquest.com/lib/gla/detail.action?docID=894584.

Morrison, T. (1992) *Playing in the Dark: Whiteness and the Literary Imagination*. Cambridge, MA: Harvard University Press.

Morrissey, L. (2001) "Eve's Otherness and the New Ethical Criticism," *New Literary History*, 32(2), pp. 327–45.

Moynihan, S. (2010) *Passing into the Present: Contemporary American Fiction of Racial and Gender Passing*. Manchester: Manchester University Press. Available at: http://ebookcentral.proquest.com/lib/gla/detail.action?docID=1069666.

Muresan, L. (2015) "Writ(h)ing Bodies: Literature and Illness in Philip Roth's Anatomy Lesson(s)," *Philip Roth Studies*, 11(1), pp. 75–90, 125.

Neelakantan, G. (2005) "Textualizing the Self: Adultery, Blatant Fictions, and Jewishness in Philip Roth's Deception," in J. L. Halio and B. Siegel (eds) *Turning up the Flame: Philip Roth's Later Novels*. Newark: University of Delaware Press, pp. 58–68.

Newlin, J. (2012) "Living on the Edge: Deconstruction, the Limits of Readability, and Philip Roth's The Counterlife," *Philip Roth Studies*, 8(2), pp. 161–77, 236.

Newman, J. (2019) "'There's Always More to a Story than a Body Can See from a Fence Line': Philip Roth and Barbara Kingsolver," *Philip Roth Studies*, 15(2), pp. 84–100.

Newman, S. (2018) "Stop Treating the Misogyny in Philip Roth's Work like a Dirty Secret," *HuffPost*. Available at: https://www.huffpost.com/entry/stop-treating-the-misogyny-in-philip-roths-work-like-a-dirty-secret_n_5b09562be4b0568a880bbda3.

Novick, P. and Novick, P. (1999) *The Holocaust and Collective Memory: The American Experience*. London: Bloomsbury.

Omer-Sherman, R. (2005) "'A Little Stranger in the House': Madness and Identity in Sabbath's Theater," in D.P. Royal (ed.) *Philip Roth: New Perspectives on an American Author*. Westport: Praeger Publishers, pp. 169–85.

Ozick, C. (1994) "America: Toward Yavneh," in H. Wirth-Nesher (ed.) *What Is Jewish Literature?* Philadelphia: Jewish Publication Society, pp. 20–36.

Parfitt, T. (2013) *Black Jews in Africa and the Americas.* Cambridge, MA: Harvard University Press. Available at: http://ebookcentral.proquest.com/lib/gla/detail.action?docID=3301201.

Paris, V. (2013) "The Queer Dialectic of Whitman's Nation: 'Let' in 'Respondez,'" *The Arizona Quarterly*, 69(3), pp. 1–22. Available at: https://doi.org/10.1353/arq.2013.0018.

Parrish, T. (2004) "Ralph Ellison: The Invisible Man in Philip Roth's The Human Stain," *Contemporary Literature*, 45, pp. 421–59. Available at: https://doi.org/10.1353/cli.2004.0026.

Parrish, T. (2011) "Autobiography and History in Roth's The Plot against America, or What Happened When Hitler Came to New Jersey," in D. Shostak (ed.) *Philip Roth: American Pastoral, the Human Stain, the Plot against America.* New York: Bloomsbury, pp. 145–61.

Pellegrini, A. (1997) *Performance Anxieties: Staging Psychoanalysis, Staging Race.* New York: Routledge.

Perelberg, R.J. (2022) "The Murder of the Dead Father: The Shoah and Contemporary Antisemitism," *The International Journal of Psychoanalysis*, 103(5), pp. 851–71. Available at: https://doi.org/10.1080/00207578.2022.2094797.

Pickard, S. (2021) "Ageism, Existential and Ontological: Reviewing Approaches toward the Abject with the Help of Millett, Hodgman, Lessing, and Roth," *University of Toronto Quarterly*, 90(2), pp. 111–26. Available at: https://doi.org/10.3138/utq.90.2.04.

Pierpont, C.R. (2014) *Roth Unbound.* London: Jonathan Cape.

Pinsker, S. (1990) *Bearing the Bad News: Contemporary American Literature and Culture.* Iowa City: University Of Iowa Press.

Pollack, E.G. (2010) *Antisemitism on the Campus: Past and Present.* Boston: Academic Studies Press. Available at: http://ebookcentral.proquest.com/lib/gla/detail.action?docID=3110421.

Posnock, R. (2006a) "On Philip Roth's The Plot against America," *Salmagundi* (150/151), pp. 270–82.

Posnock, R. (2006b) *Philip Roth's Rude Truth: The Art of Immaturity.* Princeton: Princeton University Press.

Potter, R. (2013) *Obscene Modernism: Literary Censorship and Experiment, 1900–1940.* Oxford: Oxford University Press.

Pozorski, A. (2011) *Roth and Trauma: The Problem of History in the Later Works.* New York: Continuum.

Pozorski, A. (2015) "Confronting the 'C' Word: Cancer and Death in Philip Roth's Fiction," *Philip Roth Studies*, 11(1), pp. 105–23. Available at: https://doi.org/10.5703/philrothstud.11.1.105.

Purvis, J. (2019) "Confronting the Power of Abjection: Toward a Politics of Shame," *philoSOPHIA*, 9(2), pp. 45–67. Available at: https://doi.org/10.1353/phi.2019.0020.

Rankine, P.D. (2005) "Passing as Tragedy: Philip Roth's The Human Stain, the Oedipus Myth, and the Self-Made Man," *Critique—Bolingbroke Society*, 47(1), pp. 101–2. Available at: https://doi.org/10.3200/CRIT.47.1.101-112.

Rickel, J. (2020) "The Fear of Foreign Violence and the Narrative of American Victimization: Lessons from Three Post-9/11 Coming-of-Age Novels," *Studies in the Novel*, 52(2), pp. 172–90. Available at: https://doi.org/10.1353/sdn.2020.0021.

Riess, Steven A. (2002) "From Pike to Green with Greenberg in between: Jewish Americans and the National Pastime," in L. Baldassaro and R. Johnson (eds) *The American Game: Baseball and Ethnicity*. Carbondale: Southern Illinois University Press, pp. 116–42.

Robertson, R. (1998) "Historicizing Weininger: The Nineteenth-Century German Image of the Feminized Jew," in B. Cheyette and L. Marcus (eds) *Modernity, Culture and "The Jew"*. Cambridge: Polity, pp. 23–40.

Rodwan, J.G. (2011) "The Fighting Life: Boxing and Identity in Novels by Philip Roth and Norman Mailer," *Philip Roth Studies*, 7(1), pp. 3, 83–96, 113–14.

Rosenberg, W. (2001) *Legacy of Rage: Jewish Masculinity, Violence, and Culture*. Amherst: University of Massachusetts Press.

Rosenfeld, A.H. (1997a) "The Americanization of the Holocaust," in A.H. Rosenfeld (ed.) *Thinking about the Holocaust: After Half a Century*. Bloomington: Indiana University Press, pp. 119–51.

Rosenfeld, A.H. (ed.) (1997b) *Thinking about the Holocaust: After Half a Century*. Bloomington: Indiana University Press.

Roth, Z. (2022) *Formal Matters: Embodied Experience in Modern Literature*. Edinburgh: Edinburgh University Press. Available at: https://doi.org/10.3366/edinburgh/9781474497503.001.0001.

Rothberg, M. (2007) "Roth and the Holocaust," in T. Parrish (ed.) *The Cambridge Companion to Philip Roth*. Cambridge: Cambridge University Press, pp. 52–67. Available at: https://doi.org/10.1017/CCOL0521864305.005.

Royal, D.P. (2002) "Postmodern Jewish Identity in Philip Roth's The Counterlife," *MFS Modern Fiction Studies*, 48(2), pp. 422–43. Available at: https://doi.org/10.1353/mfs.2002.0040.

Royal, D.P. (ed.) (2005) *Philip Roth: New Perspectives on an American Author*. Westport, CT: Praeger Publishers.

Rubin-Dorsky, J. and Seeley, G. (2011) "'The Pointless Meaningfulness of Living' Illuminating the Human Stain through the Scarlet Letter," in D. Shostak (ed.) *Philip Roth: American Pastoral, the Human Stain, the Plot against America*. London: Bloomsbury, pp. 93–111.

Rubinstein, W.D. and Rubinstein, H.L. (1999) *Philosemitism: Admiration and Support in the English-speaking World for Jews, 1840–1939*. London: Martin's Press.

References

Safer, E.B. (2006) *Mocking the Age: The Later Novels of Philip Roth*. Albany: State University of New York Press.

Sartre, J.-P. (1995) *Anti-Semite and Jew: An Exploration of the Etiology of Hate*. New York: Knopf Doubleday Publishing Group.

Scheurer, M. (2021) "'The Blunt Remnant of Something Whole': Living Stumps and Prosthetic Relations in Thomas Bernhard's Die Billigesser and Philip Roth's The Plot against America," in E. Grayson and M. Scheurer (eds) *Amputation in Literature and Film: Artificial Limbs, Prosthetic Relations, and the Semiotics of "Loss"*. Cham: Springer International Publishing, pp. 185–210. Available at: https://doi.org/10.1007/978-3-030-74377-2_9.

Schwartz, L. (2005) "Roth, Race, and Newark," *Cultural Logic: A Journal of Marxist Theory & Practice*, 12. Available at: https://doi.org/10.14288/clogic.v12i0.191860.

Shakespeare, W. (2006) *The Tempest*. Edited by B. Raffel and H. Bloom. New Haven: Yale University Press.

Shapiro, S.E. (1997) "The Uncanny Jew: A Brief History of an Image," *Judaism*, 46(1), p. 63.

Sharpe, R.F. and Sexon, S. (2018) "Mother's Milk and Menstrual Blood in Puncture: The Monstrous Feminine in Contemporary Horror Films and Late Medieval Imagery," *Studies in the Maternal*, 10(1), pp. 1–26. Available at: https://doi.org/10.16995/sim.256.

Shechner, M. (2003) *Up Society's Ass, Copper: Rereading Philip Roth*. Madison: University of Wisconsin Press.

Sherwood, R. (2021) "Through the Dark Mirror: Philip Roth's The Plot against America as Noir Fantasia," *Philip Roth Studies*, 17(2), pp. 3–25.

Shostak, D. (2011a) "Introduction: Roth's America," in *Philip Roth: American Pastoral, the Human Stain, the Plot against America*. London: Bloomsbury, pp. 1–15.

Shostak, D. (ed.) (2011b) *Philip Roth: American Pastoral, the Human Stain, the Plot against America*. London: Bloomsbury.

Shostak, D. (2016) "Prosthetic Fictions: Jonathan Safran Foer's Extremely Loud and Incredibly Close through Philip Roth's *The Plot against America*," in C. Morley (ed.) *9/11: Topics in Contemporary North American Literature*. London, Oxford, New York, New Delhi, and Sydney: Bloomsbury Academic, pp. 21–41.

Shostak, D.B. (2004) *Philip Roth: Countertexts, Counterlives*. Columbia: University of South Carolina Press.

Siegel, J. (2012) "*The Plot against America*: Philip Roth's Counter-Plot to American History," *MELUS: Multi-Ethnic Literature of the U.S.*, 37(1), pp. 131–54. Available at: https://doi.org/10.1353/mel.2012.0015.

Sokoloff, N. (2006) "Reading for the Plot? Philip Roth's 'The Plot against America," *Association for Jewish Studies*, 30(2), pp. 305–12.

Sontag, S. (2009) *Illness as Metaphor and AIDS and Its Metaphors*. London: Penguin Classics.

Spillers, H.J. (1987) "Mama's Baby, Papa's Maybe: An American Grammar Book," *Diacritics*, 17(2), pp. 65–81. Available at: https://doi.org/10.2307/464747.

Spiro, M. (2012) *Anti-Nazi Modernism: The Challenges of Resistance in 1930s Fiction.* Evanston, IL: Northwestern University Press.

Staudte, C. (2015) "Athleticism and Masculinity in Roth's American Trilogy and Exit Ghost," *Philip Roth Studies*, 11(2), pp. 55–66, 116.

Stone, A. (2016) "Sexual Difference," in L. Disch and M. Hawkesworth (eds) *The Oxford Handbook of Feminist Theory*. New York: Oxford University Press, pp. 874–893. Available at: https://doi.org/10.1093/oxfordhb/9780199328581.013.43.

Stratton, J. (2000) *Coming out Jewish: Constructing Ambivalent Identities.* London: Routledge.

Sundquist, E.J. (2005) *Strangers in the Land: Blacks, Jews, Post-Holocaust America.* Cambridge, MA: Harvard University Press. Available at: http://ebookcentral. proquest.com/lib/gla/detail.action?docID=3300098.

Syrkin, M. (1980) *The State of the Jews.* Washington, DC: New Republic Books.

Toker, L. (2013) "Between Dystopia and Allohistory: The Ending of Roth's *The Plot against America*," *Philip Roth Studies*, 9(1), pp. 41–50.

Tracy, M. (2012) "Philip Roth Tries to Kibosh "Great American Novel'"-Featuring Performance Art," *Tablet Magazine*. Available at: https://www.tabletmag.com/ sections/news/articles/installation-uses-roth-novel-to-roths-chagrin.

Trendel, A. (2018) "The Tribulations of American Democracy in Philip Roth's 'The Plot against America'," *Baltic Journal of English Language, Literature and Culture*, 8, pp. 120–8. Available at: https://doi.org/10.22364/BJELLC.08.2018.08.

Trepanier, L. (2023) "The Paradoxes of the Body in Philip Roth's Last Novels," *Perspectives on Political Science*, 52(3), pp. 130–44. Available at: https://doi.org/10.10 80/10457097.2023.2196224.

Tyler, I. (2009) "Against Abjection," *Feminist Theory*, 10(1), pp. 77–98. Available at: https://doi.org/10.1177/1464700108100393.

Tyler, I. (2013) *Revolting Subjects: Social Abjection and Resistance in Neoliberal Britain.* London: Zed Books.

Vanderwall, E. (2022) "Reverse Biography: The Philip Roth We Still Don't Know," *Philip Roth Studies*, 18(2), pp. 92–8.

Varvogli, A. (2007) "The Inscription of Terrorism: Philip Roth's American Pastoral," *Philip Roth Studies*, 3(2), pp. 101–13, 160.

Ward, M. (2018) "Predicting Trump and Presenting Canada in Philip Roth's The Plot against America," *Canadian Review of American Studies*, 48(S1), pp. 17–37. Available at: https://doi.org/10.3138/cras.2017.008.

Warren, C.L. (2018) *Ontological Terror: Blackness, Nihilism, and Emancipation.* Durham, NC: Duke University Press. Available at: http://ebookcentral.proquest. com/lib/gla/detail.action?docID=5389606.

References

Weininger, O. ([1903] 1906) *Sex & Character, Wellcome Collection*. Available at: https://wellcomecollection.org/works/gada7gsw/items.

Weinstock, J.A. (2014) *The Ashgate Encyclopedia of Literary and Cinematic Monsters*. Surrey: Ashgate.

Whitman, Walt (2009) *Leaves of Grass 1860: The 150th Anniversary Facsimile Edition*. Edited by J. Stacy. Chicago: University of Iowa Press. Available at: http://ebookcentral.proquest.com/lib/gla/detail.action?docID=843251.

Wilson, K.A. (2005) "The Ghosts of Zuckerman's Past: 'The Zuckerman Bound Series,'" in D.P. Royal (ed.) *Philip Roth: New Perspectives on an American Author*. Westport: Praeger, pp. 103–19.

Wilson, M. (1991) "Fathers and Sons in History: Philip Roth's 'The Counterlife,'" *Prooftexts*, 11(1), pp. 41–56.

Wirth-Nesher, H. and Wirth-Nesher, H. (eds) (1994) *What Is Jewish Literature?* Philadelphia: Jewish Publication Society.

Woeste, V.S. (2012) *Henry Ford's War on Jews and the Legal Battle against Hate Speech*. Redwood City: Stanford University Press. Available at: http://ebookcentral.proquest.com/lib/gla/detail.action?docID=928368.

Woods, G. (1987) *Articulate Flesh: Male Homo-eroticism and Modern Poetry*. New Haven: Yale University Press.

Yancy, G. (2016) *Black Bodies, White Gazes: The Continuing Significance of Race in America*. 2nd edition. Lanham: Rowman & Littlefield Publishers.

Yang, P. and Koshy, K. (2016) "The 'Becoming White Thesis' Revisited," *The Journal of Public and Professional Sociology*, 8(1). Available at: https://digitalcommons.kennesaw.edu/jpps/vol8/iss1/1.

Ziff, L. (2000) *Return Passages: Great American Travel Writing, 1780–1910*. New Haven: Yale University Press.

Zucker, D.J. (2004) "Philip Roth: Desire and Death," *Studies in American Jewish Literature*, 23, pp. 135–44.

Index

abjection theory 16–17, 17 n.16, 19, 43, 46, 60, 66–7, 70–1, 74, 76–8, 98, 117, 136, 145, 147

African Americans 7–8, 15, 21, 61 n.5, 80, 117, 120, 124, 131–7, 142, 144, 147

Ahmed, S. 19

American Jews 4–5, 7, 15–18, 24, 32, 39–40, 50, 54, 57, 59, 65–8, 78–9, 81, 84, 87–8, 137

American Pastoral (1997, Roth) 20, 57, 68, 76, 81–3, 95, 99–100, 100 n.9, 105, 107, 116, 125, 127, 132–3

The American Scene (1905, James) 13–14

The Anatomy Lesson (1983, Roth) 20, 23, 40–1

Anti-Oedipus: Capitalism and Schizophrenia (Deleuze and Guattari) 82–3

Anti-Semite and Jew (1995, Sartre) 121

antisemitism 6, 11, 13–14, 13 n.14, 18, 20–1, 23–4, 31, 33–4, 37–9, 47–52, 56–9, 62–72, 74–5, 77–9, 83, 88, 118 n.2, 119, 125, 148 n.26, 154–5

Antler, J. 28

artificial myth (Barthes) 104

Barthes, R. 103–4

Basu, A. 111

Bauman, Z. 11, 27, 51, 137

Bellow, S. 4–5, 49–50, 81–2
  Henderson the Rain King (2007) 81–2, 84

Bennett, A. 45

Bergner, G. 138–9

Berlinerblau, J. 3 n.2, 6–7, 61, 61 n.5, 62, 154
  The Philip Roth We Don't Know: Sex, Race, and Autobiography (2021) 6

Bettelheim, B. 39

Bhabha, H. K. (*The Location of Culture*, 1994) 53–4

Black body, Jewish and 61–3, 70, 79–80, 119–21, 120 n.7, 140–1

Black Skin, White Masks (1952, Fanon) 121–2, 134–5, 138

Boese, S. 74

Bousfield, C. 26, 35, 43

Brauner, D. 3 n.1, 27, 46 n.6, 47, 49, 78, 83–4, 95, 99 n.6

Bresnan, M. P. 66

Brod, H. 30 n.2

Brodkin, K. 15, 80

Butler, J. 130

Bylund, S. 109 n.11

The Cambridge Companion to the Body in Literature (2015, Hillman and Ulrika) 9

Canales, G. S. 148–9

Clarkson, S. 27–8, 30

Clinton, B. 123–4, 123 n.9

Connolly, A. 3–4, 6–7, 66–7, 132 n.13

Cooper, A. 94 n.5

Coughlan, D. 44

The Counterlife (1986, Roth) 7, 20, 49–52, 56–7, 59–61, 69–70, 78, 122, 125, 127, 129, 133

Countertexts, Counterlives (2004, Shostak) 3 n.1, 8

Cox, K. 109

Davis, B. R. 62, 117

De Boer, K. 45

Deception: A Novel (1990, Roth) 20, 49–50, 60–5, 70

Deleuze, G. (*Anti-Oedipus: Capitalism and Schizophrenia*) 82–3

Diasporism 51–2

disabled body 75–7

Douglas, C. 72

Dragulescu, L. M. 145 n.23

The Dying Animal (2002, Roth) 9

Index

Eagle, C. 109
Eilberg-Schwartz, H. 10
Emerson, R. W. 138, 142, 145–6
European Jews 42, 78, 154
Ewara, E. 17

The Facts: A Novelist's Autobiography (1988, Roth) 23–5
Fanon, F. 62–3, 117, 120–2, 124, 134–6, 138–41
  Black Skin, White Masks (1952) 121–2, 134–5, 138
Feldman, D. 11
fetishism 31, 36, 72, 78, 100–1, 112–13, 126, 138–9, 143–4, 154
Fong, T. 24
Ford, H. 14
Foucault, M. 9–10
Franco, D. 33, 144
Freud, S. 25, 27, 31, 36–8, 42, 55
  The Interpretation of Dreams (1997) 31
  Oedipal complex 25, 36–8
Friedman, M. 27

Gair, C. 85, 112 n.12
Geller, J. 11
gender 8, 23, 27–31, 33–6, 38, 43, 60, 63, 74, 95, 99–100, 109, 154–5
The Ghost Writer (1979, Roth) 38–40, 50, 124
Gilman, S. L. 10, 12–13, 15, 58–9, 118–19
  The Jew's Body (1991) 10, 118–19
Ginsberg, A. (*Howl and Other Poems*) 84–6
Godfrey, M. 143, 148 n.26
Golash-Boza, T. 4
Goodbye, Columbus and Five Short Stories (1959, Roth) 5, 7, 87
Gotanda, N. 120
The Great American Novel (1973, Roth) 7
Greenwell, G. 97–8
Grosz, E. A. 10, 33, 123
Guattari, F. (*Anti-Oedipus: Capitalism and Schizophrenia*) 82–3

HaCohen, R. 118–19
Hawthorne, N. 123–4

Henderson the Rain King (2007, Bellow) 81–2, 84
Hertzberg, A. 32
heterosexualism 86, 139
Hillman, D. (*The Cambridge Companion to the Body in Literature*, 2015) 9
Hirsch, M. (*The Mother/Daughter Plot*, 1989) 26
Hirth, B. 3, 67, 72
Hobbs, A. 78 n.10, 99 n.7
Holocaust 15, 29–31, 29 n.1, 32, 38, 42–3, 45, 50, 52, 54, 72, 78–9
Holroyd, J. 135 n.17
Hoovestol, C. 132 n.12, 146 n.24, 151
Horn, D. 6
Howe, I. 5
Howl and Other Poems (Ginsberg) 84–6
The Human Stain (2000, Roth) 4, 21, 98, 117–18, 122–4, 124 n.11, 129–31, 133, 138, 151–3
Husserl, E. 9

Illness as Metaphor (2009, Sontag) 42
The Interpretation of Dreams (1997, Freud) 31
Iragaray, L. 138–9
Itzkovitz, D. 16, 119

James, H. (*The American Scene,* 1905) 13–14
Jarvis, C. 14
Jewish Anxiety and the Novels of Philip Roth (2015, Kaplan) 8
The Jew's Body (1991, Gilman) 10, 118–19
Jews/Jewish 100–1, 144
  blackness 19, 117–24, 118 n.2, 121, 133, 135, 140, 142–4
  body 8–16, 29, 49, 51, 59, 62, 65–7, 69, 74, 78, 81, 101, 117–24, 135, 144, 154
  difference 5, 11–12, 15–17, 19–20, 23, 38, 49, 56, 59–60, 68, 70, 74, 118–19, 154
  fathers 23–7, 29–33, 36–43, 46–7, 68–71, 136–7, 147–8
  foetor Judaicus 58

174 *Index*

and gentile (non-Jews) 10, 11 n.11, 27, 39–40, 49–51, 54, 57, 59, 64–5, 70, 74, 80, 100–2, 112, 154
identity 10, 16, 19, 32–3, 36, 39, 47, 50, 52, 60, 102–3, 133, 144, 154
lives 15, 49, 64, 67–8, 118 n.2
mothers 23–8, 34, 38, 40, 43, 47–8, 154
whiteness 5, 17–18, 63, 67, 70, 80, 118–22, 120 n.5, 133–4, 136, 140–1, 151–2
Judaism 10–11, 18–20, 23, 27–9, 43, 53, 60, 73, 91 n.3, 100, 102
Just Folks program 71–2

Kaplan, B. A. 6, 8, 32, 51, 66–7, 70, 80, 95
Jewish Anxiety and the Novels of Philip Roth (2015) 8
Karasik-Updike, O. 27
Katz, J. 11 n.9
Kavitha, K. 119–20
Keller, C. 31
Kirsch, A. 4
Kirshenblatt-Gimblett, B. 10
Kolodny, A. 82, 99–100, 106, 116
Lay of the Land (1975) 82
Körper (body-object) 9
Kristeva, J. 2, 16, 17 n.16, 19, 25–6, 34–5, 43, 76, 89, 111
Powers of Horror: an Essay on Abjection (1982) 16–17

Lay of the Land (1975, Kolodny) 82
legitimate street art 85
Levine, A. 74, 76–7
Levitt, L. 16
Lewinsky, M. 123
Lewis, R. W. B. 102–3
Lindbergh, C. 65–9, 71, 73, 77–8
Lindemann, A. 11–12, 11 n.11
The Location of Culture (1994, Bhabha) 53–4

The Machine in the Garden (1964, Marx) 106–7
Marcus, L. 14
Martin-Charcot, J. 12
Marx, L. (*The Machine in the Garden*, 1964) 106–7

masculine/masculinity 2, 12, 29, 31–8, 53, 68, 77, 94 n.5, 95, 101–2, 107, 129, 136–7, 139
Maslan, M. 124 n.11, 132 n.14
maternal body 23–7, 43–4, 46, 48
Maurer, Y. 17
Mell, J. J. 12–13
Melville, H. 118
Merleau-Ponty, M. 9, 154
middle-class Jew 86–8
Mills, C. W. 2–3
Milton, J. (*Paradise Lost,* 2003) 100, 105, 108–9, 114–15
Morley, C. 75, 108
Morris, K. J. 9
Morrison, T. 151–2
Morrissey, L. 100 n.9
The Mother/Daughter Plot (1989, Hirsch) 26
Moynihan, S. 141 n.18
Muresan, L. 46 n.7

Newman, S. 6
Novick, P. 29–30

Oedipal complex (Freud) 25, 36–8
Omer-Sherman, R. 94
Ontological Terror: Blackness, Nihilism, and Emancipation (2018, Warren) 63
Operation Shylock: A Confession (1993, Roth) 50–1
Orthodox Jews 56–7
Ozick, C. 4–5

Paradise Lost (2003, Milton) 100, 105, 108–9, 114–15
Paris, V. 89
Parrish, T. 78 n.9, 133 n.15, 143, 145 n.22
Patrimony: A True Story (1991, Roth) 7, 20, 61
Perelberg, R. J. 71
persecuting spirit (Hawthorne) 123–30
The Philip Roth We Don't Know: Sex, Race, and Autobiography (2021, Berlinerblau) 6
philosemitism 13 n.14
Pickard, S. 19–20

Pierpont, C. R. 42 n.3, 58 n.3, 81, 144 n.20, 148

The Plessy v. Ferguson case (1896) 120 n.7

The Plot Against America (2004, Roth) 3, 20, 49–50, 65–8, 70, 72, 74, 78, 78 n.10, 79, 90

Posnock, R. 45 n.5, 78 n.10, 81, 84, 89, 99 n.6, 112, 149 n.28

Powers of Horror: an Essay on Abjection (1982, Kristeva) 16–17

Pozorski, A. 78 n.9, 91, 149–51

Purvis, J. 17

race/racial 2–4, 7–8, 12, 21, 38, 58, 61–3, 67, 69–74, 79–80, 119, 121–5, 133, 135–8, 143, 144 n.20, 153
   ambiguity 144
   ambivalence 118, 120
   categorization 121, 134, 137, 142
   difference 20–1, 23, 58, 120
   identity 70, 144–5
   politics 3, 17, 19

Rankine, P. D. 148–9

Riess, S. A. 14

Rosenfeld, A. H. 29 n.1

Rothberg, M. 43

Roth, P. 1–21, 153–5
   American Pastoral (1997) 20, 57, 68, 76, 81–3, 95, 99–100, 100 n.9, 105, 107, 116, 125, 127, 132–3
   The Anatomy Lesson (1983) 20, 23, 40–1
   The Counterlife (1986) 7, 20, 49–52, 56–7, 59–61, 69–70, 78, 122, 125, 127, 129, 133
   Deception: A Novel (1990) 20, 49–50, 60–5, 70
   The Dying Animal (2002) 9
   "Eli the Fanatic" 17–19
   The Facts: A Novelist's Autobiography (1988) 23–5
   The Ghost Writer (1979) 38–40, 50, 124
   Goodbye, Columbus and Five Short Stories (1959) 5, 7, 87
   The Great American Novel (1973) 7
   The Human Stain (2000) 4, 21, 98, 117–18, 122–4, 124 n.11, 129–31, 133, 138, 151–3

Operation Shylock: A Confession (1993) 50–1

Patrimony: A True Story (1991) 7, 20, 61

The Plot Against America (2004) 3, 20, 49–50, 65–8, 70, 72, 74, 78, 78 n.10, 79, 90

Portnoy's Complaint (1969) 5, 20, 23, 27–8, 34, 37–8, 45, 49–50, 83–4, 90, 91 n.3, 112–13, 133

Sabbath's Theater (1995) 20, 57, 69, 81–99, 91 n.3, 92 n.4, 94 n.5

Zuckerman Bound: A Trilogy and Epilogue (1979, 1981, 1983, 1985) 38, 40, 47, 100–1, 133

Royal, D. P. 127

Royle, N. 45

Sabbath's Theater (1995, Roth) 20, 57, 69, 81–99, 91 n.3, 92 n.4, 94 n.5

Sartre, J. -P. (*Anti-Semite and Jew,* 1995) 121

Scholem, G. 5–6

Schwartz, L. 7

Second World War 14–17, 20, 38, 66, 68, 80–1, 87, 101, 154

Sex and Character (1903, Weininger) 12

Sexon, S. 26

sex/sexual/sexuality 12–13, 29, 33, 35, 37–8, 40–1, 50, 52–3, 58, 61–2
   abundance 107
   assault 123, 123 n.9
   deviancy 50
   difference 58
   disempowerment 107–8
   divide 38
   and gendered norms 29
   pleasure 82, 110, 146
   politics 124, 130, 146
   power 83, 128
   race and 122–3, 130–1
   violence 61

Shakespeare, W. (*The Tempest,* 2006) 12, 57, 94

Sharpe, R. F. 26

Shechner, M. 124, 145 n.21

Shostak, D. 3 n.1, 8, 32, 34, 64, 67, 76, 94 n.5, 128

176 Index

Countertexts, Counterlives (2004) 3 n.1, 8
Silk, C. 117–18, 124–50
  big white thing 138–45
  "Everyone knows" 130–2
  raw singular I 130–8, 142, 145, 150
  writing in the dark 145–52
Sokoloff, N. 79
Sontag, S. (*Illness as Metaphor,* 2009) 42
Stratton, J. 10–11
street art 85
Sundquist, E. J. 15 n.15, 133 n.15
Syrkin, M. 5, 36

The Tempest (2006, Shakespeare) 12, 57, 94
Trepanier, L. 154
Trump, D. 3, 66, 155
Tyler, I. 35, 74

Ulrika, M. (*The Cambridge Companion to the Body in Literature,* 2015) 9

Varvogli, A. 99 n.8
violence 57, 61, 70–1, 73, 78–80

Warren, C. L. (*Ontological Terror: Blackness, Nihilism, and Emancipation,* 2018) 63
Weininger, O. (*Sex and Character,* 1903) 12
white Americans 5, 15–16, 18, 23, 68, 73, 77, 80, 102, 118–19, 135
white gaze 120–1, 120 n.7
white supremacy 2, 7–8, 62–3, 72–3, 80, 119, 154–5
Whitman, W. 33, 83–6, 89, 122
Wilson, M. 60
Woeste, V. S. 14
Woodenton Jewry 18
Woods, G. 84

Yancy, G. 119, 119 n.4, 120, 120 n.7, 121, 140
Yang, P. 119–20

Ziff, L. 14
Zionism 53–6, 59–60
Zuckerman Bound: A Trilogy and Epilogue (1979, 1981, 1983, 1985, Roth) 38, 40, 47, 100–1, 133

www.ingramcontent.com/pod-product-compliance
Lightning Source LLC
LaVergne TN
LVHW021604060925
820435LV00003B/38